HARVARD ECONOMIC STUDIES
VOLUME CII

Awarded the David A. Wells Prize for the year 1954–55 and published from the income of the David A. Wells fund. This prize is offered annually, in a competition open to seniors of Harvard College and graduates of any department of Harvard University of not more than three years' standing, for the best essay in certain specified fields of economics.

The studies in this series are published by the Department of Economics of Harvard University. The Department does not assume responsibility for the views expressed.

The Investment Decision

An Empirical Study

John R. Meyer & Edwin Kuh

1957
HARVARD UNIVERSITY PRESS
CAMBRIDGE, MASSACHUSETTS

© 1957
BY THE PRESIDENT AND FELLOWS OF HARVARD COLLEGE

Distributed in Great Britain by
OXFORD UNIVERSITY PRESS
LONDON

LIBRARY OF CONGRESS CATALOG CARD NUMBER: 57–7614
PRINTED IN THE UNITED STATES OF AMERICA

"For—though no one will believe it—economics is a technical and difficult subject. It is even becoming a science."
John Maynard Keynes

Preface

Dissatisfaction with the empirical foundations of existing investment theories in combination with an interest in certain aspects of statistics constitutes the underlying motivation of this study. An effort has been made to synthesize these investment findings with other recent research on business objectives and motives into a unified explanation of corporate behavior, particularly as it relates to growth.

The main intellectual stimulus to the undertaking of this study was provided by Professors Guy H. Orcutt, James S. Duesenberry, and John Lintner. We are particularly indebted to Professor Orcutt whose keen and imaginative interest in the testing of economic hypotheses shaped the procedures and content of the entire study. He lent valuable counsel on a number of technical statistical questions as well. Similarly, our conception of business behavior owes much to many helpful discussions with Professors Duesenberry and Lintner whose outlook on these matters is broadly kindred, although definitely not identical, with that presented here.

Assistance with data collection and processing was provided by many individuals. Mr. Vito Natrella and Mr. Lloyd Dollet of the Securities and Exchange Commission made available to us that agency's corporate investment figures in compact, easily accessible form and were also most helpful in answering questions about the data. Among several who assisted in obtaining supplementary information from *Moody's Industrial Manual* and individual corporate records, Mr. William Geertsema and Mrs. Lee Meyer, both of whom also did substantial amounts of additional work, were major contributors to the success of this phase of the project. Mr. John Alman, Director of the Boston University Office of Statistical and Research Services, undertook the IBM computations leading to correlation coefficients, and Professors John Harr and Kenneth Iversen of the Harvard Computation Laboratory were extremely generous in making available to us their experience and time in operating the Mark IV computer to invert the correlation matrices. The chore of typing and final checking of bibliographic references was performed by Mrs. Alice Young with an extraordinary diligence that far surpassed normal secretarial requirements.

The basic financial wherewithal for this study was provided by a McGraw-Hill Publishing Company grant to the Harvard Seminar on Quantitative Economics and a Rockefeller Foundation grant to Professor John Lintner and the Harvard Business School Division of Research for a Study of Profits and the Functioning of the Economy. Important additional assistance, particularly in the latter stages of the research, was supplied by the Massachusetts Institute of Technology School of Industrial Management.

We are also obliged to the *Review of Economics and Statistics* for permission to republish here parts of an earlier article by the authors, "Acceleration and Related Theories of Investment: An Empirical Inquiry" that appeared in the August 1955 issue of that Journal. Also Appendix C, "Correlation and Regression Estimates When the Data Are Ratios," first appeared under the same title in *Econometrica* of October 1955 and permission to republish was kindly granted by the Econometric Society.

September 1956

J. R. M.
E. K.

Contents

Part I. Introduction

Chapter   Page

  I. Purpose and Objectives   3

 II. Modern Theories of Investment: A Survey   6

      Introduction. The Marginal Theories. The Acceleration Principle. Institutional and Empirical Generalizations About the Investment Process. Summary.

      Appendix to Chapter II 23

Part II. Methods and Techniques

III. The Sample 39

      The Basic Analytical Problem and the Data Matrix. The Sample: Its Origins and Biases. The Conceptual Questions of Industry Grouping. The Unit of Observation and Some General Properties of Cross-Section Samples. Summary.

IV. The Variables 57

      Problems of Selection: General Nature and Scope. The Selection Process. Accounting and Economic Properties. Summary.

 V. The Statistical Models 73

      The Correlation Matrix and the Choice of Statistical Method. The Final Models. Statistical Problems. Summary.

Part III. The Empirical Results

VI. Echo and Senility Effects 91

      The Age of Capital and Investment: Theory and Observed Fact. The "Senility Effect." Liquidity and the Age of Capital. Summary.

CONTENTS

Chapter	Page
VII. Depreciation Expense and the Policy of Accelerated Amortization	101

The Liquidity and Tax Policy Aspects of the Depreciation Expense Variable. Causes of Within-Industry Variation in the Depreciation Expense Variable. The Empirical Results. Summary.

VIII. Profit and Acceleration Variables over the Business Cycle . . . 116

Introduction: The Cyclical Pattern 1946–1950. The Liquidity Variables. The Acceleration Variables. Capacity and Profit Variables in 1948. Costs, Profits, and the Level of Output in the Long and Short Run. Summary.

IX. Financial Patterns, Dividend Policy and Trade Position Motivation . . . 136

Introduction. A Summary of Financial Patterns in the Manufacturing Sector, 1946–1950. Industry Characteristics Associated with the Use of Outside Funds. The Relationship between the Dividend Payout and Investment. Summary.

X. The Liquidity Restraint and the Internal Growth Rates of Small and Large Firms . . . 159

Introduction. Concepts and Definitions. A Comparison of Small and Large Firm Investment Rates. The Liquidity and Financial Factor. A Comparison of Small and Large Firm Correlation Estimates. Summary.

XI. Some Marginalist Hypotheses . . . 181

Introduction. Statistical Problems in Combining Cross-Section and Time Series Estimates. The Models. The Present Application. Empirical Results. Summary.

XII. A Residual Funds Theory of Investment . . . 190

The Principal Findings. Costs, Price Policy, Market Structure, and Investment. Dividends, Inventories, and Investment in Relation to Short-Run Financial Requirements. Debt, Equity, and the Investment Process. A Theoretical Model. Summary.

Appendices

A   The Sample: Industry and Firm Coverage . . . 209

B   Cross-Section Correlation and Regression Estimates . . . 233

CONTENTS

Appendix	Page
C Correlation and Regression Estimates When the Data Are Ratios	258

Introduction. The Spurious Correlation Problem. Ratio Correlations as Estimates of Partial Correlations. Bias in Regression Estimates. A Sufficient Condition for a Regression Equation to Have a Zero Intercept.

List of Works Cited 269

Index 279

Tables

	Page
1. Summary of Empirical Results from Previous Investment Studies	23
2. Major Reasons for Excluding Observations from Regressions	42
3. Sample Coverage of Total Investment — 1948	45
4. Size Distribution of Firms in Sample	47
5. Reclassified Industry Groups	50
6. Year Averages of Correlations between Age Variable and Investment	92
7. Industry Averages of Partial Correlations between Age and Investment Variables	95
8. Simple Correlations between Liquidity Stock and Age of Equipment	97
9. Estimated Range of Average Firm Equipment Life by Industry Groupings	105
10. Partial Correlations between Investment and Depreciation Expense	110
11. Comparison of 1946–48 and 1949–50 Average Partial Correlations between Investment and Depreciation Expense	111
12. Comparisons of Durability Range and 1949–50 Average Partial Correlations between Investment and Depreciation Expense	113
13. Partial Correlations between Profits and Investment	118
14. Annual Averages of Partial Correlations between Investment and Liquidity Stock and Flow Variables	119
15. Partial Correlations between Change in Sales and Investment	121

TABLES

	Page
16. Partial Correlations between Capacity Utilization and Investment	122
17. Rank Order Correlations between Selected Liquidity, Capacity, and Sales Position Measures and Profit and Capacity Variable Performance, 1948	128
18. Liquidity, Capacity, and Sales Conditions, 1946–50	129
19. Averaged Data Partial Correlations of Investment with Profits, Sales, and Relative Capacity	133
20. Sources and Uses of Manufacturing Corporate Funds 1946–50	138
21. Relation of Stock Issues to Total Amount of New Capital Issues by Industry Groups, 1925–50 for Industrial and Miscellaneous Corporations	139
22. Aggregate Fund Source Analysis by Industry Group	140
23. A Comparison of Industry Growth and Modernization Rates	144
24. Median Dividend-Profit Ratio by Industry and Year	146
25. Concentration Indices by Industry	148
26. A Ranking of the Industries According to Market Share Rivalry	151
27. Simple Correlations between Investment and the Dividend to Profit Ratio	155
28. A Contingency Table of Positive and Negative Correlations between Dividend Payout and Investment Observed for Top Six, Middle Five, and Lowest Six Industries on Change in Age Index	156
29. Definitions of Small and Large Firm Used with Different Industry Groups	162
30. Arithmetic Average 1946–50 Growth Rates for Small and Large Firms	164
31. Median 1946–50 Growth Rates for Small and Large Firms by Industry Group	165

TABLES

	Page
32. Median Growth Rates, 1949, for Small and Large Firms	166
33. Quarterly Ratios of 1949 to 1948 Sales	168
34. Large and Small Firm Use of Outside Funds Compared with Growth Rates	171
35. A Comparison of 1949 Net New Issues with Total Net New Issues for Small and Large Firms by Industry Group	174
36. Partial Correlations for Different Size Groups between Investment and Four Explanatory Variables	177
37. Combined Cross-Section, Time Series Regressions	188

Part I

Introduction

Chapter I

Purpose and Objectives

A decade has now passed since the end of the Second World War and in retrospect it seems inevitable that the economics profession should have focused so much of its postwar attention upon the problems of industrial growth. In a Europe of destroyed factories, an Asia uprooted by resurgent nationalism, and a world divided by a bitter power struggle, the maintenance and expansion of economic productivity has become crucially important. Problems associated with business cycles have receded somewhat in immediacy, yet income and employment fluctuations remain a major concern of the economist.

Central to both theories of economic growth and, increasingly during the past fifty years, theories of business fluctuations is the rate of capital formation and its determinants. There is a plethora of theories to explain accumulation, in fact so many that selecting from among them the most worthwhile explanations has become most difficult. The importance of the problem and the unresolved status of these theoretical conflicts have been the main impetus to this study, which is, in essence, an empirical investigation designed to gain greater insight into the process of entrepreneurial decisions to purchase capital assets.

As a first step in narrowing the range of choice, a survey was made of the suggestions contained in the existing literature, both empirical and theoretical. Three principal explanations of investment motivation emerged: (1) the profit motive, which is the fundamental propelling drive in both static marginal theories and the more recent adaptations of marginalism contained in uncertainty, risk, and expectation theories; (2) the technical need for greater capacity to meet an increase in demand for final product, which is the accelerator in its original and strictest construction; and (3) the desire to keep or increase one's share of the market, that is, the trade position motive, which is so often mentioned in questionnaires or interviews of individual businessmen.

In testing and evaluating alternative hypotheses about capital investment, certain limits have been established to keep the subject matter within reasonable bounds. First, only micro-economic phenomena will be examined and therefore aggregative interaction involving other parts of the economy will not be investigated. Thus, the fascinating panorama of multiplier and multiplier-accelerator interactions is eschewed. Second, only plant and equipment investment in the following manufacturing industries will be statistically treated: machinery, metal products, primary iron and steel, pulp and paper, automobiles, textiles, petroleum, chemicals, and rubber. Obviously, many important sectors have not been included and the scope of permissible generalization is therefore immediately limited, since it is likely that different explanatory hypotheses might be required for these unincluded sectors. Third, insofar as institutional factors are germane, our conclusions will necessarily reflect the current attitudes and characteristics of the American economy and society. A theory so general as to encompass all situations in different economic environments will ordinarily have little to say about any particular milieu. Fourth, we have found it convenient to work on the assumption that business decisions are made in response to certain observable phenomena in the firm's environment. This means that we deal with psychological theories only to the extent that mental states have objective counterparts. Fifth, the emphasis has been primarily upon studying short-run influences on investment; in particular, little attention has been given to that most important exogenous factor, technological change.

The basic statistical data consist of observations for about six hundred firms in the postwar years of 1946–1950, a period containing war shortages, inflation, recession, and the beginning of a war boom. These have been supplemented by time series for several industries during the interwar and post World War II years to test hypotheses unamenable to cross-section analysis. The main analytical technique has been to use regression and correlation analysis with cross-section data of individual firm observations. By concentrating attention on cross sections, many of the conventional statistical problems, such as independence of observations and functional identification, have been minimized but not eliminated. New problems arise, moreover, because of the necessity of eliminating size effects in the cross-section data. These statistical difficulties and the limitations of the sample receive detailed consideration in Part II.

To borrow an analogy from Alfred Marshall, it is now obvious that the results, as finally reported in Part III, will pertain to the growth of the individual trees rather than to that of the entire forest — whose aggregates have been so extensively surveyed in the past. Admittedly, this choice has limited the opportunity to investigate the impact of certain factors which primarily vary over time. This could be a disabling defect if immediate quantitative prediction is sought, which it has not been in this work.

Instead, we have concentrated on testing hypotheses of investment behavior and the social consequences of that behavior. This path was followed not because prediction was thought impossible but rather because of the belief that more adequate knowledge of the actual decision process is a prerequisite to better quantitative prediction whether by econometric models or by more intuitive, less formalized techniques.

Chapter II

Modern Theories of Investment: A Survey

INTRODUCTION

Of the various domains of economics, one of the most confused and controversial has been the theory of the demand for assets. This situation contrasts sharply with that in the theory of demand for non-durable commodities which in recent decades has witnessed substantial theoretical and empirical advance. One unfortunate result is that some of the most elementary policy decisions regarding the business cycle and economic growth must, of necessity, rest on questionable, empirically unsubstantiated notions about the causes of variations in investment outlay.

Since, by definition, investment is the time rate of change in a stock of durable assets, decisions to invest are likely to involve a number of considerations including expectations about future prices, outputs and technology, current rates of capacity utilization, anticipated reactions of major rivals, as well as a variety of constraints such as technological conditions and availability of finance. In short, the investment problem is complex and requires treatment of many magnitudes, each with a variety of dimensions. Because the problem is intrinsically so difficult, the literature on the subject reports a number of different analytical approaches many of them complementary but not a few contradictory. The basic problems arise primarily from different interpretations of entrepreneurial motives and a different emphasis given to alternative constraints. In addition, new complications have arisen in recent years as several authors have abstracted from underlying entrepreneurial motivation and constructed cycle theories based upon macro-economic relations. Since such an approach immediately compounds the number of possible interactions and thereby the analytical difficulties, attention will be exclusively focused on investment at the firm level.

For purposes of discussion, investment theories can be conveniently grouped into three categories: the profit maximization or marginal theories, the more technically oriented acceleration approach, and inductive generalizations based upon institutional and empirical studies. Each of these will be discussed in turn, paying particular attention to their motivational implications and observed empirical validity.[1]

THE MARGINAL THEORIES

The marginal theories date back to the middle and end of the nineteenth century when the tools of mathematical calculus were applied to a wide range of economic problems. When the calculus was used in conjunction with an elementary hedonistic psychology, precise implications about economic behavior were readily deduced. These led to systematic, apparently pervasive models which did not seem to violate the actual facts of the economic world either too often or too violently. In the particular instance of entrepreneurial behavior, hedonistic motivation was simplified even further by equating utility to profits. The entrepreneur was thus a singularly single-purposed individual; he sought nothing but maximum possible profits from the conduct of his business affairs. Given this profit maximizing behavior, the marginal calculus indicated what the businessman would do when confronted with certain widely varying objective conditions.

Of course, the reality of these assumed conditions immediately determines the usefulness of the theories. The postulated assumptions generally have been stated in about the following way:

[1] The appendix to this chapter contains a brief summary of most previous empirical studies on investment behavior.

1. All future product prices, factor prices, and outputs are known so that future revenues accruing to a particular investment are known.

2. Current costs are known when investment takes place all at once or, when outlays are incurred over a period of time, these future costs are known.

3. Technology is constant.

4. The supply of funds is either unlimited at the going rate of interest or it is reflected in a certain known way by the interest rate structure.

Given this substantial bundle of *ceteris paribus*, it immediately follows, assuming the entrepreneur maximizes the difference between discounted revenues and costs, that the volume of investment is determined by the cost of capital equipment and the market rate of interest. Interest rates are thus central to marginal theories and their relation to the volume of investment has been the object of numerous empirical inquiries. The empirical findings, however, as summarized in the first section of the appendix, indicate that the interest rate is not important whether statistical inference, interviews, or questionnaires have been the method of investigation. About the only important exception is Klein's time series studies of the railroad and electric utility industries, thought to be among the more interest-sensitive industries.[2] The interview-questionnaire results were uniformly negative and include, moreover, substantial representation from electric utilities. While the conclusions are not as absolutely one-sided as is often suggested, the existing body of empirical knowledge does not lend much comfort to the marginalist position. And it deserves emphasis that the virtual unanimity of interview-questionnaire findings, encompassing as they do a wide range of industries, places, and time periods, should be especially valuable in ascertaining forces relevant to the decision-making process.

Numerous rationalizations of these predominantly negative results can be offered. Where imperfect capital markets are the rule, market interest rates should not be a key variable; furthermore, interest rates may have been his-

[2] See Table 1, pp. 25 and 26.

torically too low to be influential, particularly since expectations probably shift so much more than interest that the influence of interest rates has been overshadowed. In short, the really crucial determinants of investment in the real world are those "assumed objective conditions" that are put in *ceteris paribus* by the marginal theories. Therefore, of necessity, the empirical investigations have been conducted under conditions that fail to meet all the assumptions of the theory. While these objections are correct, and not all the empirical tests are beyond criticism, it seems reasonable to suppose that the theory's assumptions should, broadly speaking, conform to the real world, rather than vice versa.[3] The reverse position — that the world should be made to conform to the theoretical assumptions — holds many fascinating possibilities for philosophic speculation but has little to offer any pragmatic applications of economics. In all fairness, though, it should be recognized that the choice of what properly belongs in *ceteris paribus* is itself an institutional variable and subject to change. That is, interest and cost fluctuations may actually have been crucially important determinants of investment behavior back in the nineteenth century when the marginal theories were initially propounded.

Partial recognition of institutional changes has led in recent years to efforts to shift the theory of the firm, and consequently of plant and equipment investment, from a profit maximization orientation to that of utility maximization. Primarily, this move represents a growing belief that profit maximization is too narrow to encompass the full scope of modern entrepreneurial motives, particularly once the previously assumed objective conditions are released from *ceteris paribus,* and the theory seeks to explain a much wider range of behavioral responses. Specifically, the use of a utility maximization assumption enables the theoretician

[3] It is correct to suggest that the firms at the margin of investing are the ones which would affirm the importance of interest rates in response to surveys if the interest rate were important, and these firms would be only a small fraction of all firms at any one time. However, the unanimity of responses from hundreds of firms suggests that investments marginal to the interest rate are or have been negligible.

to bring the entrepreneurial desire for flexibility into a theoretical model, a beneficial modification since the typical businessman usually desires not only larger profits but also protection against uncertainty as evidenced, say, by a certain balance sheet structure. In other words, if uncertainty about the future exists, a premium is placed on being able to adapt to changing circumstances.[4]

Of course, all investment theories taking uncertainty into account will contain, explicitly or implicitly, some theory of expectations. These theories usually fall into two distinct categories, both of which are exemplified by the utility approach. In the first category, a set of objectives (utility or profit maximization) are characterized as the goals of behavior but in a very broad, general way. In general, these theories would have the entrepreneur maximizing either utility or profits as before, but in terms of the parameters of a probability distribution.[5] In the second category, a sub-

[4] The idea was first suggested by Jacob Marschak, "Money and the Theory of Assets," *Econometrica*, VI (October 1938), 311–325. The importance of liquidity as manifested in asset and liability composition, however, was suggested by Michael Kalecki, "The Principle of Increasing Risk," *Economica*, N. S., IV (November 1937), 440–447. Leonid Hurwicz, "Theory of the Firm and of Investment," *Econometrica*, XIV (April 1946), 109–136, extended and developed the Marschak and Kalecki ideas. Also see Lawrence R. Klein, *Economic Fluctuations in the United States, 1921–1941* (New York, 1950), Friedrich A. Lutz and Vera C. Lutz, *The Theory of Investment of the Firm* (Princeton, 1951), and Kenneth E. Boulding, *A Reconstruction of Economics* (New York, 1950).

[5] For instance, Evsey D. Domar and Richard A. Musgrave, "Proportional Income Taxation and Risk-Taking," *Quarterly Journal of Economics*, LVIII (May 1944), 388–422; Albert G. Hart, *Anticipation, Uncertainty, and Dynamic Planning* (Chicago, 1948); Lutz and Lutz, pp. 179–182; Gerhard Tintner, "A Contribution to the Non-Static Theory of Production," *Studies in Mathematical Economics and Econometrics* (Chicago, 1942), pp. 92–109; Charles F. Roos, "A Dynamical Theory of Economics," *Journal of Political Economy*, XXXV (October 1927), 632–656; William W. Cooper, "Theory of the Firm — Some Suggestions for Revision," *American Economic Review*, XVI (December 1949), 1204–1232; and Hurwicz (above, note 4). For excellent summary discussions of decision making under uncertainty, see C. R. Jung, "Business Expectations and Plant Expansion with Special Reference to the Rubber Industry," unpubl. diss. (Ohio State, 1953), or R. S. Weckstein, "On the Use of the Theory of Probability in Economics," *Review of Economic Studies*, XX (1952–53), 191–198. A slightly different approach has been proposed by G. L. S. Shackles, *Expectations in Economics* (New York, 1949), who denies the possibility of assigning probabilities because of the uniqueness of the typical entrepreneurial decision and hence the in-

jective desire, say the desire for flexibility, is linked to an objectively measurable variable presumed capable of satisfying the subjective desire, for example, a particular type of asset structure. While it would be trivial to suggest the distinction in other theoretical fields,[6] in the field of investment theorizing a clearly different situation exists since subjective utility or subjective profit anticipations depend upon another set of subjective expectations together with their estimated probability distributions — which, in turn, are often subjectively estimated. In short, the link to observable phenomena is frequently omitted. This is so for three reasons. First, several alternative sets of rules might be equally rational decision guides in the face of uncertainty,[7] and these can be made amenable to differential calculus only through the device of "certainty equivalents." [8] Second, there often is doubt about which motivational elements should be combined in the function to be maximized. Third, the constraints in a dynamic situation, like the financial, are not as obvious or likely to be so simple in problems focused on the future.

For these reasons, the second attack on the problem of expectations has eschewed a formal structure and instead has relied exclusively upon the recently observed values of those "expectational" variables which are thought to be watched by businessmen and translated into expected future values. One variant of profit theories falls into this school

applicability of probability theory. Shackles views utility as a function of "potential surprise" which in turn is a function of various outcomes, an unfavorable and a favorable outcome evoking the greatest surprise. Assigning potential surprise would seem, however, to depend in the final analysis upon some sort of probabilistic interpretation of previous experience since the likelihood of an outcome directly conditions its surprise content. Thus, despite demurs to the contrary, this approach seems to be basically very similar to the other theories.

[6] For instance, in the theory of consumer choice, the subjective utility to be maximized depends upon objective goods and leisure.

[7] Herman Chernoff, "Rational Selection of Decision Functions," *Econometrica*, XXII (October 1954), 422–443, and John Milnor, "Games Against Nature," *Decision Processes,* ed. R. M. Thrall *et al.* (New York, 1954), pp. 49–60.

[8] This term is used to denote that an uncertain value (e.g., a variable which has a probability distribution) has been made equivalent to a certain value by appropriate adjustments.

of thought as does, implicitly, the rigid acceleration principle. Such a leap — from present to expected future values — possesses a strong element of plausibility, if only because it seems hard to imagine expectations totally disjointed and unconnected with the present. There remains, however, the problem of selecting the correct variables from among a welter of candidates. Indeed, there is an embarrassment of riches. Despite these cautions, empirical studies require that some account be taken of expectations. The usual solution has been to assume that expectations are extrapolations of present experience. This is probably about as good a first approximation as can be found, since current and recent circumstances are likely to be the best available historical counterpart of the situation in the immediate future.[9] Grounds for belief in the continuity between present and future are further strengthened when consideration is given to objective variables, such as sales or prices, which are among the usual elements of decision-making. These variables are normally highly autocorrelated. In light of a tendency for profits to be concentrated in the earlier years of an investment (maintenance cost and obsolescence weigh against the older machine), it is sensible to pay closest attention to current variables, given the highly autocorrelated nature of "true" decision-making variables.

A somewhat different description of entrepreneurial response in the face of uncertainty is the minimax solution which derives from the *Theory of Games* and suggests that

[9] As Jan Tinbergen and J. J. Polak, *The Dynamics of Business Cycles, a Study in Economic Fluctuations* (Chicago, 1950), pp. 166–167, have expressed the point: "the separation of profit expectations from the entrepreneur's experience appears to be exaggerated. To a very large extent, profit expectations will be based on current facts, in particular on the actual magnitude of profits. . . . There is always a strong and well understandable tendency to extrapolate the recent past and current events into the future." For similar views see George Katona and James N. Morgan, "The Quantitative Study of Factors Determining Business Decisions," *Quarterly Journal of Economics*, LXVI (February 1952), 67–90; Robert Eisner, "Expectations, Plans and Capital Expenditures: A Synthesis of *Ex-Post* and *Ex-Ante* Data," paper delivered at joint meeting of the American Economic Association, Econometric Society and American Statistical Association (December 1953); Walter Heller, "The Anatomy of Investment Decisions," *Harvard Business Review*, XXIX (March 1951), 95–103; and Klein, *Economic Fluctuations*, pp. 27–32, 34–39.

maximum pleasure is realized when the decision-maker pursues a course which minimizes his maximum possible loss. This path, of course, may be quite different from that which maximizes his maximum possible gain.[10] A minimax solution thus implies that typical business behavior is somewhat cautious and conservative; indeed, strictly interpreted, it means that the businessman assumes that the future will be as bleak as possible and he shall behave so as to minimize the consequences. Furthermore, it departs significantly even from most other probability approaches in its implication that strict maximizing behavior, either of expected profits or utility, may not result in the greatest return in the face of uncertainty.

From what has been stated thus far, it is clear that alternative marginalist theories can be interpreted in one or both of two ways — first as a description of how businessmen actually behave, and second as a prescription of how businessmen ought to behave in order to do as well as they can. The straightforward maximization theories are usually based on the explicit assumption that the businessman is always behaving optimally so that the two ingredients have been inextricably blended. While the profit theories of investment are certainly not inconsistent with optimal actions, emphasis tends to be directed towards the description of actual behavior. Game theory, on the other hand, has moved theoretical efforts in the direction of prescribing rules of behavior which will coincide with actual behavior only in certain limited circumstances.

A theory can encompass both actual and optimal behavior when businessmen in fact behave optimally. This distinction has been blurred in traditional marginalist literature but is essential to theories intended to explain actual behavior. While comments on investment theories therefore arise mainly from an evaluation of usefulness in explaining actual behavior, the optimal and motivational aspects of theories should be mutually reinforcing.

[10] John Von Neumann and Oskar Morganstern, *Theory of Games and Economic Behavior* (Princeton, 1947). Also see Kenneth J. Arrow, "Alternative Approaches to the Theory of Choice in Risk-Taking Situations," *Econometrica,* XIX (October 1951), 404–437.

THE ACCELERATION PRINCIPLE

The acceleration principle, rigidly construed, asserts that the change in the capital stock per unit of time is a linear function of the rate of change in output. Like the quantity theory of money, the acceleration principle has little or no motivational content — a circumstance which must, particularly at the individual firm level, be counted as a substantial weakness. That is, the accelerator function simply implies that the typical entrepreneur behaves somewhat like a thermostat, noting when capacity is technically overtaxed and then initiating steps to remedy this deficiency. The theory is therefore simple, direct, and readily lends itself to empirical testing.

Primarily because of this simplicity, however, the theory has had a controversial existence that has led to numerous additions and qualifications of the original hypothesis and assumptions.[11] In fact, the process of revision has been one of the more fruitful sources of new hypotheses in the field of investment theory and this discussion of the accelerator will therefore be centered on these developments.

The most critical and basic of all accelerator assumptions postulates that firms, prior to an increase in output, must have no excess capacity.[12] Since excess capacity is frequently observed in reality, attempts have been made to adapt the accelerator to these facts. The most common solution has been to view excess capacity primarily as a cyclical phenomenon so that the accelerator works in an upswing but becomes inoperative during a downswing.[13] Others, while recognizing

[11] It should be noted, however, that the earliest complete formulation of the problem, that of John M. Clark, "Business Acceleration and the Law of Demand; A Technical Factor in Economic Cycles," *Journal of Political Economy*, XXV (March 1917), 217–235, listed numerous important qualifications that often were neglected in subsequent discussions.

[12] A linear accelerator hypothesis ordinarily assumes constant short-run returns to scale up to some point at which a fixed capital stock will give rise to a sharp increase in marginal costs. When this does not hold true, the concept of capacity becomes fuzzy. In many fields of production, however, the assumptions appear to be reasonably valid.

[13] For instance, John R. Hicks, *A Contribution to the Theory of the Trade Cycle* (Oxford, 1950); Richard M. Goodwin, "The Nonlinear Accelerator and the Persistence of Business Cycles," *Econometrica*, XIX (January 1951),

cyclical overcapacity, go further and suggest that secular excess capacity is often needed for profit maximization in an industry with increasing returns to scale and growing output.[14] Given secular overcapacity, the level of output and the firm's capital stock become the relevant variables, rather than the change in output alone.

Since the accelerator technically deals with only net investment, it might appear unwarranted to suggest that it should also take into account replacement investment. Empirically, however, it is usually difficult or impossible to distinguish net and replacement investment, like for like replacement being very rare, so that a theory which fails to recognize this fact is inaccurate to the degree that the two categories are intermingled. In recognition of this difficulty, two schools of thought have emerged, the first holding that replacement investment depends on the level of output[15] and the second that it depends on the age distribution of the capital stock.[16]

Still another major difficulty with the simple accelerator is its assumption that firms can obtain funds with little or no difficulty so that the desired rate of investment stimulated by changes in output will not be constricted by inadequate finance. Since unlimited financial availability does not exist in actuality, profits are generally the major source of business funds. As a consequence, S. C. Tsiang has suggested incorporating profits into acceleration theory.[17] Tsiang ac-

---

1–17; and Wassily Leontief, *Studies in the Structure of the American Economy* (New York, 1953).

[14] For instance, Simon Kuznets, "Relation between Capital Goods and Finished Products in the Business Cycle," in *Economic Essays in Honour of Wesley Clair Mitchell* (New York, 1935) and Hollis Chenery, "Overcapacity and the Acceleration Principle," *Econometrica*, XX (January 1952), 1–28.

[15] For instance, Clark, "Business Acceleration and the Law of Demand"; Ragnar Frisch, "The Interrelation between Capital Production and Consumer-Taking," *Journal of Political Economy*, XXXIX (October 1931), 646–654; and Kuznets.

[16] Johan Einarsen, *Reinvestment Cycles and Their Manifestation in the Norwegian Shipping Industry* (Oslo, 1938) and Kenneth E. Boulding, "An Application of Population Analysis to the Automobile Population of the United States," *Kyklos*, VIII, Fasc. ii (1955), 109–124.

[17] S. C. Tsiang, "Accelerator, Theory of the Firm, and the Business Cycle," *Quarterly Journal of Economics*, LXV (August 1951), 325–341.

cepts as a truism the basic accelerator notion that more productive capacity will usually be desired when demand presses against capacity but feels that other factors, particularly financial availability and constraints, will obscure or modify this motivation.

In sum, the original and attractively simple acceleration principle has in recent years become complex and rather confused. For the most part, these modifications and additions have aimed at giving the theory greater empirical and motivational substance, but, in addition, represent a response to the fact that the statistical tests of the simple accelerator have not been too favorable.[18] Emerging from the accelerator discussions are three basically different theories of investment: the original theory based on change in sales, a capacity oriented theory involving the ratio of absolute sales or output to capital stock, and a profit model.[19]

INSTITUTIONAL AND EMPIRICAL GENERALIZATIONS ABOUT THE INVESTMENT PROCESS

Many empirical studies of firm investment behavior have been undertaken without reference to a specific theoretical

[18] A summary of these results, as well as those for the capacity principle and capital stock, is contained in the appendix to this chapter.

[19] Recently, the view has been advanced, Harold M. Somers, *Public Finance and National Income* (Philadelphia, 1949) and Richard S. Eckaus, "The Acceleration Principle Reconsidered," *Quarterly Journal of Economics,* LXVII (May 1953), 209–230, that all three formulations are really equivalent. In fact, by using certain highly restrictive assumptions, e.g., that the capital-output relation is in equilibrium, that all functions are exactly (nonstochastically) specified in terms of the four variables, output, change in output, capital stock, and profits, that profits are an exactly linear function of output, etc., a mathematical equivalence between accelerator, profit, and capacity theories can be demonstrated. However, when the investment relations are set up in stochastic form, it is clear that the excluded variables in the different formulations are very different indeed, these excluded variables including such important elements as the influence of liquidity, expectations, and changing technology. Furthermore, the fact that output levels and profit variables consistently yield a far better statistical explanation of investment than do changes in output strongly suggests that the excluded variables are of substantial importance. Apart from stochastic considerations, it is clear that motives geared to expectations or liquidity or overtaxed capacity do not contain identical behavioral implications. All three, moreover, are likely to receive individual consideration in any particular investment decision.

model and with a minimum of preconceptions. The investigators have, of course, entertained *a priori* notions about the decision-making process, but such thoughts, for the most part, have not been rigidly systematized. Thus the difference between the work discussed in this section and that mentioned earlier is primarily a matter of degree; the "model-free investigations" have been guided by *a priori* concepts but in a somewhat more casual, flexible manner. Furthermore, in these studies, direct interview and questionnaire techniques have generally been preferred to strict econometric models. Finally, in most cases, though not all, the discovered facts have been left to speak for themselves, only occasional efforts being made to conceptualize or explain the discoveries in terms of basic psychological, institutional motivations or historical antecedents.

By far the most outstanding aspect of the direct inquiries is their virtual unanimity in finding that internal liquidity considerations and a strong preference for internal financing are prime factors in determining the volume of investment.[20] These attitudes can be explained in terms of three main causes: (1) the disadvantages that arise when a firm extends its external debt position; (2) historical events and institutional adjustments which have made outside funds difficult and expensive to obtain; and (3) the hierarchical structure and motivations of corporate management which

[20] The empirical evidence on the preference for internal funds is extensive. See, in particular, Ruth Mack, *The Flow of Business Funds and Consumer Purchasing Power* (New York, 1941), pp. 259–271; Heller, "The Anatomy of Investment Decisions"; J. Keith Butters and John Lintner, *Effects of Federal Taxes on Growing Enterprises* (Boston, 1945), pp. 62–69; Joel Dean, *Capital Budgeting* (New York, 1951), pp. 37–43; James E. Meade and Philip Walter Sawford Andrews, "Summary of Replies to Questions on the Effects of Interest Rates," *Oxford Economic Papers*, No. 1 (October 1938), 14–31; Philip Walter Sawford Andrews, "A Further Inquiry into the Effects of Rates of Interest," *Oxford Economic Papers*, No. 3 (February 1940), 33–73; and George Terborgh, *A Dynamic Equipment Policy* (New York, 1949), pp. 4–7. Further support, moreover, is derived from the findings of other studies of capital markets and general entrepreneurial motivation. With the exception of Edgar M. Hoover, "Some Institutional Factors in Business Investment Decisions," *American Economic Review* (May 1954), 201–213, however, no synthesis or theoretical integration of these scattered facts has been attempted.

make outside financing asymmetrically risky for the established or in-group.

The inherent disadvantage of using outside debt lies in the fact that all three of the principal sources of long-term external finance — debt, preferred stock, and common stock — have particular drawbacks which do not apply to internal sources. For example, debt always means a fixed interest burden and in addition is likely to involve restrictions on managerial flexibility and prerogatives. Stocks, on the other hand, tend to be a much more expensive method of raising money, particularly for the small or medium sized firm. Being a compromise, the preferred stock combines many of the best and worst features of common and bond issues, implying a relatively fixed dividend obligation which, at the same time, is not deductible as an expense for tax purposes. Conversely, while common stock involves no fixed obligation, its issue often results in control or earnings dilution. Furthermore, the possibility of earnings dilution has been greatly heightened in recent years by prolonged periods of excess profits taxation.[21]

Greatly intensifying these inherent economic disadvantages of outside financing are the institutional and attitude changes bequeathed by the great depression. For one thing, the public, ever since the 1929 crash, has become so much more safety conscious that the buyers of claims have displayed a strong preference for debt over equity, although it is true that the passage of time has apparently begun to weaken the influence of harsh memories. The ever-increasing institutionalization of savings exemplifies and, at the same time, reinforces this trend toward debt. In addition to the unfavorable psychological impact, the shock of the stock market collapse led directly to two significant institutional modifications which have made the equity market less accessible: the bank reforms of the thirties which reduced the

[21] Specifically, the excess profits tax is likely to separate original invested equity from adjusted net worth to such an extent that equity issues become increasingly forbidding, as Dan T. Smith, *Effects of Taxation: Corporate Financial Policy* (Boston, 1952), points out in his comprehensive study of the effects of taxation on financial policies.

flow of funds to the equity market and the restrictions and administrative requirements of the Securities and Exchange Act. Taken together, these developments caused the deterioration of an equity market for any but the better known stocks with the result that equity issue, except for the very largest firms, has, for some time, been a relatively expensive method of raising capital.[22]

The economic unheaval of the thirties also may have hastened and reinforced the trend, begun some years before, toward the increased professionalization of corporate management. In this development, with its strong implication of ever greater divorce of ownership and control, some see an increasing tendency for corporate decisions to eschew debt financing of risky or even remotely risky ventures.[23] The essence of the argument can be simply stated. If a debt financed project backfires and ends in bankruptcy or a substantial loss, the managerial group could readily lose everything, that is, their jobs and connection with the corporation. On the other hand, if the project is successful, they are likely to gain little because of their usually minor stock holdings and participation in extra profits. With slight modification, the same arguments can also be used to build a case for managerial retention and reinvestment of profits. Just as the divorce of ownership and control makes professional management cautious about debt financing, minor participation in dividend payments makes internal or retained funds essentially costless and risk-free from the managerial group's point of view. Thus by retaining profits, the firm can expand, reduce costs, or otherwise improve its position without any concomitant risk of losses for the managers. In short, if debt financing is asymmetrically risky for professional

[22] For data substantiating this point, see Securities and Exchange Commission, *Sales Record of Unseasoned Registered Securities, 1933–39* (Washington, 1941), release. Butters and Lintner, *Effects of Federal Taxes on Growing Enterprises*, pp. 89–116, present a summary and an interesting interpretation of the Security and Exchange Commission findings. Also see Dean, *Capital Budgeting*, pp. 49–50.

[23] For instance, Dean, p. 55, and Robert A. Gordon, *Business Leadership in the Large Corporation* (Washington, 1945), pp. 297–343.

management, expansion out of retained earnings is beneficial for exactly the same reasons.[24]

Direct investigation of investment has also focused attention on the importance of market structure in the decision-making process. The long-recognized existence of oligopoly led to theories of inter-firm rivalry, theories considered an important, if ill-mannered and discordant, adjunct to the analytically more tractable market structures usually assumed in price theory. With the exception of Kaysen,[25] theoretical recognition of market structure in the field of investment decisions has been ignored. Over and over again, however, interviewers report that businessmen seem very sensitive to what is known as "trade position," which is the businessman's term for oligopolistic rivalry.[26] Only the liquidity limitation is mentioned more often. Concern over trade position means that businessmen are driven by the desire to keep pace with rivals and investment is undertaken when and if needed to keep one's standing in the industrial hierarchy.[27]

[24] Many profit theorists have derived the raw material for their work from the institutional characteristics just noted. Since the flow of gross retained earnings is ordinarily large relative to the liquidity stock for a conventional period of time (e.g., a year), attention has been focused on the hypothesis that ordinarily gross retained earnings will set a limit to the rate of investment. Since retained profits fluctuate more than depreciation expense which displays a trend, attention has been centered either on net retained earnings or gross retained earnings rather than depreciation. In this school of theory we may include Michael Kalecki, "A New Approach to the Problem of Business Cycles," *Review of Economic Studies*, XVI (1949–50), 57–64; Jan Tinbergen and J. J. Polak, Kuznets, and Tsiang.

[25] Carl Kaysen, "A Dynamic Aspect of the Monopoly Problem," *Review of Economics and Statistics*, XXXI (May 1949), 109–113.

[26] Mrs. Mack says, *The Flow of Business Funds and Consumer Purchasing Power*, pp. 248–249, of this motive: "One hears a lot about trade position; it is the economic counterpart of keeping up with the Joneses; keeping it means not losing sales to competitors. Whether or not the onward business march will always seem so needful a way to Americans is difficult to say. This is an attitude that, if it changes, it will change slowly and it is not impossible that it will change; in fact, it may be changing now. Even today it is stronger in some industries than in others; the need to get on thrives on the opportunity to do so. . . . Be that as it may, increased sales is still an important business objective; cost reduction through equipment purchase is one way of helping achieve this goal. There are many others."

[27] Oligopoly behavior can of course take many forms. The most frequently mentioned in surveys and other research is relative market shares. William

SUMMARY

Each theory or set of institutional, empirical findings has served to focus attention on a number of important considerations.

Profit maximization theories, for example, have brought into prominence the role of expectations and cost considerations. Furthermore, it is almost tautological that in a free enterprise society the prospect of increased profit will be an important ingredient of investment decisions. Most theories in this category, however, are too general to be useful, except in a normative sense, and tend to ignore numerous features of the investor's milieu that are likely to be important to the decision-maker.

Accelerator hypotheses, in concentrating on dynamic aspects of investment, have impressed upon theoretical work the importance of growth as a determinant of investment. Pure accelerator theories are, however, incomplete since they fail to encompass important institutional constraints and generally neglect the role of expectations and profit maximization. The effort to remedy these defects has led to a number of new insights into the nature of the investment process but it has also meant presenting the accelerator in such a modified and altered form that it often cannot be distinguished from theories associated with entirely different schools of thought.

Institutional-empirical approaches have served several functions. For one thing, they have uncovered negative evidence concerning some hypotheses. More positively, they have stressed the importance of the liquidity restraint. Also, they have suggested a distinctly different motivation for

---

Fellner, *Competition among the Few; Oligopoly and Similar Market Structures* (New York, 1949), has shown that this criterion may conflict with joint profit maximization and, needless to say, the same holds true for individual firm profit maximization in the static case. When an industry "maverick" upsets a stable market situation, we have clear *prima facie* evidence that individual firm profit maximization does not accord with the group-oriented behavior of joint profit maximization or maintenance of relative market shares. The absence of a maverick, however, does not necessarily insure an absence of such rivalry, e.g., in young or dynamic industries, an absolutely stable market pattern may never develop.

investment, a desire to keep trade position, which appears to be of widespread importance in the business community. The main shortcomings of this general approach have been an absence of a theoretical framework for explaining the investment process — although this has not been an avowed objective of these investigators. Until more precisely qualified, however, neither trade position motivation nor liquidity restraints provide a satisfactory theory.

In sum, simple conceptualization of the investment process is called into question, both by conflicting views among economists themselves and by businessmen's expression of their own ideas of the investment process.

Appendix to Chapter II

TABLE 1

SUMMARY OF EMPIRICAL RESULTS FROM PREVIOUS INVESTMENT STUDIES: EXPLANATORY NOTE

A. Interpretation of the results has been done in the following manner:

   1. When regression parameters or correlation coefficients have been used, a "Yes" in the "Significance" column means that the computed values are significant at the 5 per cent level and a "No" indicates insignificance at the 5 per cent level. Numerous regressions that did not report standard errors have not been included in the tables.
   2. Interview, questionnaire, and other analyses that did not use statistical inference have been recorded as "Important," "Not Important," etc., to enable the reader to distinguish quickly the nature of this type of investigation, the results of which are ordinarily qualitative.

B. The tables do not contain sufficient information to permit the reader fully to evaluate the results of these studies, which vary widely in method, quality of research, and quality of data. The purpose of presenting these tables has been to offer the reader a broad, rapid summary of results and not a detailed criticism of each investigator's results.

C. Results by Avram Kisselgoff shown in this Table have been reported in an abstract in *Econometrica,* 1951, as preliminary findings of a forthcoming paper written in collaboration with Franco Modigliani. The statistical findings of Robert Eisner presented in this Table have been drawn from a preliminary report in his unpublished paper, "Expectations, Plans and Capital Expenditures: A Synthesis of Ex Post and Ex Ante Data," presented at a joint session of the American Statistical Association, American Economic Association and Econometric Society in 1953. The study has since then been extended considerably and a revised report has been prepared for a projected volume which is being prepared by Mary Jean Bowman on the basis of the

Conference on Expectations, Uncertainty and Business Behavior held by the Committee on Business Enterprise Research of the Social Science Research Council in October, 1955. We are obliged to the authors for their permission to report on their research prior to publication.

D. Because of an unfortunate oversight, the number of observations listed for the time series analyses in the fourth column of the following tables are one less than they properly should be.

SYMBOLS*

Investment

DGI	=	deflated gross investment
DNI	=	deflated net investment
GI	=	gross investment
NI	=	net investment

Explanatory Variables

A	=	per cent of freight cars less than 20 years old
C	=	ratio of idle to total freight cars
K_1	=	capital stock
K_2	=	ratio of capital stock to car miles
K_3	=	railroad capital stock
K_4	=	generating capacity
O	=	current operating cost
P_1	=	price index of capital goods
P_2	=	price index of building costs
P_3	=	price index of pig iron
P_4	=	price index of railroad capital goods
P_1/W	=	ratio of capital cost index to labor cost index
r_1	=	interest rate
r_2	=	share yield
t	=	trend
W	=	price index of labor costs
x	=	output
Y_1	=	non-labor income
Y_2	=	profits
Y_3	=	non-operating profit
Y_4	=	unappropriated surplus

*Unless industries are specifically mentioned, the data refer to a particular national economy.

SUMMARY OF EMPIRICAL FINDINGS: *INTEREST RATES*

Source	Dependent Variable	Other Explanatory Vars.	Number of Observations	Significance	Country	Time Period	Estimation Technique
Tinbergen (1938) p. 78-9	Producers and consumers durables (excluding building)	Y_2, P_1, r_2	14	Yes	U.S.	1919-1933	Least Squares
p. 78-9	Pig iron consumption	Y_1, P_1	24	No	U.K.	1871-1895	Least Squares
p. 78-9	Pig iron consumption	Y_1, P_1,	39	No	U.K.	1871-1910	Least Squares
p. 78-9	Pig iron consumption	Y_2, P_1	13	No	U.K.	1920-1933	Least Squares
p. 78-9	Pig iron consumption	$Y_2, \Delta Y_2, P_1$	41	No	Germany	1871-1912	Least Squares
Klein (1951) p. 250	DGI by railroads	K_3, Y_2	19	Yes	U.S.	1922-1941	Least Squares
p. 253	DGI by railroads	K_3, P_4, Y_2	19	Yes	U.S.	1922-1941	Least Squares
p. 255	DGI by railroads	Y_3, K_1, Y_4	19	No	U.S.	1922-1941	Least Squares
p. 256	DGI by railroads	$P_1/W, K_1, Y_2$	19	Yes	U.S.	1922-1941	Least Squares
p. 256	DGI by railroads	$P_1/W, K_2, Y_2$	19	Yes	U.S.	1922-1941	Least Squares
p. 270 (a)	DGI by railroads	W, O	43	No	U.S.	1936	Least Squares
p. 272	DGI by railroads	Y_2, K_1, A	37	No	U.S.	1936	Least Squares

(a) All data in logs

- continued

SUMMARY OF EMPIRICAL FINDINGS: INTEREST RATES

Source	Dependent Variable	Other Explanatory Vars.	Number of Observations	Significance	Country	Time Period	Estimation Technique
Klein (1951) p. 273	DGI by railroads	Y_2, I_3, A, K_1	36	No	U.S.	1936	Least Squares
p. 278	GI by Electrical Utilities	Y_2, K_1	20	Yes	U.S.	1921–1941	Least Squares
p. 280	GI by Electrical Utilities	r_2, K_4	19	Yes	U.S.	1922–1941	Least Squares
J.E. Meade and P.W.S. Andrews (1938)	GI	Not applicable	37	Very slight	U.K.	1938	Interview
P.W.S. Andrews (1940)	GI	Not applicable	309	Very slight	U.K.	1940	Questionnaire
J. Franklin Ebersole (1938)	GI	Not applicable	93	Very slight	U.S.	Various times 1920 to 1937	Interview–Harvard Business School Case Studies
Ruth P. Mack (1941)	GI in Manufacturing	Not applicable	58	None	U.S.	Late 1930's	Interview
Michael Gort (1951)	GI in Electrical Utilities	Not applicable	25	Very slight	U.S.	1950	Interview

SUMMARY OF EMPIRICAL FINDINGS: *PROFITS, INTERNAL LIQUIDITY* *

Source	Dependent Variable	Other Explanatory Vars.	Number of Observations	Significance	Country	Time Period	Estimation Technique
Tinbergen p. 78-9	Producers and Consumers durables, except building	r_1, P_1, r_2	14	Yes	U.S.	1919-1933	Least Squares
p. 78-9 (a)	Pig iron consumption	r_1, P_1	24	Yes	U.K.	1871-1895	Least Squares
p. 78-9 (a)	Pig iron consumption	r_1, P_1	39	Yes	U.K.	1871-1910	Least Squares
p. 78-9	Pig iron consumption	r_1, P_1	13	Yes	U.K.	1920-1933	Least Squares
p. 78-9	Pig iron consumption	$\Delta Y_2, r_1, P_1$	41	Yes	Germany	1871-1912	Least Squares
Klein(1951) p. 250	DGI by railroads	K_3, r_1	19	Yes	U.S.	1922-1941	Least Squares
p. 253	DGI by railroads	K_3, P_4, Y_2	19	Yes	U.S.	1922-1941	Least Squares
p. 255	DGI by railroads	Y_3, K_1, Y_4, r_1	19	Yes	U.S.	1922-1941	Least Squares
p. 256	DGI by railroads	$P_1/W, K_1, r_1$	19	Yes	U.S.	1922-1941	Least Squares
p. 256	DGI by railroads	$P_1/W, K_2, r_1$	19	Yes	U.S.	1922-1941	Least Squares
p. 272	DGI by railroads	K_1, A, r_1	19	Yes	U.S.	1922-1941	Least Squares

Notes: (a) Explanatory variable is non-labor income.
* Profits have been used in the regressions while interview-questionnaire results refer mainly to liquidity.

- continued

SUMMARY OF EMPIRICAL FINDINGS: *PROFITS, INTERNAL LIQUIDITY*

Source	Dependent Variable	Other Explanatory Vars.	Number of Observations	Significance	Country	Time Period	Estimation Technique
Klein (1951) p. 273	DGI by railroads	Y_4, K_1, A, Y_3	37	Yes	U.S.	1936	Least Squares
p. 274	DGI by railroads	Y_4, K_1, A, r_1	36	Yes	U.S.	1935 and 1936	Least Squares
p. 274	DGI by railroads	Y_4, K_1, A, Y_3	36	Yes	U.S.	1935 and 1936	Least Squares
p. 275	DGI by railroads	A	39	Yes	U.S.	1928	Least Squares
Liu and Chang (1950)	GI	K	10	Yes	U.S.	1930–1940	Least Squares
Klein (1950) p. 71	DGI	K_1	19	No-unlagged Yes-lagged	U.S.	1921–1940	Reduced form
p. 73	DGI	none	19	No-unlagged Yes-lagged	U.S.	1921–1940	Reduced form
p. 75	DGI	none	19	Yes-unlagged Yes-lagged	U.S.	1921–1940	Least Squares
Tinbergen (1938) p. 51	GI plus consumer durables except housing	r_2, P_1, r_1	19	Yes	U.S.	1919–1938	Least Squares
p. 51	Iron and steel consumption	none	39	Yes	U.K.	1871–1910	Least Squares
p. 53	DGI	none	14	Yes	U.S.	1919–1933	Least Squares
p. 124	$\frac{\Delta K_1}{K_1}$ Railroads	none	17	Yes	U.S.	1896–1913	Least Squares

— continued

SUMMARY OF EMPIRICAL FINDINGS: PROFITS, INTERNAL LIQUIDITY

Source	Dependent Variable	Other Explanatory Vars.	Number of Observations	Significance	Country	Time Period	Estimation Technique
Tinbergen p. 124	$\frac{\Delta K_1}{K_1}$ Railroads	None	38	Yes	U.S.	1873-1911	Least Squares
p. 124	$\frac{\Delta K_1}{K_1}$ Railroads	None	34	Yes	Germany	1874-1908	Least Squares
p. 124	$\frac{\Delta K_1}{K_1}$ Railroads	None	32	Yes	France	1876-1908	Least Squares
Kisselgoff (1951)(a)	DGI by electrical utilities	$\frac{X}{P}, \frac{\Delta X}{K_1}$	15	Yes	U.S.	1926-1941	Least Squares
Heller (1951)	GI	Not applicable	Several dozen	Very Important	U.S.	1950	Interview
Friend and Bronfenbrenner (1950)	GI in manufacturing	Not applicable	Several thousand	Quite Important	U.S.	1949	Analysis of SEC-Dept. Commerce Questionnaire
Andrews and Brunner (1951)	GI	Not applicable	One large firm	Important Sometimes	England	1918-1948	Analysis of a large steel company
Mack (1941)	GI	Not applicable	58	Very Important	U.S.	Late 1930's	Interview
Butters and Lintner (1945) pp. 58-69	GI	Not applicable	Not applicable	Very Important	U.S.	Twenties to early forties	Firm analyses and SEC industry data
Terborgh (1949)(b)	GI	Not applicable	512	Quite Important	U.S.	1948 or 1949	Questionnaire

Notes: (a) Numerous similar regressions show similar results.
(b) Iron Age survey regarding depreciation.

SUMMARY OF EMPIRICAL FINDINGS: *ACCELERATION PRINCIPLE*

Source	Dependent Variable	Other Explanatory Vars.	Number of Observations	Significance	Country	Time Period	Estimation Technique
Tinbergen (1938) pp.51-3	Tinbergen used regressions including the change in consumers' goods, output to explain the investment or its proxy, iron and steel consumption, for the United States, United Kingdom, and Germany. No standard errors are given, but judging by the increase in the multiple correlation coefficient, the acceleration variable is generally unimportant.
Tinbergen (1938) p. 124	$\frac{\Delta K_1}{K_1}$ Railroads	None	17	Yes	U.S.	1896-1913	Least Squares
(a) p. 124	$\frac{\Delta K_1}{K_1}$ Railroads	None	38	Yes	U.K.	1873-1911	Least Squares
(a) p. 124	$\frac{\Delta K_1}{K_1}$ Railroads	None	34	Yes	Germany	1874-1908	Least Squares
(a) p. 124	$\frac{\Delta K_1}{K_1}$ Railroads	None	32	Yes	France	1876-1908	Least Squares
Chenery (1952) (b) p. 20	$\frac{\Delta K_1}{K_1}$ Electric Power	None	20	Yes	U.S.	1921-1941	Least Squares
(b) p. 20	$\frac{\Delta K_1}{K_1}$ Steel	None	18	No	U.S.	1921-1939	Least Squares
(b) p. 20	$\frac{\Delta K_1}{K_1}$ Portland cement	None	19	Yes	U.S.	1920-1939	Least Squares
(b) p. 20	$\frac{\Delta K_1}{K_1}$ Zinc	None	15	No	U.S.	1925-1940	Least Squares
(b) p. 20	$\frac{\Delta K_1}{K_1}$ Petroleum Refining	None	20	Yes	U.S.	1921-1941	Least Squares
(b) p. 20	$\frac{\Delta K_1}{K_1}$ Paper and paper board	None	10	Yes	U.S.	1927-1937	Least Squares

Notes: (a) Tinbergen found the regression coefficients to be lower than those required by the rigid acceleration principle.
(b) Both variables measured in capacity units.

- continued

SUMMARY OF EMPIRICAL FINDINGS: *ACCELERATION PRINCIPLE*

Source	Dependent Variable	Other Explanatory Vars.	Number of Observations	Significance	Country	Time Period	Estimation Technique
Eisner (1953b) (a) pp. 9-10	$GI \div K_1$	None	254	Yes	U.S.	1950	Least Squares
(a) p. 13	$GI \div K_1$; Machinery Inv.	None	68	Yes	U.S.	1950	Least Squares
(a) p. 13	$GI \div K_1$; Other Durables Goods	None	55	Yes	U.S.	1950	Least Squares
(a) p. 13	$GI \div K_1$; Textiles and Apparel	None	22	No	U.S.	1950	Least Squares
(a) p. 13	$GI \div K_1$; Food, alcoholic beverages and tobacco	None	23	No	U.S.	1950	Least Squares
(a) p. 13	$GI \div K_1$; All other non-durables	None	49	Yes	U.S.	1950	Least Squares
(a) p. 13	$GI \div K_1$; Utilities, Transportation, other non-mfgr.	None	36	No	U.S.	1950	Least Squares
(b) p. 15	$GI \div K_1$	None	254	Yes	U.S.	1950	Least Squares
(b) p. 19	$GI \div K_1$	None	244	Yes	U.S.	1949	Least Squares
(b) p. 19	$GI \div K_1$; Small firms	None	56	No	U.S.	1949	Least Squares
(b) p. 19	$GI \div K_1$; Medium firms	None	118	No	U.S.	1949	Least Squares
(b) p. 19	$GI \div K_1$; Large firms	None	70	Yes	U.S.	1949	Least Squares

Notes: (a) McGraw-Hill sample survey data. Independent variable = $\frac{\Delta X}{X}(t-1)$.
(b) Independent variable is current year's change in sales.

continued

SUMMARY OF EMPIRICAL FINDINGS: *ACCELERATION PRINCIPLE*

Source	Dependent Variable	Other Explanatory Vars.	Number of Observations	Significance	Country	Time Period	Estimation Technique
Eisner (1953b) (a) p. 39	$GI \div K_1$	None	251	Yes	U.S.	1949	Least Squares
(b) p. 39	$GI \div K_1$	None	258	Yes	U.S.	1950	Least Squares
(a) p. 39	$GI \div K_1$	$Y_2 \div K_1$	251	No	U.S.	1949	Least Squares
(b) p. 39	$GI \div K_1$	$Y_2 \div K_1$	258	Yes	U.S.	1950	Least Squares
Manne (1945)	$\frac{\Delta K_1}{K_1}$ Railroads	C	20	No	U.S.	1919-1939	Least Squares
Kisselgoff (c)(d) (1951)	DGI of Electrical Utilities	None	15	Unlagged–Yes Lagged–Yes	U.S.	1926-1941	Least Squares
(c)	DGI of Electrical Utilities	$Y_2, t, \frac{X}{P_1}$	15	Yes	U.S.	1926-1941	Least Squares
(e)	$GI \div X$	None	28	Unlagged–No Lagged–No	U.S.	1940	Least Squares
Kuznets (1935) (f)	New orders for railroad cars	Not applicable	39	Not Important	U.S.	1891-1930	Time Series Inspection

Notes: (a) Independent variable = $\frac{\Delta X}{Y}(t)$ (b) Independent variable = $\frac{\Delta X}{Y}(t-1)$

(c) Independent variable = $\frac{\Delta X}{P_1}$ (d) Other similar regressions showed similar results.

(e) Independent variable is change in capacity utilization.

(f) Explanatory variable is car miles.

SUMMARY OF EMPIRICAL FINDINGS: OUTPUT

Source	Dependent Variable	Other Explanatory Vars.	Number of Observations	Significance	Country	Time Period	Estimation Technique
Klein (1950) (a) p. 112	NI	K_1	20	Unlagged-Yes Lagged-Yes	U.S.	1921-1941	Least Squares
Liu and Chang (1951)	GI	Y_2	10	Yes	U.S.	1930-1940	Least Squares
Katona and Morgan (1952) p. 84	NI by large manufacturing firms	Not applicable	109	Quite Important	U.S. (Mich.)	1950	Interview
Gort (1951)	GI by electrical utilities	Not applicable	22	Quite Important	U.S.	1920-1945	Interview
Friend and Bronfenbrenner (1950)	GI	Not applicable	Several thousand firms	Quite Important	U.S.	1948-1949	Analysis of SEC Dept. Commerce surveys
Andrews and Brunner (1951)	GI	Not applicable	One firm: 30 years	Important	England	1918-1948	Analysis of large steel firm
O.J. Firestone (1951) p. 35 cited Eisner (1953a)	GI	Not applicable	17,000	Important in some situations only	Canada	1950-1951	Questionnaire
Leontief (1951) p. 312	DGI by railroads	K_1, r_1	19	Yes	U.S.	1922-1941	Least Squares
Kuznets (b) (1935)	New orders for railroad cars	Not applicable	39	Quite Important	U.S.	1891-1930	Inspection of Time Series

Notes: (a) Independent variable: Value of national income minus excise taxes divided by price index.
(b) Explanatory variable is car miles.

SUMMARY OF EMPIRICAL FINDINGS: *CAPITAL STOCK*

Source	Dependent Variable	Other Explanatory Vars.	Number of Observations	Significance	Country	Time Period	Estimation Technique
Klein (1951) p. 250	DGI of railroads	I_2, r_1	19	Yes	U.S.	1922–1941	Least Squares
p. 253	DGI of railroads	I_2, r_1, P_4	19	Yes	U.S.	1922–1941	Least Squares
p. 255	DGI of railroads	$I_2, Y_3, r_1, P_1/W$	19	Yes	U.S.	1922–1941	Least Squares
p. 256	DGI of railroads	$I_2, r_1, P_1/W$	19	No	U.S.	1922–1941	Least Squares
p. 272	DGI of railroads	I_2, r_1, A	37	No	U.S.	1937	Least Squares
p. 273	DGI of railroads	I_2, Y_3, A, Y_4, r_1	36	No	U.S.	1936–1937	Least Squares
p. 274	DGI of railroads	I_2, Y_3, A, Y_4	36	No	U.S.	1936–1937	Least Squares
p. 276	DGI of railroads	I_2, Y_3, A, Y_4	37	No	U.S.	1940	Least Squares
p. 278	DGI by Electric Utilities	I_2, r_1	20	Yes	U.S.	1921–1941	Least Squares
Klein (1950) p. 71	NI	$Y_2, r_2(t-1)$	19	Yes	U.S.	1921–1941	Reduced Form
p. 75	NI	$I_2, r_2(t-1)$	19	Yes	U.S.	1921–1941	Least Squares
p. 112	NI	$\frac{X}{P_1}, \frac{X}{P_1}(t-1)$	19	Yes	U.S.	1921–1941	Least Squares

SUMMARY OF EMPIRICAL FINDINGS: *CAPACITY PRINCIPLE*

Source	Dependent Variable	Other Explanatory Vars.	Number of Observations	Significance	Country	Time Period	Estimation Technique
Chenery (1952) p. 20	$\frac{\Delta K_1}{K_1}$ Electric Utilities	None	20	Yes	U.S.	1921–1941	Least Squares
p. 20	$\frac{\Delta K_1}{K_1}$ Steel	None	19	Yes	U.S.	1920–1939	Least Squares
p. 20	$\frac{\Delta K_1}{K_1}$ Portland Cement	None	19	Yes	U.S.	1920–1939	Least Squares
p. 20	$\frac{\Delta K_1}{K_1}$ Zinc	None	15	Yes	U.S.	1925–1940	Least Squares
p. 20	$\frac{\Delta K_1}{K_1}$ Petroleum Refining	None	15	Yes	U.S.	1924–1940	Least Squares
p. 20	$\frac{\Delta K_1}{K_1}$ Paper and Paper Board	None	11	Yes	U.S.	1927–1938	Least Squares
Manne (1945)	$\frac{\Delta K_1}{K_1}$ Railroads	X	20	Yes	U.S.	1919–1939	Least Squares
Kisselgoff (1951)(a)	DGI by Electric Utilities	$Y_2, t, \left[\frac{X}{Y_1(t)} - \frac{X}{Y_1(t-1)}\right]$	15	Yes	U.S.	1926–1941	Least Squares
Klein (1951) p. 256	DGI by Railroads	$Y_2, r_1, P_1/W$	19	No	U.S.	1922–1941	Least Squares

Note: (a) Similar regressions showed similar results.

Part II

Methods and Techniques

Chapter III

The Sample

THE BASIC ANALYTICAL PROBLEM AND THE DATA MATRIX

The analytical problems of this study belong to that branch of modern statistics known as multivariate analysis. In essence, a matrix of observations on a large number of different variates has been collected; so, with "n" observations and "p" variates there exists an "n" by "p" matrix of data whose information is to be reduced to interpretable dimensions. This and the following two chapters will be concerned with the technical choices associated with the achievement of this goal. Specifically, this chapter presents a review of the sources and the limitations of the sample. The next chapter is devoted to the choice and character of the variables. Finally, the last of the three chapters in Part II contains a brief discussion of the general advantages and disadvantages of alternative methods of multivariate analysis, followed by an exact statement of the models actually chosen for this study and the rationale underlying these selections.

THE SAMPLE: ITS ORIGINS AND BIASES

Initially, the sample included five years of observation, 1946 through 1950, on slightly less than 750 firms in twelve manufacturing industries[1] whose securities were registered with the Securities and Exchange Commission. Thus the basic sample contained about 3,750 observations.[2] The limitation

---

[1] Textiles, chemicals, petroleum, rubber, clothing, pulp and paper, electrical machinery, other machinery, iron and steel, automotive vehicles and suppliers, fabricated metal products, and nonferrous metals.

[2] Particular analytical problems that arose in the treatment of the time series will be discussed in Chapter IV.

to registered corporations was dictated by the greater availability of data on such firms. Of particular importance, since this is a study of investment motivation and behavior, is the fact that registered firms must submit annually the Securities and Exchange Commission Form 10-K which contains, among other items, separate reporting of new and used investment goods purchased during the previous year. By the very nature of the selection process, however, the sample is bound from the beginning to have certain biases as a sample of the larger universe of all corporations. Furthermore, for a number of inevitable and good reasons, even this sample had to be reduced. For the most part, these reasons can be placed in two general categories: (1) cases where crucial information was not obtainable on many of the variables; and (2) instances where firms had exceptional experiences, like a number of large mergers, in the historical period under study.

The first category of exclusion is primarily due to accounting peculiarities found in the independent variables used in the study. For example, one of the more important reasons for excluding firms was failure to report depreciation expense, an especially common occurrence with the smaller firms that often lumped depreciation in with a general expense category. Similarly, net sales created problems in cases like International Business Machines Corporation and the United Shoe Machinery Corporation, which rent but do not sell their product. Such firms were removed from the sample on this as well as other grounds stemming from the peculiarities implicit in their position as lessors rather than sellers of machinery.[3]

Of the items obtained from the balance sheet, only the property account raised any real accounting difficulties. To maintain symmetry between firms that consolidate their

[3] For example, when the United Shoe Machinery Corporation invests in more rental equipment, an act which would be recorded in the Securities and Exchange Commission investment figures, the firm is actually investing for almost the whole *shoe-making* industry. Obviously, many conventional investment theory concepts, like capacity-accelerator effects, lose virtually all meaning when applied to such data. Further difficulties are introduced by the special market structure of such industries.

property accounts and those that do not, construction, tools, and land were added into the plant account where these were recorded separately. In very few cases did the land component of the property account add more than 10 per cent to the property account value excluding land. Complications arose only in connection with the property accounts of mineral, petroleum, and timber product industries. The confusion in the primary nonferrous metal group, occasioned by the fact that some companies holding mineral deposits choose to capitalize at high rates while others do not, led to highly capricious variations which, for the time being, led to the outright rejection of this industry from the sample universe. Relatively symmetrical treatment of petroleum reserves by the oil companies allowed their inclusion. The pulp and paper group invariably reported timber lands as a separate item where they were of any substance so these were deducted from the property accounts when recorded. A final complication arose where firms leased considerable amounts of property or equipment for production purposes. Such firms were eliminated from the sample. One of the main reasons firms were rejected, however, and once more this held true mostly for smaller firms, was the reporting of the property account at net rather than gross values.[4]

In the second category of reasons for exclusion, those pertaining to special experiences of certain firms, were such diverse items as mergers, large acquisitions of government property, reorganization, and abrupt modifications in productive structure. All of these factors usually cause violent changes in the property account which are not immediately reflected in the values of other variables, and would, therefore, give a misleading picture. In these cases, firms were dropped for the year or years in question, that is, the year or years of abrupt changes, but data on previous and subsequent years were utilized. Similar inconsistencies among different variables for the same firm occurred when the income statement was a consolidated return and the balance sheet was not, and when firms altered their fiscal closing dates so

[4] Actually, this category of exclusions has a better than 85 per cent overlap with those eliminated because of no reported depreciation expense.

TABLE 2

MAJOR REASONS FOR EXCLUDING OBSERVATIONS FROM REGRESSIONS [1]

Industry & Year	Excluded, No Deprec. Charge	Total No. in Sample	Excluded from Annual Regressions Investment Rate ≥ 500	Midyear Closings	No. in Annual Regressions
Textile					
1946	2	40	1	3	36
1947	2	42	0	7	35
1948	2	47	1	7	39
1949	2	45	0	7	38
1950	2	45	1	6	38
Total	10	219	3	30	186
Chemical					
1946	10	79	6	9	64
1947	11	86	6	11	69
1948	11	82	0	11	71
1949	12	80	0	11	69
1950	10	84	1	14	69
Total	54	411	13	56	342
Petroleum					
1946	1	36	0	4	32
1947	1	39	0	6	33
1948	1	40	2	6	32
1949	1	38	0	6	32
1950	1	41	0	0	32
Total	5	194	2	31	161
Rubber					
1946	2	14	0	0	14
1947	1	17	1	0	16
1948	3	15	0	0	15
1949	4	15	0	0	15
1950	4	16	1	0	15
Total	14	77	2	0	75
Primary Iron & Steel					
1946	2	62	3	5	54
1947	3	61	1	5	55
1948	2	64	3	5	56
1949	2	65	1	5	59
1950	2	62	2	5	57
Total	11	314	10	25	281
Fabricated Metal Products					
1946	15	66	6	8	50
1947	16	61	3	8	50
1948	14	64	1	9	54
1949	12	66	0	10	56
1950	8	70	1	10	59
Total	65	327	11	45	269

[1] a. The firms have been classified according to Bureau of Internal Revenue classification procedures by the SEC.
b. While simple correlations were computed for the clothing industry and the radio and television section of the electrical industry, these had too few degrees of freedom to be used in the regressions and were therefore excluded.

TABLE 2, *continued*

Industry & Year	Excluded, No Deprec. Charge	Total No. in Sample	Excluded from Annual Regressions Investment Rate >.500	Mid-year Closings	No. in Annual Regressions
Electrical Machinery					
1946	16	55	6	1	48
1947	17	66	4	5	57
1948	15	70	6	7	57
1949	14	69	1	9	59
1950	17	70	4	11	55
Total	79	330	21	33	276
Other Machinery					
1946	14	141	12	12	117
1947	14	132	4	16	112
1948	14	140	8	19	113
1949	13	137	4	19	114
1950	11	138	2	20	116
Total	67	688	30	86	572
Motor Vehicles & Equipment					
1946	8	62	10	11	41
1947	8	61	5	11	45
1948	9	61	3	13	45
1949	7	63	3	15	45
1950	5	63	1	17	45
Total	37	310	22	67	221
Pulp & Paper					
1946	4	52	3	2	47
1947	5	54	3	5	46
1948	8	53	0	5	48
1949	8	52	0	4	48
1950	6	54	1	6	47
Total	31	265	7	22	236
Clothing					
1946	5	10	0	0	10
1947	5	13	1	1	11
1948	6	12	1	2	9
1949	7	11	0	2	9
1950	4	15	1	4	11
Total	27	61	3	9	50
Annual Totals					
1946	79	615	47	55	513
1947	83	632	28	75	529
1948	85	648	25	84	539
1949	82	641	9	88	544
1950	71	661	15	102	544
Grand Total	400	3,073	124	404	2,669

that the income statement in the year of change covered only a few months rather than a year. Just as with mergers, the year of change was the only one stricken from the sample.

Also excluded were newly organized firms in the first two or three years of their lives. It appeared unreasonable to suppose that new firm investment was, at least initially, governed by the data in the same way as that of established firms since the behavior of new firms would appear to be almost completely autonomous.

To maintain time homogeneity, analysis of annual cross-section data included firms with closing dates ranging from September 30 to March 31. Firms with closing dates after January 1, of course, were included in the previous calendar year's activities. When, on the other hand, statistical operations were carried out on five-year averages of annual observations,[5] firms with midyear fiscal closings, from April 1 to September 30, were reintroduced into the sample since the time overlap would at most be six months at either end of the five-year span.

Finally, the patent implausibility of explaining extremely large rates of growth in capital assets led to the exclusion from annual data of those observations which had gross investment rates greater than 50 per cent of gross fixed assets. Although arbitrary, even the 50 per cent cutoff is a large figure, so that possibilities of bias through censoring have been minimized. Few firms in any one year were excluded on this ground. When the variables were averaged over a five-year period, high values of investment previously excluded were re-entered into the sample. The effect of the most important of these operations is summarized in Table 2.

Although the firm coverage of the original Securities and Exchange Commission industry groups in the sample used in this study is not complete, it is still quite extensive. This is indicated in Table 3, where number of firms and value of investment for 1948 in the study sample are compared to the original Securities and Exchange Commission sample. The Securities and Exchange Commission's estimates on the

[5] See Chapter V for a full discussion of specific averaged data problems.

TABLE 3
SAMPLE COVERAGE OF TOTAL INVESTMENT — 1948

Industry	Investment This Sample ($Millions)	Investment Securities and Exchange Commission Sample ($Millions)	Total Estimated Investment* ($Millions)	Investment This Sample as Percentage of Estimated Total	Securities and Exchange Commission Investment as Percentage of Estimated Total
Textile	198	212	618	32	34
Chemical	640	661	941	68	70
Petroleum	1,839	1,949	2,100	90	93
Rubber	86	89	102	84	87
Primary Iron and Steel	707	690	772	92**	85
Fabricated Metal Products	118	130	343	34	38
Electrical Machinery	242	265	289	84	92
Other Machinery	268	329	528	51	62
Pulp and Paper	229	241	383	60	63
Motor Vehicles and Suppliers	456	408	474	96**	86

*Estimate based on proportion of total corporate assets in Securities and Exchange Commission sample in 1948. See Lawrence Bridge, "Capital Expenditures by Manufacturing Industries in the Postwar Period," Survey of Current Business, XXXI (December 1951), 21.

**The Securities and Exchange Commission has reduced its recorded investment for this industry by eliminating some consolidated companies which belonged to other industries. Our data is a larger fraction of total estimated investment in this industry since we have not eliminated these subsidiaries from our data.

percentage coverage of their sample to the totality of industry is also given. The final column which represents the product of this figure with the ratio of the study to the Securities and Exchange Commission's sample yields a good approximation of the per cent of total manufacturing investment covered in this investigation. The extent of coverage using fixed assets as a measure indicates that all the two digit groupings have more than a two-fifths coverage of their field, while five of the twelve industries have four-fifths or more coverage. In short, the sample appears reasonably extensive.

There were biases, of course, in the original Securities and Exchange Commission sample and perhaps a few more were introduced by the operations just outlined. Inclusion in the Securities and Exchange Commission sample means that the firm has entered the open capital markets which implies that the included firm will be larger on the average than the unincluded. Further, the bulk of our deletions were caused by insufficient reporting which will again bias the sample in favor of large firms. That this is not a serious flaw for many purposes follows from the fact that it is the larger firms that do most of the investing. Ideally, size should have been represented in the sample in proportion to the size distribution of investment outlays existing in the parent distribution, almost enumerating the largest firms and decreasing the sample size in proportion to the decline in size of firms.[6] In fact this ideal is approached for most size strata except the small firm end of the distribution, and even there the coverage is considerable, as shown in Table 4.

An alternative to speaking of a biased sample is to say that we have very nearly enumerated a specific universe. It is, of course, the universe in which the typical firm is incorporated, well established, fairly large, and frequently selling in an oligopolistic market. Strictly interpreted, probability statements are impermissible if we consider our

[6] See William G. Cochran, *Sampling Techniques* (New York, 1953), pp. 65–110. For an optimum sample, strata variance and number of items per strata would also have to be taken into account in addition to sampling probabilities proportional to size (Cochran, pp. 206–213 and 239–243).

enumeration as complete. Short of complete enumeration, the effect is one of sampling from a finite universe which, if the sampling were random, would imply a narrower confidence region than that associated with samples drawn from an infinite universe. It can be argued that the lack of randomness and the finite nature of the universe tend to offset one another.

Whatever interpretation is made, however, the computation of probability measures would seem advisable. In short, while they may be bad or imperfect guides, they may also be

TABLE 4

SIZE DISTRIBUTION OF FIRMS IN SAMPLE *

1945 Fixed Assets $Millions	Number of Firms	Per Cent of Total
0 - 4.9	292	46
5 - 14.9	155	24
15 - 29.9	84	13
30 - 74.9	44	7
75 - 299.9	35	6
300 and up	20	3
	Total 630	

*This distribution is based on 1945 gross fixed assets with a few exceptions. It contains about 50 fewer firms than appeared at one place or another in the sample.

the only ones available. For one thing, if parameter estimates fail to pass probability tests, they are not likely to be of substantial importance. At the other extreme, should the estimates prove highly significant, it is unlikely that the biases of selectivity and non-randomness will nullify the findings based on a probability approach. Finally, interpretation of the correlation results by no means depends wholly on a probability finding. The fact that a high correlation indicates small unexplained variation is a useful fact in and of itself, provided that known causes of bias have been taken into account.

THE CONCEPTUAL QUESTIONS
OF INDUSTRY GROUPING

As the gathering of the data proceeded, some important causes of variation in investment outlay were noted that could not be adequately accounted for by any of the variates. Some of these involved qualitative rather than quantitative aspects of behavior and therefore could not be readily measured by the purely quantitative variates being recorded. For the most part these qualitative properties were closely associated with the peculiarities and practices which come to be associated with a specific industry group, for example, production and market structure, trade credit practices, durability or perishability of product, consumer attitudes, etc. There are two basic methods of handling such a situation: (a) stratifying the observations into sub-groups defined by conventional industry definitions; and (b) creating a dummy variable which assumes different values for the different industry groups. There is much to be said in favor of both approaches. We chose to proceed on the basis of the first approach, stratification, in order to facilitate comparisons between industries of the parameter estimates associated with the same variables.

Setting boundaries to industry groups, however, posed a number of difficulties. Since an industry is, at best, an arbitrary concept, any set of boundaries might be picked that were reasonably consistent. It was found convenient and advantageous to proceed along conventional lines set up by the three established government classification manuals: (1) that of the Securities and Exchange Commission; (2) the Standard Industrial Classification, which is general throughout most of the government; and (3) that of the Bureau of Internal Revenue. When the Securities and Exchange Commission data were obtained, they had already been placed on a Bureau of Internal Revenue basis for large industry groupings such as chemicals, fabricated metal products, rubber products, etc. In determining these large groups, the decision on where to put any particular multi-product firm was decided by that product whose value was the largest share of total sales value in 1948. Unfortunately, in large industrial groups, there may be a tremendous range of diversity. The Chemical industry, for instance, encompasses Du Pont and Helena Rubenstein, while the Electrical Machinery industry ranges from General Electric to Silex.

It soon became apparent that the conventional industry definitions established by the government bureaus gathering the statistics would be too gross for present purposes. Above all, there was too much within industry heterogeneity in the capital intensity of physical production processes. Should industries with widely different capital intensities be included in the same sample, the same value of a variable for firms with disparate capital intensities would imply different fixed investment decisions.

Again the difficulty could be handled by defining a new variable which in this case would have to be an index of capital intensity. Optimally, values would be assigned to each individual firm according to the nature of its productive processes. Unfortunately, the detailed information necessary accurately to carry out such an operation is not available. As an alternative, we broke the industry groups into their component smaller industries and then regrouped until statistically insignificant differences in the central tendency of capital intensity were found for all classifications. The specific procedure was as follows. Each large (two-digit) industry was set up with its constituent small (three-digit) industries as column components.[7] A 5 per cent level of significance was then used with the F or variance ratio to test the homogeneity of the column means. If the test led to the rejection of the null hypothesis of no differences between the means, the small industry with the largest deviation from the grand mean was rejected and the F statistic recomputed. This process was continued until the null hypothesis that the small industry means did not differ significantly could

---

[7] In the parlance of classification manuals, large industry groupings are referred to as two-digit industries, the small industry groups as three-digit industries. In this work the small (three-digit) industry definitions of the Securities and Exchange Commission have been followed and although not identical with those of the Standard Industrial Classification or the Bureau of Internal Revenue, they are sufficiently close for most practical purposes.

TABLE 5
RECLASSIFIED INDUSTRY GROUPS

Bureau of Internal Revenue Two Digit Industry	Reclassified Industry	Component Securities and Exchange Commission Three Digit Industries
26 Pulp and Paper	Pulp and Paper	231 Pulp and Paper
28 Chemicals and Products	Light Chemicals	261 Cleaning, Polishing Preparations and Household Disinfectants 271 Paints and Varnishes 272 Vegetable Oils 281 Drugs and Medicines 282 Toilet Preparations 283 Soap
22 Textiles 29 Petroleum 30 Rubber 28 Chemicals	Heavy Chemicals	191 Yarn Mills (synthetic fibres) 251 Chemicals 251 Chemicals 251 Chemicals 252 Potash 253 Fertilizer 351 Non-ferrous Metals 466 Vulcanized Fibre and Misc. Fabricated Plastics
29 Petroleum	Petroleum	291 Oil Refiners and Distributors with Producing Facilities
30 Rubber	Rubber	301 Tires and Tubes 302 Rubber Products - Misc. 303 Rubber-Asbestos Products
33 (43) Basic Iron and Steel	Heavy Steel	341 Pig Iron Producers 342a Steel Producers with Blast Furnaces 342b Steel Producers without Blast Furnaces 343 Rolling Mills without Steel Making Facilities 344 Iron and Steel Foundry Products 345a Iron and Steel Forgings 412 Railroad Parts and Equipment
33 (43) Basic Iron and Steel 34 Metal Products	Metal Products	433 Parts and Accessories-Motor Vehicles 352 Non-ferrous Metal Products-Producers and Fabricators 349 Steel-Wire, Springs and Rope 363 Metal Working Machinery 261 Cleaning, Polishing Preparations and Household Disinfectants 325 Heating, Air Conditioning and Plumbers Supplies 327 Locks and Builders Hardware 328 Building Materials and Equipment-Misc. 343 Rolling Mills without Steel Making Facilities 345b Misc. Iron and Steel Products 347 Bolts, Nuts and Rivets 346 Metal Stamping, Coating and Plating 349 Steel-Wire, Springs and Rope 352 Non-ferrous Metal Products-Producers and Fabricators

THE SAMPLE

		367 General Industrial Machinery and Equipment
		382 Electrical Supplies and Equipment
		395 Household Machines
		397 Household Utensils and Table Cutlery
		431 Frames, Bodies and Wheels- Motor Vehicles
		433 Parts and Accessories- Motor Vehicles
		471 Metal and Glass Containers
35 Other Machinery		369 Ball and Roller Bearings
36 Electrical Machinery		352 Non-ferrous Metal Products- Fabricators and Producers
	Other Machinery	
35 Non-electrical Machinery		361 Construction, Mining and Related Equipment
		362 Engines and Turbines
		364a Printing Trades Machinery
		364b Food Trades Machinery
		366 Special Industry Machinery
		367 General Industry Machinery and Equipment
		368 Automobile Service Station Equipment
		371 Agricultural Machinery and Tractors
36 Electrical Machinery		363 Metal Working Machinery
47 Automotive and Suppliers		362 Engines and Suppliers
	Light Electrical Machinery	
35 Non-electrical Machinery		391 Office Machines and Equipment
36 Electrical Machinery		383 Batteries
		412 Railroad Parts and Equipment
		433 Parts and Accessories - Motor Vehicles
		462 Radio and Television and Equipment
	Heavy Electrical Machinery	
37 Electrical Machinery		382 Electrical Supplies and Equipment
	Vehicles and Suppliers	
35 Non-electrical Machinery		432 Pistons, Piston Rings and Bushings
		367 General Industrial Machinery and Equipment
47 Automobiles and Suppliers		421 Automobiles
		422 Commercial Cars and Trucks
		431 Frames, Bodies and Wheels - Motor Vehicles
		432 Pistons, Piston Rings and Bushings
		433 Parts and Accessories - Motor Vehicles
		434 Trailers
	Consumer Durables	
34 Metal Products		326 Household Ranges and Stoves
		476 Safety Razors
35 Other Machinery		325 Heating, Air Conditioning Equipment and Plumbers Supplies
		395 Household Machines
36 Electrical Machinery		396 Household Appliances
		397 Household Utensils and Table Cutlery
	Machine Tools	
34 Metal Products		363 Metal Working Machinery
	Basic Textiles	
22 Textiles		171 Textile Fabrics
	Other Textiles	
22 Textiles		181 Carpets, Rugs and Other Floor Coverings
		201 Hosiery

not be rejected.[8] Later the small industries which had been rejected from their original two-digit classifications were regrouped, wherever possible, with fellows of like intensity and products. In this way, the number of industry groups was expanded from the original eleven to seventeen, so, essentially, capital intensity influences have been isolated, at least partially, by using a finer industry stratification. The results, that is, the revised limits set for the large industry groups, are shown in Table 5.

THE UNIT OF OBSERVATION AND SOME GENERAL PROPERTIES OF CROSS-SECTION SAMPLES

In addition to the non-trivial questions of reliability and availability just discussed, two considerations will generally determine the selection of data for any study: (1) the nature of the hypothesis to be tested; and (2) the characteristics of available statistical models. A hypothesis usually will set limits to the categories of data that can be used and sometimes will determine the exact series within a category. For example, when testing a consumption-income hypothesis, an investigator might decide on the basis of existing knowledge that personal income after taxes and personal consumption expenditures are the two sets of information to relate. On the basis of the hypothesis alone one could go no further.

At this point statistical considerations must enter since there are almost always a variety of universes representing the variables chosen. These universes can be classified and cross-classified by a series of characteristics, sociological attributes, etc. If the hypothesis has been narrowed down to cover just a few of these universes, the area of discretionary selection will be reduced but usually not eliminated.

The firm, of course, is not the smallest or the largest potentially appropriate unit for an investment study: such units would start with the machine and go from there, in an as-

---

[8] While this procedure lacks the elegance and precision of that proposed by John W. Tukey in "Comparing Individual Means in the Analysis of Variance," *Biometrics*, V (June 1949), 99–114, essentially the same results are obtained.

cending hierarchy, to processes, plants, the firm, the industry, and finally the sector. It would be of great interest to work with units smaller than the firm but several considerations counseled against such a course of action. The explicit purpose of this study is to test hypotheses concerning investment decisions; these for the most part are made at the firm level. Furthermore, financial considerations figure prominently in most modern investment hypotheses and allocating monetary variables such as profits or cash assets to any one process or piece of equipment is an impossibility. Given this decision not to use a smaller unit of observation, all investment and supporting data refer to a consolidated statement of the firm's position. Only in the case of the very largest firms, where decision-making is frequently decentralized, could this prove a serious drawback. For all except this handful, the consolidated statements should be the most accurate representation of the situation existing at the point of actual decision.[9]

These then were the reasons, mainly economic in origin, for using the firm as the particular unit of observation. In contrast, the primary rationale for using a cross-section sample in preference to other alternatives rests as much on statistical as on economic grounds. In fact, the major reason for using cross sections was to better meet the underlying assumptions of the available probability models. Specifically, micro data are much less likely to grossly violate the assumption of independence in successive observations, or to be damagingly collinear, or to require simultaneous equation techniques because of interdependencies between error terms and explanatory variables.

A further advantage lies in the greater likelihood of stability in the universe from which the sample values are drawn, since only a few rather than the usual fifteen or twenty years are involved. It has sometimes been argued that if only longer time series were available, say with fifty to one hundred or more observations, meaningful estimates

[9] Some economists who have studied large firm behavior are convinced that the capital budget is almost invariably controlled at the center, while production and marketing problems are more decentralized.

could be made from such data. Insofar as these series are composed of annual observations, it is absurd in all but the rarest instance to suppose that the qualitative content of the included variables has remained unchanged, or for that matter, the relative importance of included and excluded variables has remained invariant over time. Tastes, preferences, production techniques, market structure are just a few of the many factors whose changes over time will be sufficient to invalidate the presumption of stable structure upon which statistical estimates using aggregate time series are based.

The use of cross sections based on one or a few years also permits the statistician to sharply augment his supply of recent information relative to that available in time series. For example, with forty observations *per annum* pooled for three years, the investigator who has reason to believe that institutional or structural changes have been occurring can drop the earliest year, incorporate the latest year's observations, and recompute the parameters. Speaking roughly, the investigator can refresh one-third of his information in any one year. An investigator with a twenty-item time series could, by a similar procedure, garner only 5 per cent new information.

The two previous points are just special illustrations of the general advantages that accrue to cross sections because of their disaggregative nature. Aggregation usually affects the structure of time series, obscuring compositional shifts and suppressing data on the sampling distributions of the observations. Similarly, when predicting with aggregates, it must be assumed that the relative proportion between the component elements will in the future be the same as they were on the average during the period in which parameters were estimated. Furthermore, the use of micro data widens the scope of the information that can be applied. For one thing, variables especially pertinent to any one industry may be meaningless with reference to others. Analogously, there is a great deal of existing information about the special characteristics of certain markets and industries which can be used to interpret the results observed on individual firm basis.

Despite these many desirable properties, it must be recognized that cross-section data cannot be used to test some hypotheses of great importance in economics. In particular, variables that change only over time, such as prices, are not subject to measurement on a cross-section basis — just as variables which differ between individuals but not over time cannot be subjected to tests with time series data. Some of these variables will be investigated in Chapter XI. The advantages of micro data, however, would seem to far outweigh the disadvantages.

SUMMARY

The basic analytical problem of this study has been set forth as that typically associated with the statistical subject of multivariate analysis; that is, reducing and interpreting the data embodied in a matrix of "n" observations on "p" variates. In this chapter we have discussed the nature and character of the observation dimension of this matrix.

We found that our data as a sample of the universe of manufacturing firms would be biased in the following important senses: (1) it includes only corporations and registered ones at that; (2) it has absolutely no representatives from certain important industries in the manufacturing sector; (3) it includes few truly small firms; (4) it excludes from the annual data those firms which are expanding most rapidly; (5) it does not contain firms which acquired the bulk of their assets at postwar surplus sales; (6) it ignores firms which lease most of their equipment; and (7) it does not include firms which rent rather than sell their products. These considerations limit the generality of any conclusions or findings that will later be reported. Despite the nonrandom nature of the sampling procedure, it was felt that a probability approach should be adopted to the interpretation of the results even though admitting that the data do not perfectly fit the usual statistical models. Such perfection is rarely if ever obtained and a probabilistic approach at the very least requires a rigor and consistency in the proceedings that at least should guarantee against the graver offenses of more casual empiricism.

Furthermore, the properties of cross-section samples are such that, at the least, less violence is done to the underlying statistical assumptions than is the case with time series data. Cross-section samples also enable the investigator to discover regularities which would be obscured by aggregation and to bring a good deal of additional knowledge to bear on the testing of most economic hypotheses.

Chapter IV

The Variables

PROBLEMS OF SELECTION: GENERAL NATURE AND SCOPE

In the variate dimension of the basic data matrix, it was necessary to choose between a multiplicity of available possibilities. These choices were, of course, extraordinarily crucial since they determined the basic ingredients of the final hypotheses or models to be tested.

To be explicit, descriptive data for every included firm were initially collected on the following accounting values: (1) new equipment purchases; (2) used equipment purchases; (3) total assets; (4) gross fixed assets; (5) depreciation reserves; (6) current assets; (7) inventories; (8) current liabilities; (9) total tax liabilities; (10) short-term bank debt; (11) accounts payable; (12) long-term bank and mortgage liabilities, (13) tax note holdings; (14) bonded debt; (15) total paid-in capital; (16) total capital surplus which was defined to include all special reserves for contingencies, inventory losses, and similar items; (17) total net sales; (18) allowances for depreciation; (19) net operating profits; (20) estimated current income tax liability; (21) net income to surplus; and (22) total cash dividend declarations for the current year.

Considering such possibilities as non-linearities, joint functions, and distributed time lags, these twenty-two values obviously could be assembled in a number of different combinations that would yield many more than twenty-two possible variables for final analysis. Such a number, however, is probably far more than is necessary and certainly more than could be handled conveniently in any statistical model.

Therefore the number was pared on the basis of: (1) existing knowledge of the system; (2) general theoretical considerations; and (3) additional empirical information that was gathered by performing preliminary analysis of the data. This chapter describes these procedures in detail and provides a summary of the accounting and measurement characteristics of the variables finally selected.

THE SELECTION PROCESS

In any econometric study there are usually distinct clusters of closely related variables defined by the various hypotheses under test. For example, in the present study such clusters are formed by the liquidity, accelerator, age of capital, market share, profit expectation, and size of firm hypotheses. While within each of these clusters further sub-classification is often possible, there are, in most instances, still a number of variables which will represent any given hypothesis. Consider for illustrative purposes the two distinct sub-universes of liquidity hypotheses, those associated with stocks and those associated with flows, each of which has a number of possible measures. On the one hand, liquidity stocks could be represented by any one of the following: cash, cash and government bonds, cash and government bonds and other marketable securities, cash and government bonds and other marketable securities and accounts receivable, all of the above plus inventories, and any combination of the above minus various combinations of current liabilities. In the same way, liquidity inflow has a wide number of similar manifestations, for example, gross operating profit, gross operating profit plus other income, operating profit net of depreciation, operating profit net of depreciation and gross of taxes, net income to surplus, and retained earnings.

Most theories will fail to specify exactly which of the many possibilities is most appropriate. Furthermore, even if each of the various measures belonging to one cluster represented distinctly different theoretical concepts, statistical properties will ordinarily frustrate efforts to make empirical distinctions. The common influences often tend to swamp individual differences between the concepts and the forces they represent.[1] Hence, at the conceptual level, variable choice is largely a matter of establishing homogeneous clusters within which selection may be made on such grounds as convenience, accounting properties, and availability. Unfortunately, even after the clusters have been defined and the conceptual problems settled, multicollinearity may remain because of common "between-cluster" influences. In the present study, this turned out to be the case with profits and sales which were therefore analyzed separately.

Once limited to choosing between the representatives of specified clusters, further narrowing was performed on a strictly empirical basis. The procedure initially proposed was quite straightforward: the simple correlations between investment and candidate independent variables were computed and those independent variables recording the highest values retained. A preliminary scrutiny of the data, however, revealed the presence of several properties in conflict with the underlying assumptions of most statistical models, for example, wide differences between observations on the large and just ordinary sized firms that made any assumption of normality questionable. These difficulties and methods of meeting them are discussed in detail in the next chapter and Appendix C. The basic decision, however, was that deflation by a size variable, gross fixed assets, was the best and simplest way to amend the data to conform better with the probability assumptions.

Various combinations of variables were initially tried with four test industries: textiles, other machinery, electrical machinery, and machine tools.[2] Not only were simple additive variable combinations tried but also curvilinear and joint forms,[3] the latter two by using the Ezekiel graphic approxi-

[1] For example, the use of two or more profit figures in the same estimating equation would, because of common elements, usually lead to multicollinearity and meaningless parameter estimates.

[2] These industries were chosen because they represented a wide spectrum of market structures, size compositions, products, durabilities, and cyclical experiences in the postwar period.

[3] A curvilinear function specifies that an independent variable's effect upon the dependent variables changes with the independent variable's *own* absolute size. The joint function is a particular type of non-linearity in which the effect of changes in certain independent variables differs with different

mation method.[4] In addition, lagged as well as unlagged values were tried for all flow variables except depreciation expense.[5] Stock variables were used only in lagged form, that is, their values were taken as they existed at the beginning of the time period. Use of unlagged stock variables would mean hypothesizing that conditions at the end of the current period influenced behavior during the period. For similar reasons, the deflator, gross fixed assets, also was lagged in every instance. Only one-year lags were tried because any greater lag than a year seemed inconsistent with existing knowledge of corporate budget policies;[6] a finer or more sensitive lag, on the other hand, would have required semiannual or quarterly data that would be almost impossible to obtain for most firms.

As a result of theoretical considerations and preliminary explorations on the four selected industries, twenty independent variables, including simple and joint forms, were chosen for further study. These were: (1) current net profits (that is, net income to surplus); (2) lagged net profits; (3) current sales; (4) lagged sales; (5) a capacity measure (to be explained in detail shortly) based on the product of current sales times the 1946 to 1949 peak in the gross fixed

---

combinations of absolute values for *other* independent variables. *Ex-ante* considerations suggested that the sales, profit, depreciation, and age variables are the most likely candidates for such non-linearities in the present study.

[4] Mordecai Ezekiel, *Methods of Correlation Analysis,* 2nd ed. (New York, 1950), pp. 220–258, 268–298.

[5] In the case of depreciation expense it was not a matter of great importance except for the year 1946 whether lagged or unlagged values were used since, under normal conditions, firms do not drastically modify write-off rates over the years. The year 1946 was an exception because 1945 depreciation charges contained large amounts of wartime accelerated amortization not in the 1946 figures.

[6] See Michael Gort, "The Planning of Investment: A Study of Capital Budgeting in the Electric Power Industry," *The Journal of Business of the University of Chicago,* XXIV (April 1951), 85: Joel Dean, *Capital Budgeting* (New York, 1951), pp. 37–43; Ruth Mack, *The Flow of Business Funds and Consumer Purchasing Power* (New York, 1941); Walter Heller, "The Anatomy of Investment Decisions," *Harvard Business Review,* XXIX (March 1951), 95–103; and Martin Segal, "Some Economic Aspects of Adjustment to Technological Change," unpublished dissertation (Harvard, 1953).

assets to sales ratio; (6) a lagged capacity measure, based on lagged sales times the 1946–1949 peak gross fixed assets to sales ratio; (7) current change in sales; (8) lagged change in sales; (9) the ratio of current profits to current sales; (10) the ratio of lagged profits to lagged sales; (11) depreciation reserves; (12) lagged depreciation expense; (13) net quick liquidity defined as total current assets less inventories less total current liabilities; (14) the ratio of current dividend declarations to net income to surplus; (15) the product of current net profit times current depreciation expense; (16) the product of current net profit times net quick liquidity; (17) the product of current net profit times current depreciation expense times net quick liquidity; (18) the product of the capacity measure, (5) above, times net quick liquidity; (19) the product of the capacity measure times depreciation reserves; and (20) the product of the current change in sales times current profits. With the exception of (9), (10), and (14), which were already in ratio form, every quantity was deflated by lagged gross fixed assets before any further computations were performed; in the case of the cross-product or joint forms (15) through (20) the deflator was raised to the power of the multiplication performed, that is, squared in every case except (17) when the cube was used.

The only curvilinear form to be employed involved depreciation reserves; from the graphic applications it was found that when the ratio of depreciation reserves to gross fixed assets was below .55, that is, less than 55 per cent of the assets were written off, there was little influence on investment. Beyond .55, however, the relationship was often very pronounced. Specifically, above the "kink" at .55, another relationship seemed to rule which could be approximated by a straight line. Values below .55 were therefore all coded as zero and .55 was subtracted from all above.

After this preliminary analysis was completed, the simple zero-order correlations between the dependent investment variable (also deflated by lagged gross fixed assets) and each of the twenty possible independent variables were computed.[7] This was done for every industry grouping for each of the years between 1946 and 1950 inclusive.[8] Since there were fifteen[9] industry groupings, this meant that seventy-five correlation coefficients were obtained for each independent variable; in each case these were arranged into frequency distributions for further analysis.[10] If the bulk of the distribution for any one variable was positive, say 80 per cent or more, this was taken as *ipso-facto* evidence that it was worth inclusion.[11] Failing this, appeal had to be made either to overriding theoretical reasons demanding inclusion or further evidence had to be obtained such as the

[7] The use of correlation coefficients in this context does not prejudice the final choice of analytical techniques since the correlation matrix is the point of departure for most multivariate analyses.

[8] It might appear as a proper economy to use the correlation coefficient for the pool of all annual observations combined together in preference to the coefficient for each and every year obtained separately since pooling would cut the computation load by roughly one-fifth. Such a procedure would be perfectly legitimate so long as the annual observations did not form distinct clusters, in which case the pool results would depend only on the average values of the five clusters. In this situation it would be very possible to have five annual positive correlations and end up with a negative pool correlation or vice versa. Similarly, one cluster distinct from the other observations would have an unduly heavy influence on the final results.

[9] Only fifteen industries were used because of the limited degrees of freedom available in the Radio and Television, and Clothing industries.

[10] The shape of these distributions will depend to a minor degree on the weighting scheme employed. Three were tried in the present case: (1) equal weight for every coefficient; (2) weighting by number of observations per coefficient; and (3) weighting by value of gross fixed assets per coefficient. The choice of which is the best scheme depends on the objective. In the present case where the emphasis is on firm investment parameters, weighting by number of observations appears most promising. If quantitative predictive accuracy were sought, on the other hand, the size of gross fixed asset weighting might be superior since the large industries with the greatest stock of fixed assets and doing the greater part of the investing would be more heavily emphasized. Actually, comparison of the results achieved using the different weights suggests that the choice makes little difference, measures of central tendency being particularly unaffected.

[11] Since in general the ex-ante expectation favored positive coefficients, high positive values are spoken of here as a favorable attribute. Of course, in cases where negative coefficients were expected, the standards were just reversed. This procedure does not depend so strongly on "goodness of fit" that significant results are bound to occur a high proportion of the time. Rather, this step gives some assurance that empirically weak variables which ought to be given consideration on theoretical grounds will be eliminated early in the investigation process.

intercorrelations of the questionable independent variables with those independent variables already accepted. High negative correlations in such cases meant that inclusion could be desirable either because the variable actually has a high positive partial correlation with investment once the influence of other variables was held constant or because its inclusion would help reveal the true significance of another variable.

For example, depreciation reserves, contrary to expectation, displayed a strong tendency toward negative zero-order correlations with investment; it appeared that the greater the percentage of equipment written off, that is, the older the equipment, the less investment undertaken. There are good reasons, however, for suspecting that the older the equipment the lower were sales and profits, both of which in turn had a high positive simple correlation with capital accumulation. When obtained, these correlations in fact did have a high negative central tendency. Furthermore, low negative correlations between age and investment were associated with high positive correlations between investment and sales or profits. In short, firms with high sales also had a high investment rate and new equipment; consequently, while the zero-order correlation coefficients between age and investment were negative, positive partial correlation coefficients might appear if each of these variables' impact was measured in isolation from the others.

Thus no variable was eliminated until there was a high degree of certainty that it contributed little or nothing to the explanation in a majority of the cases. Furthermore, it was found that unlagged values were generally superior to lagged values — which agrees with the implications of previous empirical findings on corporate budget policies. The only exceptions occurred with the profit variable in the pulp and paper, petroleum, and fabricated metal products industries. The profit variable was therefore lagged in these three instances. For all other industries and flow variables, except depreciation expense, unlagged values were used. When the whole process was completed, nine basic variables remained for cross-section study: (1) **gross investment** or rate of capital accumulation; (2) unlagged sales; (3) either lagged or unlagged net profits, as explained above; (4) lagged depreciation expense; (5) the product of current sales times the 1946 to 1949 peak gross fixed assets to sales ratio; (6) current change in sales; (7) depreciation reserves; (8) net quick liquidity; and (9) the ratio of current dividend declarations to net profits.

Additional variables, which vary primarily over time, were included only in the time series section of this study. These variables were chosen almost exclusively on the grounds that they represented price effects deemed important in marginalist investment theory. Specifically, they were the interest rate, stock price, and the relative cost of labor compared to capital goods costs. While previous empirical results have cast some doubts on the weight which can be attached to these influences, theoretical interest, as well as the fact that comparatively few disaggregative studies have been made with these variables, counseled their inclusion.

ACCOUNTING AND ECONOMIC PROPERTIES

Almost every variable has its own special characteristics and features. Of particular importance are those accounting properties which condition the economic interpretation of the variables.

1. *Investment.* The investment data, as explained earlier, came from the Securities and Exchange Commission's Form 10-K, which requires the annual reporting of new and used investment goods purchased during the previous year. For Securities and Exchange Commission purposes it is the fact of chargeability to the property account which determines that a piece of equipment or plant is an investment good. This differs from the physical characteristic criterion employed in National Income commodity flow estimates. From the firm's point of view the purchase of used plant and equipment is essentially the same operation and involves similar considerations as buying new equipment; the two have, therefore, been lumped together to derive total

investment for the firm. There are two rare situations in which this procedure would be incorrect: (1) where the firm buys old plants on a speculative basis; (2) where a firm acquires other firms in an attempt to garner an assured market position. No important or obvious cases of the former were detected in the sample; the latter were also very infrequent and when found were treated as mergers and therefore excluded in the particular years of such behavior.

2. *Sales.* Output and sales measure the expectational and capacity utilization effects embodied in current levels of operation and as such represent trade position, expectational, and accelerator hypotheses. Their use on a cross-section basis involves a number of assumptions, the most important of which are: (1) that after stratification by industry groups firms have essentially similar physical capital intensities; and (2) that current prices affect the valuation of sales for all firms within the same cross-section grouping about equally. The industry stratification and regrouping, discussed earlier, represented an effort to satisfy the first condition and would seem to have eliminated the more serious violations. Realization of assumption (2) is less certain since some of our groupings are rather heterogeneous with respect to product. Despite these weaknesses, no superior alternative is immediately evident. For example, physical units might be used, but to be appropriately applied this requires extensive disaggregation; furthermore, in industries where product is homogeneous enough to permit this alternative the price difficulty would never have arisen.

3. *Net Profit (Net Income to Surplus).* This variable has a close and obvious relationship with the sales variable. Indeed, the two are the opposite ends of the income statement, net income being that final or ultimate profit figure left after accounting for all possible costs, non-recurring additions and deductions, corporate income taxes, etc. As such, it is about as pure a current measure of a firm's profit expectations as is available.[12] Net income also accounts for

---

[12] This proposition depends, of course, on the assumption that either the average current profit rate is not far different from the marginal anticipated

a large proportion of the liquidity flowing into the firm during the year. Thus, while related to sales, net profit tends to be distinctly different in a conceptual sense and therefore offers a limited opportunity for comparing the relative importance of liquidity, profit expectation, and accelerator hypotheses of investment. A pronounced tendency for one or the other of these two, profits and sales, to display a consistently closer relation with investment would shed some illumination upon the still unresolved theoretical debates discussed earlier.

4. *Depreciation Expense.* This variable is something of a crossbreed in that it combines both durability and financial factors, two very different concepts since one is primarily technical and the other economic. The total value of a firm's equipment and hence its capital intensity is a function of the durability as well as the quantity of equipment employed; therefore, since firms using "less hardy breeds" of equipment tend to write off more quickly, depreciation expense is at least a limited measure of capital intensity. Just how pronounced this effect might be depends on the extent to which the industry stratification and reclassification discussed in the last chapter accounted for within industry differences in capital durability. This residual capital intensity factor is undoubtedly important in some of our industry groupings, as shown in Chapter VII below. In other cases a marked dispersion in depreciation rates was observable even though physical durability was fairly homogeneous. Such differences seem best accounted for by differences in accounting techniques, maintenance policies, amounts of wartime equipment acquired under accelerated amortization, and, for the year 1946, the amount of rapid write-off grants remaining at the end of the emergency. These sources of variation are obviously more economic than technical and will have a pronounced effect on firm liquidity since depreciation expense is

---

rate or that the two are closely related. In general, the marginal profit rate would tend to be somewhat higher than the average rate since the latter might be lowered to some extent by overcapacity operations on worked-out and inefficient capital stock. With infrequent exceptions, however, it is hard to imagine radical or capricious variations in the two rates.

second only to profits as a source of funds for manufacturing firms.[13]

5. *The Product of Current Sales Times the 1946 to 1949 Minimum Gross Fixed Assets to Sales Ratio.* In order to meet some of the difficulties inherent in using sales as a measure of capacity utilization, an attempt was made with this variable to estimate currently needed capacity in terms of previous peak utilization. Basically, this amounts to using a bench mark in conjunction with ratio estimation techniques, a fact which becomes obvious when we rewrite this variable as $(S_t/S_m)K_m$ where S denotes sales, K gross fixed assets, t the current year, and m the year in the 1946–1949 period during which the gross fixed assets to sales ratio was at its minimum.[14] In short, this variable (which hereafter will be referred to as the capacity variable) is based on the assumption that more or less capacity is needed in direct proportion to how much present sales exceed or fall short of sales in the postwar year of peak ultilization for the firm. Thus, as a measure of needed capacity, this variable, once it is deflated by existing gross fixed assets, becomes a measure of capacity utilization unique to the individual firm and its experience. By putting each firm on an individual basis, it avoids difficulties accruing from different concepts of capacity existing within the same industry. A new assumption, however, is introduced by this changed formulation: namely, that every firm within the same industry achieved approximately the same peak of peacetime capacity utilization between 1946 and 1949. In view of the general prosperity of the period, this does not appear too unreasonable. However,

---

[13] Besides the usual reasons, gross fixed assets as a deflator had the added advantage in this case (and also that of depreciation reserves) of eliminating most price effects. Given the rather plausible assumption that a firm pursues reasonably consistent straight-line depreciation policies over time with respect to assets of the same general type or kind, the numerator of the depreciation expense to gross fixed assets ratio will have the same composition and weighting of price elements as the denominator, except for acquisitions made within the current accounting period and equipment still being used but already fully written off.

[14] The years 1945 and 1950 were excluded as peak year possibilities because of the abnormally inflated sales valuations in these war or national emergency years.

because the peak values could have been achieved in so many different ways (for example, by operating beyond desired capacity, reducing inventories, etc.), some distortions are undoubtedly present.

6. *Change in Sales.* While recognizable as the most conventional of all formulations of the accelerator hypothesis, changes in sales when entered in the same estimating equation with the previous variable (capital requirements) become as much measures of changing profit expectations and trade position pressures as of technical need for greater capacity. For obvious reasons, the accounting difficulties with this variable are of the same kind as those previously discussed in connection with the sales variable.

7. *Depreciation Reserves.* This variable becomes a measure of the age of a firm's equipment to the extent that, within a given industry, firms with older equipment will have a higher proportion of original cost written off the books. As such, it shall subsequently be referred to as the age variable. The primary instance in which depreciation reserves will not be a good within industry measure of equipment age occurs when a firm enjoyed disproportionate participation in wartime accelerated write-off privileges. For example, say a firm has a plant usually good for twenty years which is now four years old and 80 per cent written off because of accelerated amortization; obviously, it could not be expected to behave as if it possessed antiquated, obsolete facilities. Fortunately, such extreme cases were exceptional and were removed from the sample when discovered. It should be noted that this variable, as well as the next, differs from the previous variables in that it represents a stock rather than a flow.

8. *Net Quick Liquidity.* This variable is intended as a measure of net working capital or stock of quick liquidity and equals total current assets less inventories and current liabilities. The removal of inventories was dictated by three considerations: (1) problems arising from differences in inventory valuation techniques were thereby eliminated since it makes little difference whether inventories are recorded at market or cost, fifo or lifo, as long as they are not included;

(2) a certain inventory level is necessary for the proper conduct of business and such basic stocks do not represent assets ordinarily available for other purposes; and (3) the removal of inventories eliminates the possibility of a spurious appearance of affluence on the part of firms caught with unintended inventory accumulations.

9. *The Ratio of Dividends to Net Profits.* This is the well-known dividend pay-out ratio which indicates how much of current profits are distributed as dividends rather than reinvested as earned surplus. It can be used to test certain liquidity hypotheses since firms with a more generous dividend policy, everything else equal, would not be in as favorable a liquidity position and might, therefore, modify their investment plans accordingly. This variable has not been included in any of the final regression models because its influence is extremely irregular. In addition, the fact that this variable is in ratio form raises certain technical problems if included in an estimating equation whose error term is already weighted by gross fixed assets. Consequently, the analysis of this dividend pay-out variable has been undertaken only as it relates to the investigation of manufacturing financial sources undertaken in Chapter IX. In addition, since firms making dividend payments out of negative income cannot be expected to follow a mere linear or symmetric extension of the behavior observed for firms having positive income, this variable's analysis has been further restricted to include only those firms showing a positive net profit.

10. *Time Series Variables.* The theoretical implications of these variables are straightforward and well-known. One expects, *ceteris paribus,* investment and share prices to be positively related, investment and interest rates to be negatively related, investment and wage rates to be positively related, and investment and sales or profits to be positively related. Time series applications were limited to three industries, pulp and paper, textiles, and rubber. The dependent variable, gross investment values, for the interwar years, came from Chawner's estimates, and postwar investment from the joint Department of Commerce and Securities and

Exchange Commission estimates.[15] These were reduced to constant dollar figures with a capital goods price index constructed in the following manner. For the years 1920–1929, Terborgh's estimates of plant and equipment investment were used to weight Fabricant's price indices for each of these components.[16] For all subsequent years, the implicit price indices of the Department of Commerce for plant and equipment were value weighted with current dollar values of the respective components. The two series were spliced and placed on the common base year, 1926, as were all other price indices.[17] Sales and profit data were derived from the Bureau of Internal Revenue's *Statistics of Income*. These were then price corrected by dividing each series with the Bureau of Labor Statistics wholesale price index for the particular industry's output.[18] Stock price figures were based upon indices for the prices of several leading stocks in each industry.[19] For several variables, it was diffi-

[15] Lowell J. Chawner, "Capital Expenditures in Selected Manufacturing Industries," *Survey of Current Business,* Part I, XXI (December 1941), 19–26 and *ibid.,* Part II, XXII (May 1942), 14–23, for the years 1920–1941; and Lawrence Bridge, "Capital Expenditures by Manufacturing Industries in the Postwar Period," *Survey of Current Business,* XXXI (December 1951), 15–22 for the years 1946–1950; and U. S. Securities and Exchange Commission Statistical Series Release No. 1202, December 10, 1953, for 1951. The first source used commodity flow estimates, while the second source used the capitalized expenditures approach, a matter partly compensated for by the dummy trend variable.

[16] George Terborgh, "Estimated Expenditures for New Durable Goods 1919–1938," *Federal Reserve Bulletin,* XXV (September 1939), 731–736; Solomon Fabricant, *Capital Consumption and Adjustment* (New York, 1938), pp. 178–179.

[17] U. S. Department of Commerce, *National Income, 1954 Edition: A Supplement to the Survey of Current Business* (Washington, 1954), Table 41, 216–217.

[18] The profit and sales figures were recorded for all firms filing income taxes reported in U. S. Treasury Department, Bureau of Internal Revenue, *Statistics of Income* for the years 1920–1954. Wholesale price indices for all interwar years came from U. S. Department of Commerce, *Survey of Current Business: 1942 Supplement* (Washington, 1942), p. 30, and for all postwar years, from U. S. Department of Commerce, *Business Statistics, 1953 Bi-Annual Edition: Statistical Supplement to the Survey of Current Business* (Washington, 1953), pp. 30–31.

[19] Standard and Poor's Corporation, *Standard and Poor's Trade and Securities Statistics: Security Price Index Record, 1952 Edition* (New York, 1952): Textiles, p. 92, based on eight stocks; Pulp and Paper, p. 68, based on seven stocks; and Rubber, p. 94, based on five stocks.

cult to obtain information on an industry basis in a uniform manner. In these instances information at the level of total manufacturing industry was perforce used. Such proved to be the case for interest rates and wage rates as well as the previously discussed capital goods price index. For interest rates, Standard and Poor's index of high-grade industrial bond yields was used.[20] Since the covariation among yields for all grades, as well as among most industries, is very high, resort to a single composite index should not prove detrimental. The covariant aspects of composite wage indices among industries are noticeable but not as strong as with bond yields. However, because of limitations on the uniformity of available data, an index of average hourly earnings for all industry was used.[21] This series divided by the capital goods price index supplies a measure of pressures for substitution of capital for labor. Certain unavoidable limitations of these series should be borne in mind. Most important of all, no two series used for the same industry do in fact represent the same universe. While great care was devoted to obtaining as much conformity as existing sources of information permit, moderate discrepancies were unavoidable. Second, the series are of widely varying quality; the Chawner investment series, for instance, because of data limitations, necessarily contains much more guesswork than the sales and profits statistics.

SUMMARY

In this chapter we have dealt with the problem of narrowing the variate dimension of the original data matrix to more manageable proportions. This has meant choosing, from the many available alternatives, just a few specific variables, functional forms, and time lags for inclusion in the final statistical models. In making these choices, reliance has been placed on a combination of theoretical considerations,

[20] Standard and Poor's Corporation, *Standard and Poor's Trade and Securities Statistics: Security Price Index Record, 1952 Edition* (New York, 1952), p. 154.
[21] U. S. Department of Commerce, *Survey of Current Business: 1942 Supplement*, p. 55, for the years 1920–1941; U. S. Department of Commerce, *Business Statistics, 1953 Bi-Annual Edition*, p. 73, for the years 1946–1951.

existing knowledge of investment practices, and a preliminary empirical analysis of this study's sample data.

The following explicit decisions were made: (1) to accept for inclusion in further cross-section analyses seven independent or explanatory variables: sales, profits, depreciation expense, current sales times the 1946 to 1949 peak gross fixed assets to sales ratio, current change in sales, depreciation reserves, and net quick liquidity; (2) to accept the dividend pay-out ratio as a variable in our later analysis of the interrelationships between corporate financial practices and capital outlays; (3) to always lag the two stock variables, net quick liquidity and depreciation reserves, and the highly auto-correlated flow variable, depreciation expense; (4) not to lag all the rest of the flow variables with the exception of profits in the case of three industries: pulp and paper, petroleum, and fabricated metal products; (5) to reject all curvilinear formulations except in the case of depreciation reserves which were coded as zero whenever the percentage of assets written off fell below 0.55 and reduced by 0.55 of gross fixed assets whenever above this critical level; and (6) to reject all joint functional formulations with the exception of the sales times peak gross fixed assets to sales ratio variable. Interest rates, stock prices, and relative labor costs were used only in the experimental time series analyses of the pulp and paper, textiles, and rubber industries.

After outlining the techniques and the general nature of these choices, the accounting properties and economic meaning of the "surviving" variables were discussed. For the most part, this amounted to a list of qualifications or considerations that must be borne in mind when interpreting later results and conclusions.

Chapter V

The Statistical Models

THE CORRELATION MATRIX AND THE CHOICE OF STATISTICAL METHOD

The basic matrix of cross-section data has now been reduced to an observation dimension of just over three thousand and a variate dimension of eight, investment plus seven "explanatory" variables. Furthermore, the observation dimension has been stratified by industry and year so there are actually seventy-five sub-matrices of data to analyze. With few exceptions, all multivariate techniques operate upon the variance-covariance matrix or, in standardized form, the correlation matrix, so the problem is reduced to that of analyzing seventy-five such correlation matrices, which in the present case are all of rank eight, corresponding to the number of variables.

There are, however, many methods for proceeding with a multivariate analysis and therefore the necessity again arises of making explicit choices from among a number of available alternatives. For example, any of the following multivariate techniques might be used: principal components, regression, factor analysis, correlation, canonical correlation, variance and covariance analysis, discriminant functions, etc. Most of these categories, moreover, might be further subdivided, for example, regression parameters can be estimated by many different methods. Each technique, however, has properties which make it uniquely advantageous in particular applications,[1] so that choice of technique will be at least partially determined by the objectives, particularly if these are uniquely specified and known. In addition, there are other matters to be considered such as problems of understandability and interpretation, the availability of appropriate probability tests, and sufficient degrees of freedom.

On the basis of these various considerations, correlation and regression techniques have been used almost exclusively in this study. The particular advantages of so doing are: (1) the statistical procedures are familiar and well known; (2) the interpretation of results is straightforward and permits a maximum use of outside, existing information; (3) an economical use is made of available degrees of freedom; and (4) the probability tests and inferential procedures are relatively well defined and complete. While each one of these advantages may also be present in certain of the alternatives, the combination is not.

Thus far no distinction has been made between regression and correlation models. The principal disadvantage of the correlation model lies in its assumption of multivariate normality, only conditional normality in the dependent variable being needed for regression applications. Also, the correlation coefficient directly describes only the closeness of fit and not the extent or importance of the relation. On the other hand, "identifiable" unbiased regression coefficients will be found only if the error term of the regression equation is uncorrelated with the explanatory variables. For reasons which will soon be explained, such identification difficulties are present in a few industries and years of this study. In addition, use of the regression model implies knowing the direction of causation between two variables whereas a correlation analysis is concerned only with measuring association or

[1] For instance, if our primary objective was to classify firms into two categories, growth and non-growth (defined, say, in terms of unknown future investment rates), discriminant functions would probably best serve our purposes; again, if we wished to *predict* a whole complex of behavior of which investment was but one measure, canonical correlation would be most appropriate.

interdependence while assuming no knowledge of causation.

This property of correlation models is desirable in the present study because a primary objective has been to minimize the number of *a priori* assumptions about the direction of causation in economic relations. In other words, an effort has been made to empirically test the "causation assumptions" wherever possible. Given this objective, the use of regression coefficients, which immediately entails the assumption that the direction of causation is known, would have meant prejudging the outcome. For making such tests, it seems much more logical to use a measure of changes in the proportion of variation accounted for by the various variables rather than a measure of the change in one variable associated with a given change in another. Therefore, most subsequent cross-section analyses are based upon correlations. A strict regression model has been used only in the second to the last chapter when time series and cross-section results have been used in the same model to test the so-called marginalist or price variables, like the interest rate and stock prices.[2] Consequently, this investigation has been conducted in two distinct parts: (1) a preliminary study of possible structural relationships which is based entirely on a cross-section analysis of interrelationships and associations between the different variables; and (2) a testing of the various structural hypotheses suggested by the preliminary analysis. At this second stage, causal dependence is assumed, regression techniques are used, and time series as well as cross-section data are employed.

[2] In addition to a complete résumé of the partial correlation coefficients, the normalized regression coefficients (sometimes called "beta" coefficients), as well as the ratio of these to their standard error, are presented in Appendix B. A useful result from analysis of variance is that the squared beta coefficient is the proportion of the dependent variable's variation "explained" by the particular independent variable, provided that the independent variables are uncorrelated. This assumption is approximately met in this cross-section data. Thus, the beta coefficients provided a convenient further check on the relative importance of the different explanatory variables. Moreover, later work will involve many inter-year and inter-industry comparisons and the standard deviations are very different in different years and industries. Comparisons will therefore be facilitated through the use of standardized regression coefficients rather than the raw regression coefficients.

THE FINAL MODELS

Since the objectives of the initial section of the study are limited to testing and discovering the pattern of interdependencies between investment and the other variables, a traditional least-squares correlation analysis obviously offers the most appropriate model. Therefore, all the partial correlations between investment and the various independent variables were obtained, with the one exception that profits and sales were never included in the analysis at the same time. To have considered both these variables simultaneously would in many instances have led to indeterminacy because of their high collinearity.

The separation of the profit and sales analyses means that two distinct sets of estimates of the partial correlation between investment and the five variables other than profits and sales were obtained. In one of these sets, the influence of the other four variables and profits was held constant while, in the other, the influence of the other four variables and sales was held constant. For the profit and sales variables, only one set apiece of partial correlations with investment was obtained and, in each case, identically the same set of five other variables was held constant.

Supplementing the results obtained for the year-industry groups, similar partial correlations were obtained for every industry group for the five-year (1946 through 1950) averages of selected flow variables (profits, sales, depreciation expense, and capacity utilization) and the end of 1945 values for the stock variables (net quick liquidity and age). Again, sales and profits were not analyzed simultaneously. Actually, the only difference between these models and the preceding applications to industry-year groups is the use of the averaged data and elimination of the change in sales variable. In addition to the industry groupings, the averaged data were used with six different size strata.[3] These stratifications permit testing whether significantly different

[3] Grouped as follows according to millions of dollars' worth of total 1945 gross fixed assets: (1) 0 to 4.9; (2) 5 to 14.9; (3) 15 to 29.9; (4) 30 to 74.9; (5) 75 to 299.9; (6) 300 and up.

patterns of behavior are associated with differences in size, for example, the hypothesis that liquidity restraints hamper small firms more than large firms.

In fact, this is just one illustration of the way in which all of these partial correlations have been used as the basis for further study of the structure of investment motivation by linking observed correlation results to other known facts about the economy and its component parts. Special attention has been focused on the discovery of any pattern in the correlation results and the possible explanation of such observed relationships in terms of "outside" or other knowledge of the economy. The phrase "other knowledge" is interpreted broadly to include virtually all forms of empirical information gained from previous studies or well-established, reported experience.[4] The term designates a host of quantitative and qualitative facts about such diverse matters as the differences in the market structures, financial policies, growth possibilities, and cyclical fortunes of different industries and the character of consumer and producer inventories and assets at different points of time during the postwar period. The disaggregation of the results into industry and year groups is clearly a prerequisite to using such knowledge.

The second stage of the investigation has been less intensive and the results correspondingly more tentative than the previous phase. Information gleaned from the initial correlation analysis has been translated into specific hypotheses which, in turn, have been tested by regression techniques. Variables from the preliminary analyses that showed most promise have been retained and the cross-section estimates of their regression coefficients used as so-called "extraneous" estimates in a further investigation based on time series data for three specific industries: rubber, pulp and paper, and textiles. The procedures employed combined cross-section, time series analysis and are basically those described by Marschak, Tobin, Stone, Durbin, and Wold.[5]

[4] Such knowledge is commonly designated, although perhaps not with perfect semantic accuracy, as "a priori" information.

[5] Jacob Marschak, "On Combining Market and Budget Data in Demand Studies: A Suggestion," *Econometrica*, VII (October 1939), 332–335; James

The principal advantages of these methods are frequently more efficient estimates and the opportunity to estimate more accurately certain coefficients otherwise obscured by collinearities. This approach means, of course, that certain of the cross-section analyses are ultimately treated as regression models and, at this stage, the previous position of no *a priori* assumption about the direction of causation is clearly relaxed. The essential point, however, is that this assumption is only relaxed as seems merited by the empirical information about the structural characteristics of investment motivation obtained from the cross-section analyses.

These extended models can be specified in general functional notation as follows:

Cross-Section Models:

$$[I_t = f_1(S_t, D_{t-1}, A_{t-1}, S_t', C_t, L_{t-1}, u_t)] \frac{1}{K_{t-1}} \qquad (1)$$

$$[I_t = f_2(P_t \text{ or } P_{t-1}, D_{t-1}, A_{t-1}, S_t', C_t, L_{t-1}, u_t)] \frac{1}{K_{t-1}} \qquad (2)$$

Time Series Models:

$$I_t = g_1(S_t, R_t, E_{t-1}, W_{t-1}, u_t) \qquad (3)$$

$$I_t = g_2(P_t \text{ or } P_{t-1}, R_t, E_{t-1}, W_{t-1}, u_t) \qquad (4)$$

where

- I equals gross investment in both new and old plant and equipment;
- S equals sales;
- P equals net profits, that is, net income to surplus;
- D equals depreciation expense;
- A equals depreciation reserves which is taken as a measure of equipment age;

Tobin, "A Statistical Demand Function for Food in the U. S. A.," *Journal of the Royal Statistical Society,* Series A, CXIII (Part II, 1950), 113–141; Richard Stone, *Measurement of Consumers' Expenditure and Behavior in the United Kingdom 1920–1938,* Volume I (Cambridge, Eng., 1954); J. Durbin, "A Note on Regression When There Is Extraneous Information about One of the Coefficients," *Journal of the American Statistical Association,* XLVIII (December 1953), 799–808; Herman Wold and Lars Jureen, *Demand Analysis* (New York, 1953).

S' equals change in sales;[6]
C equals needed capacity as measured by the cross-product of current sales times the peak gross fixed assets to sales ratio reached between 1946 and 1949;
L equals the stock of net quick liquidity, i.e., current assets less inventory and current liabilities;
K equals gross fixed assets;
R equals the interest rate as measured by the yield on Grade A Industrial bonds;
E equals the stock price index for a particular industry;
W equals the relative price of labor as measured by the ratio of labor to capital cost indices;
u equals a stochastic term representing the influence, assumed random, of the unincluded variables;[7]
t equals the time period so that as a subscript it denotes the year to which a particular flow variable refers and the end of year value for stock variables.

In no case was either model executed in its entirety. Basically, the eliminations were made on the empirical basis of how important the variable appeared to be in the partial correlation tests executed in the first stage of the study. All terms were included additively so the functions are completely linear except for the cross-product capacity variable, C, and the age variable, A. Both functions are identical except for the interchange of profits and sales. The parameters of the last three variables, which are essentially price factors that vary only over time, were obtained from the time series analysis. The other variables were analyzed only on a cross-section basis.

STATISTICAL PROBLEMS

The principal statistical problems associated with the application of these models are of four general types: (1) those due to using stratification schemes based on other

---

[6] A subscript t for the change in sales variable denotes the change from time period t-1 to period t.

[7] In addition, it is usually assumed that this variable is distributed independently of the included independent variables and has a zero mean. Furthermore, if this error term is distributed normally, a least-squares estimate is also a maximum likelihood estimate.

than industry groups; (2) those arising from the use of averaged data; (3) those associated with the identification problem that occurs when the usual regression assumption of independence between explanatory variables and error term is inappropriate; and (4) those created by the great skewness of distributions of firm observations which leads to serious non-normality in correlation applications and heteroscedasticity in regression applications. In addition, there exist a number of minor, miscellaneous statistical difficulties that affect the interpretation and use of the observed parameters.

Stratification schemes. The main difficulty with using size or any other non-industry stratification is that the effects of certain important but unwanted influences no longer are held even approximately constant. Explicitly, one cannot so safely assume uniform capital intensity, product durability, and financial policy for a cross section not based on an industry classification. Within a size group encompassing firms from many different industries, all sorts of sundry influences could cause variation in the observed values of the independent variables; some might be associated with causes of variations in investment levels, others not. For example, under such conditions a high sales level could indicate both high-level activity and low capital intensity. In general, broader scatter and lower correlation would be the usual result for most variables. Indeed, there are only two obvious exceptions: depreciation expense and capacity; the former might record higher values because of greater within group capital intensity heterogeneity while the latter would be unaffected since it is standardized in terms of each firm's individual performance.

Averaged data. If all the observations for a given firm were independent through time, the effect of averaging would be an equiproportional reduction in the variance of both included and excluded variables, leaving all correlations essentially unchanged. However, the averaged data results indicate that, generally speaking, the reduction in unexplained variance through the averaging process is substantially more than proportional to the reduction in the variance of the included variables, a fact that is immediately reflected in the higher relative magnitude of the correlation coefficients obtained from the averaged data. One very plausible explanation of this result is that the explanatory variables for specific firms were more autocorrelated than the investment variable so that averaging led to a greater reduction in the investment variable's variance than in the variance of the other variables. In other words, the average rate of investment associated with the average rate of some explanatory variable, say profits, might differ more between firms within a given year than between years within a given firm. Each firm, then, could tend to have relatively consistent high, intermediate, or low associated values of investment and explanatory variables. Around this consistently observed position there will be year-to-year variations, but these will tend to be smaller than the variations between the firms in the sample.[8]

In essence, it seems that for many purposes a time period longer than a year may better reveal underlying behavior than the conventional one-year period. The choice will depend at least in part upon the nature of the economic hypothesis to be investigated; for example, in studies of inventory behavior, the appropriate unit will usually be quarterly or even monthly data; on the other hand, when durable goods and "lumpy" sorts of expenditure are involved and one is seeking an explanation of long-run behavior, the correct unit may be an average or aggregate taken over many years.

The identification problem. Identification difficulties are least likely to occur with the variables that are lagged, that is, net quick liquidity, depreciation reserves, and depreciation expenses. Indeed, it is often maintained that any lagged variable, whether endogenous or exogenous, is essentially

[8] Still another way of expressing this point is to recall that the variance of sample means is equal to $1/n$ times the variance of the parent population, n being the sample size. With complete independence of successive firm observations, n is correctly taken as equal to five and the variance of the means is therefore one-fifth of the population variance. On the other hand, when successive observations are completely autocorrelated, we effectively have only one observation and the variance of "means" equals the population variance.

predetermined and therefore free of any correlation with the unincluded variables. Obviously, such an assumption is correct only so long as there is little autocorrelation in the endogenous variables of the system.

The situation with respect to the four flow variables — sales, profits, change in sales, and capacity — is not so readily obvious although it has already been observed that the use of cross sections greatly reduces the probability of positive correlation between included and unincluded variables. Still, it would be presumptuous to assume that the use of such data completely solves the problem. To say that a high level of current sales creates a high level of investment, and not vice versa, certainly is not so obviously foolish when the firm rather than the whole economy is the basic unit of observation. In fact, it is doubtful whether even General Motors, with its gigantic scope of operations, is large enough so that its investment policy significantly influences the demand for its own goods.

However, in the sellers' markets so common after the war, production, not demand, was the main limitation on sales. Therefore, it might be argued that a firm which made a large investment in plant and equipment would also be best able to produce and sell more goods. Even in such instances, however, it was high level sales or at least the expectation of higher sales which called forth the greater investment; consequently, the hypothesized direction of causation was left basically unmodified, although the correlations would be higher than they would have been in the absence of excess demand.

Much more serious is the fact that even in the absence of a sellers' market, improved efficiency or products arising from the introduction of modern plant and machinery might just as readily cause high profits or sales as react conversely. In such a situation, least-squares regression could yield investment as a function of sales, sales as a function of investment, or neither function.[9] Fortunately, it is much more

---

[9] In subsequent discussion in this section all that is said of sales would also hold for the other flow variables in question, profits, change in sales, and capacity.

likely that direct regression will uncover investment as a function of sales rather than vice versa since, of the two, the sales function will usually be subject to the larger "random" shifts. This situation is analogous to the old supply, demand problem of agricultural economics in which it was assumed that the volatile shifts in supply traced out the relatively stable demand function. In the present case, this means that the observed residuals for the investment function (as approximations of the true errors) should be relatively small as compared with those for the sales function whose most important determinants, consumer income, and prices, will not be included. In short, the variance of the investment function's error term should be small relative to that of a profit or sales function, so that the observed relation is that of the investment function.

Skewness. Corporation data generally follow a skewed distribution in which there are many representatives of small firms and few representatives of the large, corporate giants. This, in turn, leads to such violations of the statistical assumptions as extreme values, non-normality, and heteroscedasticity of error terms. The usual and also the simplest method to eliminate the worst aspects of these difficulties is to use an appropriate transformation or weighting scheme for the observed variables and regression residuals. In the present study, several possibilities were considered [10] and the conclusion reached that from both the economic and statistical standpoint deflation by a size measure, specifically gross fixed assets,[11] was the best available alternative. The deflated values were found to yield both better approximations to normality[12] and more homoscedastic error vari-

---

[10] For example, use of percentage changes, deviations from group means, finer stratification, etc.

[11] Sales and profits were also used as deflators in a few cases where the resulting ratio had intrinsic economic meaning in this form; e.g., the profit realization ratio (profits divided by net sales) and the dividend payment ratio (dividends over net income to surplus).

[12] While it is difficult to check this outcome in any rigid manner because of the scarcity of observations in any given interval of the correlation table for a particular industry-year group, a rough check was obtained by making a Chi-square test on randomly selected intervals of the correlation table for all industries pooled together. Similarly, the total, that is non-conditional,

ances.[13] Furthermore, by eliminating the extreme values associated with large firms, deflation also reduced the possibility of the regression or correlation results being determined by a few exceptional values.

On the other hand, deflation raises the possibility of so-called "spurious index correlation," that is, finding positive correlation between two ratios with a common denominator even when there is no organic correlation in the population sampled. There are good reasons, however, for believing that the results of this study are essentially free from such biases. To avoid spurious correlation, the variables to be deflated must be homogeneously related to the deflator, an assumption which is reasonably well met in the present study.[14]

From the economic standpoint, it is clear that the size deflator should not fluctuate much over the business cycle. Whatever is meant by size, it stretches the imagination to assert that a firm this year is half as large as it was last year merely because its sales or some other flow variable from the income statement dropped in half. Thus, the deflating series should either have a smooth trend interrupted only by changes reflecting fundamental alterations in the structure of the firm or be a constant factor. For similar reasons, the deflator should not be subject to abrupt changes or

---

distributions were checked in several industries. The Chi-square values generally fell between the 30 and 15 per cent points of significance which, while not completely encouraging, were no cause for great alarm. A good discussion of the problem involved in checking for normality in a correlation table will be found in G. Udny Yule and Maurice G. Kendall, *An Introduction to the Theory of Statistics,* 14th ed. (London, 1950), pp. 237–246.

[13] If the constant in the multivariate function equals zero, regressing on the deflated values amounts to weighting the error variances by $1/Z^2$ where Z is the deflating variable. In other words, instead of minimizing $\Sigma(Y - a - b_1X_1 - \cdots - b_nX_n)^2$, the investigator minimizes $\Sigma(1/Z)(Y - b_1X_1 - \cdots - b_nX_n)$, the whole quantity squared, where Y is the dependent variable, the X's independent variables, and the b's regression coefficients. If the undeflated error variances increased as $1/Z^2$, as they approximately do in this study, then F. N. David and Jerzy Neyman, "Extension of the Markoff Theorem of Least Squares," *Statistical Research Memoirs,* II (1938), 105–116, have shown that the least-squares regression estimates on the deflated data are the most efficient linear unbiased estimates. For a full discussion of this point see Appendix C.

[14] Elaboration of these points will be found in Appendix C.

affected by firm differences in accounting procedures, especially those of a purely financial character that have nothing to do with size as such. On both these counts — relative immunity to capricious accounting changes and stability over the business cycle — gross fixed assets was found superior to any other alternative deflator.

Miscellaneous problems. In much of what follows, interpretation of the results will depend vitally upon inter-industry comparisons. The basic procedure for effectuating these comparisons will be to rank or classify the industries with respect to observed correlation values and then test these ranks or classifications by well-known non-parametric methods, primarily rank order correlation and Chi-square contingency tests.[15]

In making these applications, one difficulty immediately arises: How to eliminate observed differences due solely to differences in sample size? The objective, of course, is to obtain from the observed results a ranking or classification of the industries which corresponds as nearly as possible to the ranking that would have been arrived at if the true population values were known. Thus given two industries with the same population parameters, one industry being small in number of observations and one large, it would be desirable to have a ranking scheme which on the basis of sample values would give us a 50–50 chance of putting large ahead of small or vice versa. If the sampling distribution is symmetric, such a result is readily obtained by using ranks based on unbiased point estimates.

Unfortunately, most of the ranks will be based upon correlation coefficients whose sampling distribution is not generally symmetric; explicitly, this distribution becomes more skewed as sample size decreases and true parental correlation increases.[16] In such a situation, there is no scheme which will

[15] Procedures suggested by Maurice G. Kendall, *Rank Correlation Methods* (London, 1948) for rank order methods and William G. Cochran, "The Chi-Square Test of Goodness of Fit," *Annals of Mathematical Statistics,* XXIII (September 1952), 315–345, for Chi-square contingency tests have been followed.

[16] A full account of these matters will be found in F. N. David, *Tables of the Ordinates and Probability Integral of the Distribution of the Correlation Coefficient in Small Samples* (London, 1938).

be perfectly unbiased in the 50–50 sense previously outlined. For example, one could rank according to the best unbiased point estimates which are obtained by correcting the constituent variances of the correlation for differences in degrees of freedom.[17] But, if n_1 (greater than 30 but finite) is the number of observations in the large industry and n_2 (less than 30) the number in the small, and the sample is from an infinite population, as n_2 approaches the number of estimated parameters, the probability of ranking the small industry over the large approaches unity; on the other hand, if n_2 is greater than 2 and finite, as n_1 approaches infinity the probability of the small industry being ranked over the large industry approaches the probability of the small sample correlation being greater than the parental correlation and this will be greater than 0.5, just how much greater depending on the size of the true correlation and n_2.

As an alternative, the industries can be ranked according to the probability that their true parental correlation is greater than zero. This would be done by finding how many standard deviations (for true value zero and given n) that an observed result differs from zero. Using this method, however, as the ratio n_1/n_2 approaches infinity, the probability of ranking the large industry over the small approaches unity. Consequently, this method discriminates against the small industry just as the previous method did against the large.

Actually, the industry orderings obtained by the two methods will be the same, or virtually so, except when the results are closely bunched. As a consequence, it usually makes little difference just which method is used insofar as final conclusions go, the observed rank order and Chi-square probabilities being only slightly altered in most instances.

[17] The formula used is:

$$r^{2\prime}_{12.34\ldots p} = 1 - (1 - r^2_{12.34\ldots p})(n - p + 1)/(n - p)$$

where the r's are partial correlation coefficients, the prime denotes a corrected (unbiased) correlation, n is the number of observations, and p is the number of variables. This formula, insofar as the authors know, is not presented elsewhere but it can be easily derived by the methods outlined in Mordecai Ezekiel, *Methods of Correlation Analysis,* 2nd ed. (New York, 1950).

In a broader vein, some may wonder about the general advisability of using non-parametric techniques which are generally considered less "powerful" than other available tools. Actually, such advice seems unduly cautious. Even when the more restrictive assumptions of the other procedures are fully met, the rank order or distribution free analogue used in this study (Kendall's rank order correlation coefficient) is 98 per cent as asymtotically efficient as the more exact method.[18] Furthermore, since the relative efficiency of non-parametric techniques seems to improve as sample size decreases and since we have used small samples, any decline in efficiency because of non-symmetry is probably offset to some extent. All in all, the loss in efficiency would hardly seem to be substantial enough to forego the computational simplicity of these techniques.

SUMMARY

In this chapter some of the alternative methods of performing a multivariate analysis of a covariance-variance or correlation matrix have been briefly outlined and the reasons indicated why regression and correlation techniques were chosen for this study. Essentially, the choice was based on the fact that these methods are well known and have a combination of desirable technical properties not closely approximated in any of the alternatives. The study itself was divided into two different conceptual stages: (1) an initial investigation of possible structural hypotheses based on cross-section data and employing correlation as the principal analytical tool; and (2) a tentative testing of structural hypotheses suggested by the preceding cross-section analysis; at this latter stage, both cross-section and time series estimates are employed and the regression model is the basic statistical tool. The next step was to specify the regression

[18] Alan Stuart, "The Efficiencies of Tests of Randomness against Normal Regression," *Journal of the American Statistical Association,* LI (June 1956), 285–287 and "Asymtotic Relative Efficiencies of Distribution-Free Tests of Randomness against Normal Alternates," *Journal of the American Statistical Association,* XLIX (March 1954), 147–157, and Harold Hotelling and Margaret R. Pabst, "Rank Correlation and Tests of Significance Involving No Assumption of Normality," *Annals of Mathematical Statistics,* XII (1936), 29–43.

and correlation models to be used in this investigation. Once formalized in this fashion, several technical or statistical difficulties became apparent. These were of four general types: (1) the meaning of regression and correlation parameters obtained from cross sections stratified according to size classes; (2) interpreting results obtained from data averaged over a period of several years; (3) identifying regression parameters when there is some doubt about the independence of error term and included variables; and (4) amending the data to minimize the discrepancies between data and statistical models created by the extreme skewness of cross sections of firm observations. Broadly speaking, these considerations led to certain explicit cautions about the interpretation of the results in several situations. Finally, some miscellaneous problems concerning the use of non-parametric methods and the necessity of correcting for differences in sample size when comparing the regression and correlation results obtained from the different industries were considered; it was pointed out that there is no perfect method of eliminating or correcting for the size differences but, in practice, this made little difference because the usual alternative methods yielded virtually identical results.

This concludes the basic discussion of methods and techniques. Succeeding chapters will be concerned with the reporting and interpretation of the actual empirical results. In general these chapters will be organized about particular or closely related hypotheses so that findings will be loosely grouped by variable or variables rather than by overall models. For those impatient to see particular parameters or wishing to get a quick general impression of the overall results, all the findings for each cross-section model, industry, and year group have been reported in Appendix B.

Part III

The Empirical Results

Chapter VI

Echo and Senility Effects

THE AGE OF CAPITAL AND INVESTMENT:
THEORY AND OBSERVED FACT

According to "echo effect" theories of investment, the older the existing capital stock, the greater will be investment demanded for replacement. Variants of this intuitively plausible hypothesis have been incorporated into several business cycle theories. Einarsen suggests that lumpy investments in a previous period cause lumped replacement waves in subsequent years. An early contributor to business cycle theory, Karl Marx, urged the possibility that an unequal age distribution of the capital stock can initiate and perpetuate a cyclical investment pattern.[1] To the extent that depreciation reserve size measures relative equipment age, these theories have been decisively rejected by our statistical findings, although certain industries are exceptions, mainly the machine tool industry, and, to a lesser degree, the basic textile group.

Specifically, the simple correlations of the age variable with investment were low and consistently negative for all years in the sample, although noticeably less negative from 1948 on. As pointed out in Chapter IV, firms with old assets usually have low profits, sales, and depreciation expenses too. These negative correlations with the other explanatory variables were sufficient in some instances, like the basic textile and machine tool industries, to yield significantly positive partial correlations between age and investment. But, outside these few exceptions, the main results were partial

[1] For critical comment and attribution of this concept to Marx, see Joan Robinson, *An Essay in Marxian Economics* (London, 1942), p. 54.

correlations in the neighborhood of zero with negative values noticeably predominating. This broad picture is portrayed by the averages of partial and simple correlations presented in Table 6.

There is no particular point in presenting a detailed comparison of the age variable's partial correlations with investment *vis-à-vis* those of the other variables; in each year it is uniformly least by a substantial amount. These remarks about the annual regressions also apply to the averaged data results where with few exceptions the partial correla-

TABLE 6

YEAR AVERAGES OF CORRELATIONS BETWEEN AGE VARIABLE AND INVESTMENT [+]

	\multicolumn{5}{c	}{Annual Data}	Averaged Data
	1946	1947	1948	1949	1950	
Simple Correlations	-.240	-.255	-.048	-.146	-.140	-.307
Partial Correlations[++]	-.169	-.051	-.054	-.031	-.037	-.207

[+] The hypothesis of homogeneity of correlations included in the average correlation could not be rejected at the 10 per cent level of significance for any average. Correlations were averaged by Fisher's method as described in George Snedecor, Statistical Methods, 4th ed. (Ames, 1946), p. 155.

[++] Values associated with the profit model.

tions of age with investment are negative and, in some cases, strongly so.

The behavior of the depreciation reserve variable and its relevance to the echo effect require careful interpretation. Explicitly, two possibilities present themselves: (1) the test of the echo effect is incomplete and if properly supplemented would show a significantly positive relationship between age and investment outlay; or (2) these findings correctly represent the true cross-section relationship which is explicable in terms of existing knowledge about manufacturing market structure and corporate institutions. While there is an element of truth in both propositions, the second appears to be the sounder of the two alternatives.

Before the first alternative can be safely minimized, however, it deserves careful attention since at least three arguments can be made as to the inadequacy of these results as tests of the echo effect. First, gross investment has been used as the dependent variable when, strictly interpreted, the echo effect refers only to replacement investment. Second, the measure of age might be inadequate: perhaps the variance of the age distribution of a firm's equipment should have been included as an additional independent variable. Finally, a complete test of the echo effect should be based on time series in addition to cross-section analysis. It might turn out, for example, that while different firms within a cross section are habituated to given investment rates and equipment ages, an increase through time in the age of a given firm's capital stock would cause an increase in that firm's investment rates.

In answer to these inadequacy arguments, it is obvious that since replacement investment is included in gross investment, the net impact of the echo effect should be ascertainable even when using gross investment as the dependent variable — although perhaps not as precisely as would be desirable. Furthermore, replacement investment is such a nebulous concept that it is doubtful whether a satisfactory measure of such outlays could ever be found, particularly in the manufacturing sector. While desirable, data for effectuating the second suggestion, expansion of the model to include the variance of the equipment age distribution, would be very difficult to obtain. As for the need to use a time series analysis, limited information on this matter has been obtained from the cross-section results. This is particularly evidenced by the great extent of negative values in the early years when, if ever, the cross-section age distributions should have been out of equilibrium because of wartime restrictions. Conditions, moreover, were propitious for rectifying such imbalances. While it could still turn out that the relationship would be reversed in a time series analysis of individual firm behavior,[2] none of these objections

---

[2] One exception to this expectation might occur with firms in declining industries.

are sufficient to deny the strong probability that the *true cross-section* relationship between age and investment is, as our results indicate, more often negative than positive. Indeed, an economic rationale for such behavior can be readily developed.

THE "SENILITY EFFECT"

The negative cross-section results can be plausibly explained as the result of a time continuity in a firm's investment behavior; this explanation will be entitled, for want of a better sobriquet, the "senility effect." Explicitly, firms which on the average have older equipment may have had it that way for some time and intend, or are forced, to keep it that way. A company that has been investing at a low rate in the past will tend to have old equipment. If such a firm continues to invest at a low rate, the age of equipment will continue on the average to be old. In short, the senescent, unambitious firm will remain in decline, as exhibited by the negative relationships, while the newer, growing firm will, to a point, decrease the age of its capital stock.[3]

In a secularly declining industry, of course, we would normally expect a negative relation between age of capital stock and additions to that stock. The important point is that the same considerations apply, it appears, with equal strength to the declining individual firm whether or not it is in a growing or declining industry. Firms that in the past have let their capital stock grow old will by and large continue to do so in the present, while those who in the past had "middle aged" or newer equipment were on the average investing at greater rates.[4]

The long-run behavior of the age variable lends further

---

[3] It should be recalled that in the annual models the age variable had practically no relation with investment for firms with a ratio of depreciation reserves to gross-fixed assets less than .550 so that these remarks can be applied only to firms which have middle-aged equipment with an age ratio of at least .550.

[4] The fact that the *a priori* (positive) sign of the echo effect occurred most frequently in 1950 should be viewed as an important qualification to the "senility effect" theory. Possibly investment behavior after 1950 continued to reverse the negative investment-age reactions that were so pronounced throughout most of the sample period.

TABLE 7
INDUSTRY AVERAGES OF PARTIAL CORRELATIONS BETWEEN AGE AND INVESTMENT VARIABLES [+]

Industry	Annual Data — Five Year Average Simple Correlations	Annual Data — Five Year Average Partial[++] Correlations	Averaged Data — Simple Correlations	Averaged Data — Partial[+*] Correlations
Pulp and Paper	-.159	-.230	-.093	-.116
Light Chemicals	-.217	-.199	-.597	-.575
Heavy Chemicals	-.161	-.019	-.031	-.057
Petroleum	-.183	-.146	-.263	-.376
Rubber	-.254	-.141	-.523	.021
Heavy Steel	.014	.012	-.079	-.210
Metal Products	-.225	-.093	-.043	-.074
Other Machinery	-.221	-.031	-.080	-.088
Light Electrical Machinery	-.216	-.125	-.372	-.292
Heavy Electrical Machinery	-.310	-.399	.067	.040
Vehicles and Suppliers	-.138	-.030	-.567	-.668
Consumer Durables	-.193	-.251	.019	-.021
Machine Tools	-.107	.230	.270	.251
Basic Textiles	.058	.228	-.067	-.139
Other Textiles	-.248	-.222	-.149	-.093

[+] The hypothesis of homogeneity of correlations included in the average correlation could not be rejected at the 10 per cent level of significance for any average. Correlations were averaged by Fisher's method as described in George Snedecor, *Statistical Methods*, 4th ed. (Ames, 1946), p. 155.

[++] Values associated with the profit model.

support to the senility effect. Unlike the flow variables in the average data regressions, the age variable has not been averaged over the five-year period but instead is the 1945 value.[5] As can be seen from the last two columns of Table

---
[5] Because there was no evidence of non-linearity in the averaged data, moreover, the variable was included without subtraction of .55 of gross fixed assets. The results thus have special significance since they indicate that the negative relationship is not a quirk due to the non-linear form used.

7, the partial correlations are overwhelmingly negative and except in the case of machine tools the few positive values are small. Thus, the typical firm which entered the postwar period with older plant and equipment invested less throughout the period than the firm with newer plant and equipment. Furthermore, the same pattern is found in the five-year industry averages of the simple and partial annual correlations between depreciation reserves and investment; again, almost all industries show consistent negative tendencies with the exception of machine tools, and to a lesser extent, basic textiles. It is difficult to explain why, from the economic standpoint, these two industries should be particular exceptions to the senility effect. The most plausible explanation would seem to lie in the nature of the sample: these two are the worst industries for scope of coverage so that the biases of the sample being what they are, there is probably little or no representation from the non-dynamic, senile elements in these industries.

Thus, while there is little doubt that the true cross-section relationship is more likely negative than positive, it must be stressed that this is not necessarily inconsistent with an echo effect. The echo effect theory is essentially concerned with behavior over time and time series analysis might show that this concept does have validity. The results do suggest, however, that echo effects probably are not important determinants of investment since, if they were, the senility effect should have been a little less prominent, particularly in the early postwar years. In addition, there is a strong possibility that for the truly declining firm the senility effect will dominate even over time. Full confirmation, however, must await examination of time series data; it is possible that once within- and between-firm effects were isolated both the echo and senility theories would show greater empirical strength.

Finally, the more important implications of the senility effect are reasonably obvious. Essentially, it indicates that success tends to feed on itself. Furthermore, it lends further substance to the importance of trade position motivation: once involved in market rivalry, a business firm must apparently keep pace or else face the possibility of eventual extinction.

LIQUIDITY AND THE AGE OF CAPITAL

While this chapter initially was designed to explore the relationship between capital stock and investment, the associations between the age variable and other explanatory variables also provide some interesting results and contrasts.

TABLE 8

SIMPLE CORRELATIONS BETWEEN LIQUIDITY STOCK AND AGE OF EQUIPMENT

Industry	\multicolumn{5}{c}{Annual Data}
	1946	1947	1948	1949	1950
Pulp and Paper	.154	.334	.249	.083	.070
Light Chemicals	.455	.558	.491	.211	.439
Heavy Chemicals	.198	-.007	.060	-.053	-.077
Petroleum	.006	-.019	-.025	-.107	.008
Rubber	-.208	-.189	.037	.045	.138
Heavy Steel	.002	-.039	.190	.122	.349
Metal Products	.236	.013	.076	.019	.037
Other Machinery	.176	.083	.137	.142	-.015
Light Electrical Machinery	.050	.455	.536	.651	.424
Heavy Electrical Machinery	.056	.041	-.110	-.210	-.222
Vehicles and Suppliers	-.331	-.063	-.149	.090	-.095
Consumer Durables	-.091	-.214	-.164	-.273	.108
Machine Tools	.284	.303	.329	.374	.309
Basic Textiles	.415	.196	.028	.003	-.083
Other Textiles	-.471	-.218	.041	.149	.149

Most striking of all is the comparatively high correlation between age and the stock of net quick liquidity. In every year and for nearly all industries, the age measure is positively correlated with the net quick liquidity variable. These findings, reported in detail in Table 8, lend decisive support to one side of conflicting arguments that *a priori* seem equally plausible. Specifically, firms with older equipment might have been those in such straitened circumstances that they were incapable of acquiring additional fixed assets; such a state of affairs would be evidenced by an inverse relationship between investment and liquidity stock. On the other hand, dependence on old equipment might be an indication among many of a conservative, caution dominated management that accumulates liquid assets at the expense of modernization and expansion. On this hypothesis one would expect to find, as indeed have been found, positive correlations.

In fact, only six industries report negative correlations and these, with the exception of consumer durables, are quite small values.[6] Noticeably large positive correlations are observable for the light chemical and light electrical machinery industries. The weighted average for all years and the usual fifteen industries is .100. This can only be viewed as an illustrative figure since the Chi-square for this pooled figure indicates highly significant divergences among the correlations averaged.

The observed relation really presents an aspect of senile firm attitudes that complements investment actions of the older equipped firm. More fully, the desired asset composition of the older asset firm differs from that of the younger firm. At one extreme, the older firm might wish to liquidate its fixed assets and then go out of business, an act that could be most advantageously carried out by restricting investment and accumulating liquid assets. The more typical motivation favoring larger liquid balances could be the desire on the part of the older, and presumably less efficient, firms to maintain larger contingency balances.

While caution or liquidity consciousness provides the most reasonable explanation of the observed age-liquidity stock positive correlations, attributing this to an "irrational" penchant for liquid balances might be premature. In particular, the two liquidity flows, profits and depreciation expense,

---

[6] All the other industry values are very homogeneous over the years. The pooling and test procedure (based on Chi-square) were devised by R. A. Fisher and are clearly described in George Snedecor, *Statistical Methods*, 4th ed. (Ames, 1946), p. 155.

are predominantly negatively correlated with age so that large stocks of liquid assets may supply badly needed insurance. In the case of profits, the explanation of the negative results is fairly simple and obvious: firms with aged equipment are likely to be inefficient and less profitable than firms with younger equipment. There is an equally obvious reason for the age-depreciation expense relationship: firms with aged equipment will have a comparatively high proportion of completely written off fixed assets in their accounts. Consequently, financial resources available from current operations are less for firms with aged capital, so that maintenance of more substantial liquidity stocks constitutes a reasonable course of action. Yet it should be noted that the "vicious" cycle commented upon in the previous section is reinforced, or perhaps forced, by such financial stringency. The firms with old capital stock generate less current funds; this tends to weaken access to the capital markets, and at the same time, internal funds are less adequate and perhaps insufficient in comparison with the more recently equipped firms.

SUMMARY

In this chapter the results associated with the depreciation reserve variable have been analyzed. It was found that, with few exceptions, the parameters are negative and not very large. While these results conflicted with *ex ante* expectations based on echo effect theories, no important technical reasons for doubting the empirical validity of these results were found.

In fact, these negative findings are consistent with a theory of behavior that has been called the "senility effect." When analyzing cross-section data, the senility effect is more than strong enough to generally overcome any echo effects upon investment. The senility effect suggests that firms tend to behave in a continuous manner related to their previous history. Firms that had old equipment achieved that result by investing at a low rate in the past. The findings show that these same firms continued to act in the same way during the years in the sample. Firms that are on the downgrade as indicated by an aged capital stock typically do not reverse the trend, while the more dynamic firms continue to "rejuvenate" their capital stock by investing at higher rates.

Relations of aged capital stock to the firm's financial behavior were also surveyed. It was found that firms with older plant and equipment also had larger stocks of net liquid assets. This suggests a policy of financial conservatism. In addition, the liquidity flows, depreciation expense and profits, had strong negative correlations with the age variable. Financial conservatism regarding liquidity stocks appears sensible in light of these negative flow relations since larger stocks are probably viewed as needed insurance against financial crises occasioned by inadequate liquidity flows.

Chapter VII

Depreciation Expense and the Policy of Accelerated Amortization

THE LIQUIDITY AND TAX POLICY ASPECTS
OF THE DEPRECIATION EXPENSE VARIABLE

Depreciation expense represents a significant portion of the new liquidity accruing to a firm in any given time period and unlike the other liquidity flow variable, net profits, it is not complicated by the fact of also being a measure of changing expectations. Differences in investment behavior associated with fluctuations in this variable are, moreover, of added importance today because the existence or nonexistence of a causal relationship between these two variables is crucially associated with the effectiveness or ineffectiveness of a major proposal in tax policy, the grant of accelerated amortization as a means to promote economic growth and stability.

Those supporting such a tax policy have argued that it stimulates private investment by: (1) placing greater liquidity in the hands of the investing entrepreneur; (2) hastening the recovery of funds tied up in plant and equipment and thereby reducing the risk involved; (3) increasing the rate of return on investment outlays through lowering interest cost; and (4) reducing the incidence of businessmen irrationally postponing profitable replacements because of a psychological aversion to throwing away equipment which still has undepreciated book value. In addition, rapid write-off has the appeal of minimum intervention in the private sphere of the economy and somewhat greater administrative flexibility than many alternative forms of granting tax relief.

Objections to accelerated amortization also have been raised on several grounds.[1] For example, it is argued that freer choice of depreciation rates, unmodified in the light of changing circumstances, might intensify cyclical swings since business could be expected to seek and obtain the largest write-offs during inflationary periods with a consequent increase in liquidity and investment at just the wrong time. Problems of resource allocation are involved, too, since continued emphasis on industrial plant expansion might or might not lead to that allocation which would maximize community welfare. Furthermore, such a policy could tend, under certain likely circumstances,[2] to benefit the existing large firm at the expense of the small and new enterprise.

It is not the purpose of this chapter to evaluate these conflicting claims and arguments. Instead, that which has not been evaluated in the previous arguments is questioned: Does a grant of accelerated amortization really stimulate a firm to undertake larger investment outlays? With only occasional exceptions, even those who have had misgivings

---

[1] Expositions of different viewpoints on the consequences of such a policy can be found in: Edgar Cary Brown, *Effects of Taxation: Depreciation Adjustments for Price Changes,* Division of Research, Graduate School of Business Administration, Harvard University (Boston, 1952), pp. 63–92; George Terborgh, *A Dynamic Equipment Policy* (New York, 1949) and *Amortization of Defense Facilities* (Chicago, 1952); L. H. Kimmel, *Depreciation Policy and Postwar Expansion* (Washington, 1946); and Evsey David Domar, "Depreciation, Replacement and Growth," *Economic Journal,* LXIII (March 1953), 1–32.

[2] Examples of such circumstances would be: (1) that small firms rent a greater proportion of their plants and equipment; (2) that to counteract the cyclical effects the allowances might be varied inversely with the cycle so that small firms which experience greater swings in income with changes in the economic climate find themselves unable to take advantage of the most lucrative write-off grants; (3) that new firms may, when they start, go several years without making a positive net operating profit, etc.

about the policy have generally accepted the premise that granting more generous depreciation allowances will stimulate investment. With the importance currently attached to this kind of tax concession, more extensive empirical consideration of its quantitative effectiveness seems appropriate.

Perhaps the explanation for the empirical neglect is that, at first glance, the available historical and empirical evidence would seem to leave little doubt that a policy of accelerated amortization does stimulate investment. For example, in both World Wars and the Korean emergency grants of special write-off privileges were readily sought and capital formation underwent notable spurts after institution of such provisions. Furthermore, in questionnaire studies businessmen have repeatedly expressed the belief that they would invest more if given permission to write off facilities more rapidly.[3]

Both bits of evidence can be questioned, however, on the grounds that the influence of other factors, such as sales expectations, over-taxed capacity, and high level profits, was not partitioned out or held constant. Actually, the influence of such collinear variables might have been primarily responsible for the observed increases in investment. War conditions of high-level unsatiated demand, urgent military needs, and available cost-plus government contracts hardly tend to dampen the investment outlook; in addition, high marginal tax rates during the war made any immediate tax concession, such as rapid amortization, particularly desirable. In the same way, most of the questionnaire studies were conducted in prosperous times and were ill-designed to elicit responses rendered in abstraction from current conditions. Furthermore, there is always the danger that respondents are giving the answer which is thought to be desired by the interrogators, particularly when the question is hypothetical and the answer consequently uncertain. Thus,

[3] *Business Week,* January 22, 1949, p. 55, reports that two-thirds of the firms in their annual Survey of Capital Plans state that they would increase investment if given increased depreciation allowances. Terborgh, *A Dynamic Equipment Policy,* p. 4, cites an *Iron Age* survey in which 306 of 512 respondents say that they would increase investment outlays if allowed to pick their own depreciation rates.

while the war experiences and the questionnaire studies are most suggestive and indicative, the possibility remains that rapid amortization might have little impact when economic conditions are less encouraging.

CAUSES OF WITHIN-INDUSTRY VARIATION IN THE DEPRECIATION EXPENSE VARIABLE

There are several reasons why the depreciation variable will assume different values for different firms within a given industry group; whether or not these sources of variation are financial and economic in character and thus of a type to test appropriately the effectiveness of a policy of accelerated amortization is a matter which is not patently obvious but certainly crucial to the later evaluation of the results. It is therefore necessary to consider the more important of these sources, paying particular attention to their accounting and technical properties.

(1) *Differences in useful life due to different products and physical processes being contained within a given industry group*.[4] When present, these differences represent an unavoidable imperfection in the industrial classification due to the industry groups not being defined narrowly enough to guarantee perfect product and physical process homogeneity.[5] As pointed out in Chapter V, a certain amount of within-group capital intensity heterogeneity remains and such residual differences will be at least partially measured by the depreciation expense variable. This will be particularly true in certain industries as can be seen from Table 9, which presents very rough estimates of the range in average equipment lives which might be expected between firms within the

---

[4] These differences should be sharply distinguished from those differences in durability which result from the exercise of entrepreneurial choice and which may be present even when identical physical processes are involved; such differences are discussed under heading (2) below.

[5] Both product and process homogeneity are emphasized because it is economically useful life rather than physical durability which is of primary interest. Although the two life spans will usually be equivalent, useful life will sometimes be less than physical life because of product and related market structure peculiarities, e.g., automobile body dies have a physical life greater than their useful life of about four years, a limit probably dictated by the exigencies of market rivalry.

specified industry groupings. These estimates were made by matching the Bureau of Internal Revenue estimates of normal obsolescence and depreciation for the machinery involved in specified industrial activities to the reported activi-

TABLE 9

ESTIMATED RANGE OF AVERAGE FIRM EQUIPMENT LIFE BY INDUSTRY GROUPINGS

Industry	Estimated Range of Average Life in Years
Pulp and Paper	17 to 21
Light Chemicals	20
Heavy Chemicals	16 to 21
Petroleum	**
Rubber	17*
Heavy Steel	24 to 26
Metal Products	17 to 26
Other Machinery	20 to 28
Light Electrical Machinery	17 to 21
Heavy Electrical Machinery	20 to 25
Vehicles and Suppliers	15 to 20
Consumer Durables	12 to 25
Machine Tools	17 to 20
Basic Textiles	25
Other Textiles	15 to 18

*Exclusive of molds which should have a life of about three years.

**Absolutely impossible to estimate due to the well-known special factors involved in this industry's depreciation policies.

Source: Bureau of Internal Revenue, Bulletin F: Income Tax Depreciation and Obsolescence Estimated Useful Lives and Depreciation Rates (Washington, 1942).

ties of firms in the sample. For example, in Consumer Durables the upper limit was determined by those manufacturers producing only cutlery and the lower limit by those who are producers of washing machines only, since *Bulletin*

"F" reports that cutlery manufacturing equipment has a useful life of about 25 years and washing-machine manufacturers' equipment a life of about 12 years, all other products and processes in the group lying somewhere in between.[6] In short, the figures of Table 9 were determined by considering only the extremes in each industry, a procedure which is appropriate since it is the range of variation which is important for the present analysis.

(2) *Differences in durability due to the exercise of entrepreneurial choice.* Plant flexibility has more dimensions than those usually recognized in much current economic literature since in a dynamic situation a variety of alternatives with differing write-off rates are open to business management. For example, operations can be conducted within more cramped quarters to reduce the proportion of slow write-off floor space and thereby increase the overall depreciation rate for a firm. Or, firms can stint on machine maintenance and repairs and thus legitimately claim higher depreciation deductions. Similarly, cheaper but less durable equipment can be used which will often give rise to higher depreciation rates or repair costs over the years. Such a practice, while it may seem somewhat irrational, can be necessary because of capital scarcity within the firm or for other equally good reasons. Furthermore, higher depreciation deductions may be claimed if machines are used unusually intensively, particularly if the firm has adopted a unit product method of depreciation accounting.

(3) *Differences in accounting techniques.* Accounting differences may arise from the use of different techniques in computing the depreciation charge since the Bureau of Internal Revenue recognizes four different methods of apportionment[7] and four different ways of keeping depreciable property accounts.[8] The method chosen must be reasonable

---

[6] U. S. Treasury Department, Bureau of Internal Revenue, *Bulletin F: Income Tax Depreciation and Obsolescence Estimated Useful Lives and Depreciation Rates* (Washington, 1942).

[7] Straight line, unit of production, declining balance, and retirement accounting (Bureau of Internal Revenue, *Bulletin F,* pp. 4, 5).

[8] Composite accounts, classified accounts, group accounts, and item accounts (Bureau of Internal Revenue, *Bulletin F,* p. 6).

and cannot be changed without consent of the Internal Revenue Commissioner. While an overwhelming percentage of most firms use straight line for the sake of simplicity, an imaginative accountant, by using an appropriate choice of alternatives, can do a great deal to modify or change his firm's level of depreciation expense; this would be particularly true under lenient or business oriented administration of the tax laws.[9]

(4) *Differences in the amount of usable equipment acquired under war grants of accelerated amortization.* Where such equipment was totally written off during the war years and is still carried in the property account the effect will be to reduce the depreciation rate by decreasing the level of current depreciation expense relatively more than gross fixed assets.[10] Firms in this position would pay a higher tax, *ceteris paribus,* than competing firms who did not acquire capital assets under the war write-off privileges. Such firms would be making partial restitutions for the tax exemptions they received during the war years.[11] A special source of variation in the year 1945 resulted from the fact that the wartime grants of accelerated amortization were set up so that write-off could be taken for tax purposes either in five

---

[9] In 1947 a special source of accounting discrepancy occurred because about 5 to 10 per cent of corporate managements increased depreciation expenses to a level thought to be more commensurate with increased replacement costs, their apparent objective being to discourage stockholder demands for higher dividends at a time when management felt the profit figure to be deceptively inflated. This practice was challenged late in 1947 by the American Institute of Accountants, which indicated disapproval of any depreciation expense figure based on other than original cost, although allowing surplus adjustments to indicate that certain profits have been earmarked for expansion or replacement expenditures. Consequently, whenever indulged, the certifying accountants almost invariably took note of price adjustments in depreciation expense and usually indicated exception; moreover, Securities and Exchange Commission regulations require that the method used for computing the depreciation charge be explained. Most cases were therefore readily recognized and have been corrected in our data.

[10] This same effect would occur where there are pronounced differences between firms in the age distribution of assets. This possibility is strongest in textiles where firms confining all their activities to the South are likely to have newer equipment than those operating partially or entirely in New England.

[11] Only partial, of course, because the marginal tax rate was much lower postwar.

years or the duration of the emergency, whichever period was the shorter. Thus, many firms came to the end of hostilities without having used all of their allowance and claimed the remainder in 1945. Since the depreciation variable is lagged, this will show up in the 1946 correlations. It seems fairly certain that such privileges would not be taken unless the depreciation expense was earned; therefore, tax payments should have been substantially less and the liquidity inflow substantially greater for those firms with residual allowances to be deducted.

In sum, causes of depreciation rate variation between firms in the same industry grouping fall into four general categories. Only the first, concerned with the concept of useful life, is associated with technical or market elements which should be eliminated or held constant when evaluating the liquidity aspects of the depreciation variable since these influences automatically tend to create their own demand for any extra free liquidity. By contrast, the other three sources or kinds of variation measure differences in liquidity which are less likely to be accompanied by such demands so that the disposal or application of the funds is much more a matter for managerial decision and discretion.

Ideally, the best method for eliminating the unwanted useful life effects would be to create an index of such durability and assign values thereof to every firm in the sample. Such a process, however, would involve not only a great expenditure of effort but a large addition to the number of arbitrary assumptions already involved. Since the range of durability variation in the different industries is roughly known, moreover, its approximate influence can be determined from a comparison of inter-industry results, that is, by determining whether the higher investment, depreciation expense correlations are associated with the industries of greater range in useful lives. More formally, rejection of the null hypothesis that differences in past depreciation rates have had no economically significant influence upon the investment rate would require that the large majority of the partial correlation coefficients be significantly positive and, in particular, that significant, positive differences from zero be found in those industries with least durability spread. Similarly, rejection of the hypothesis for a particular year or industry would require that the same conditions hold in these special instances.

THE EMPIRICAL RESULTS

In general, we shall find that the null hypothesis of no relationship between investment and depreciation expense can be rejected for the years 1949 and 1950 when general economic conditions were stable or slightly declining. Moreover, there is little evidence, particularly in the short run, that the durability factor has much influence on the investment, depreciation expense relationship. The significance of this is twofold since it indicates: (1) that the grant of accelerated amortization privileges has an influence on investment decisions even in noninflationary times — if not more so; and (2) that the liquidity aspect of depreciation expense seems to be the variable's dominant characteristic.[12]

In order to simplify the analysis, only the profit model partial correlations between investment and depreciation, as reproduced in Table 10, will be used. Since the results of the two models are substantially the same, none of the conclusions would be materially altered if the partial correlations from the sales model had been used instead. Annual partial correlations with one asterisk differ significantly from zero at the 5 per cent level and those with two at the 1 per cent level. The average correlations were obtained by the weighted Z method.[13] An "(X)" beside any average indicates that Chi-square values were sufficient, at the 5 per cent point, to reject the null hypothesis that there were no significant differences between the correlations pooled to get that average. The averages in such cases should be construed as indicative of tendencies only and not represen-

[12] This second point will take on added significance when in Chapter VIII it will be shown that the behavior of the other liquidity flow variable, profits, follows very much the same cyclical pattern as that for depreciation expense.
[13] This method is outlined by George Snedecor, *Statistical Methods*, 4th ed. (Ames, 1946), pp. 151–155.

tative of any true, constant correlation in the universe sampled.

The most striking feature of the results is how much closer the relationship between depreciation expense and investment is in 1949 and 1950 than in the earlier years.

TABLE 10

PARTIAL CORRELATIONS BETWEEN INVESTMENT AND DEPRECIATION EXPENSE +

Industry	1946	1947	1948	1949	1950	Average Correlation
Pulp and Paper	.042	.083	-.034	.094	.242	.086
Light Chemicals	-.070	.053	.214	.579**	.463*	.081(X)
Heavy Chemicals	-.075	-.132	.022	.427**	.204	.103
Petroleum	-.225	-.174	-.192	.165	.328	.054
Rubber	-.477	-.085	-.075	.775*	.748*	.251(X)
Heavy Steel	.033	-.090	-.056	-.053	-.106	-.056
Metal Products	.267	-.120	.044	.378**	.147	.154
Other Machinery	.141	.140	.066	.115	.353**	.166
Light Electrical Machinery	.158	-.047	.154	.228	.727**	.285*
Heavy Electrical Machinery	.392	-.207	.664*	.170	.000	.238
Vehicles and Suppliers	.166	.182	.293	.287	.336*	.260**
Consumer Durables	.348	.305	-.033	.290	.130	.215
Machine Tools	.366	.362	.277	.317	.512**	.376**
Basic Textiles	-.281	.436	.491	.463	.808**	.464(X)
Other Textiles	-.151	.087	-.037	.375	-.012	.061
Average Correlation	.082	.065	.093*	.260**	.281(X)	

+ Profit model results only.

* Significant at the 5 per cent level.

** Significant at the 1 per cent level.

(X) Averages based on heterogeneous component correlations.

This is illustrated first of all by the much higher average correlations for the last two years, the jump from 1948 to 1949 being threefold.[14] An even better indication of the

[14] This break in behavior pattern is also reassuring with respect to the identification problem since if higher depreciation rates cause more rapid investment the changed behavior is much more readily explained than if the causality ran in the reverse direction.

improvement is given by Table 11, which compares the 1946 through 1948 average correlation for each industry with that for 1949–50. Only three industries (heavy electrical machinery, heavy steel, and consumer durables) had higher

TABLE 11

COMPARISON OF 1946–48 AND 1949–50 AVERAGE PARTIAL CORRELATIONS BETWEEN INVESTMENT AND DEPRECIATION EXPENSE [+]

Industry	Average Sample Size[++]	Average Correlation 1946–48	Average Correlation 1949–50
Pulp and Paper	44	.028	.168
Light Chemicals	27	.079	.525**
Heavy Chemicals	42	-.058	.320**
Petroleum	31	-.210	.244*
Rubber	13	-.208	.762**
Heavy Steel	48	-.041	-.078
Metal Products	54	.061	.263**
Other Machinery	66	.058	.237**
Light Electrical Machinery	18	.080	.513**
Heavy Electrical Machinery	20	.357	.083
Vehicles and Suppliers	41	.220	.313**
Consumer Durables	28	.219	.207
Machine Tools	23	.336	.428**
Basic Textiles	18	.260	.673**
Other Textiles	18	-.037	.207

[+] Values associated with profit model.

[++] Average of observations in the annual sample industries.

[*] Significant at the 5 per cent level.

[**] Significant at the 1 per cent level.

average correlations in the 1946 to 1948 period than 1949 to 1950; only in the case of heavy electrical machinery, moreover, is this 1946–1948 edge substantial. Furthermore, nine out of the fifteen 1949–50 industry averages are significant at the 1 per cent level and ten out of fifteen at the 5 per cent point; in addition, two more of the 1949–50 results, those for pulp and paper and consumer durables, would be significant at 10 per cent. By contrast, almost all of the 1946–1948 results are effectively zero. In a few cases, for example, rubber and petroleum — where large amounts of special amortization grants were left at war's end — it would appear that the depreciation variable was mainly a measure of age: the larger the residual 1945 write-off, the newer was the firm's equipment with substantial negative correlations resulting.

The increased importance of depreciation expense in the last two years is undoubtedly due to the working of several forces — forces only imperfectly represented in the models. These matters will be considered in greater detail in the next chapter. For now, it is worth noting that at the end of World War II there had been a five-year moratorium on investment intended solely for peacetime use. The boom that followed the war, therefore, sorely taxed existing productive capacity in many lines. Demand was not only growing rapidly but productive plant was often old and in poor repair. Liquidity, moreover, was more than adequate, not only because of large corporate holdings of government bonds, but also because of price decontrol, low interest rate policies, etc.

By 1949, of course, conditions had drastically changed. Pent-up, excess war liquidity had long since been spent. Prices had stabilized and in some cases were dropping so that windfall losses replaced windfall gains with a resultant strain on liquidity. But perhaps most important of all was the changed position of productive capacity *vis-à-vis* demand. By the end of 1948 most firms had completed a fairly significant portion of their postwar programs for plant modernization, expansion, and rehabilitation which meant greater flexibility in meeting new orders. In short, at the same time that most firms were experiencing declining sales, capacity was much more adequate than it had been in some while.

In this situation, firms might be expected to pay greater attention to the so-called liquidity restraint and confine investment more rigidly to replacement needs. To at least a limited degree depreciation expense clearly measures both of these factors; hence the sharp upturn in the depreciation partials in the late years seems readily explainable. This is further borne out by the fact that two of the five industries with nonsignificant correlations in 1949–50 did not suffer

TABLE 12

COMPARISONS OF DURABILITY RANGE AND 1949–50 AVERAGE PARTIAL CORRELATIONS BETWEEN INVESTMENT AND DEPRECIATION EXPENSE

Industry	(1) Rank by Probability that Average Correlation Exceeds Zero	(2) Durability Range Rank
Pulp and Paper	10	7.5
Light Chemicals	2	13.0
Heavy Chemicals	4	5.0
Rubber	3	13.0
Heavy Steel	14	11.0
Metal Products	6	2.0
Other Machinery	8	3.0
Light Electrical Machinery	5	7.5
Heavy Electrical Machinery	13	5.0
Vehicles and Suppliers	7	5.0
Consumer Durables	11	1.0
Machine Tools	9	9.5
Basic Textiles	1	13.0
Other Textiles	12	9.5

much from the 1949 recession, namely, pulp and paper and heavy electrical machinery.

But the really notable feature of the 1949–50 results is that the industries of low durability range have as high correlations as the others. For example, note the high values for light chemicals, machine tools, and basic textiles. In fact, this observation can be given formal empirical content by comparing industry rank orders based on the size adjusted

1949–50 average partial correlations with those founded on durability range; these ranks are presented in Column (1) of Table 12. In Column (2) the industries are ranked according to the within-industry range of variation in useful equipment life, using the data of Table 9. Consumer durables is ranked first because within this industry average equipment life varies from 12 to 25 years for a total span of 13 years; ranked last, on the other hand, are industries like heavy steel and machine tools, in which almost all firms have approximately the same rate of equipment obsolescence.

The importance of the durability factor can now be determined from the rank order correlations between the two columns. If durability is important, one should obtain a value which is large and positive and, conversely, if unimportant, a value which is low or even negative. Actually, the rank order correlation (based on the number of inversions) equals -0.185 so it may be safely concluded that durability is of little apparent importance. Indeed, so emphatic are the results that even if the durability range rankings are not perfectly accurate, which they may very well not be, it is doubtful that the removal of the mistakes would be sufficiently large to reverse this finding.

SUMMARY

In this chapter interrelationships between the depreciation expense and investment variables have been analyzed. Depreciation expense represents an amalgam of liquidity, market, and technical factors that might influence the investment rate. The empirical relationship between depreciation and investment assumes special importance at the present time because it constitutes evidence as to the possible effectiveness of tax policies aimed at stimulating investment via grants of accelerated amortization. Since the primary interest of this study is in entrepreneurial investment decisions which are consciously motivated, attention has been focused on those changes in depreciation levels which create or reduce freely available internal funds. In particular, an effort has been made to exclude from the analysis variations due solely to differences in useful equipment life.

The investigation of the correlation results yielded two principal conclusions: (1) that the relationship between investment and depreciation expense is counter cyclical, being significant in economic situations of stability or deceleration and insignificant under converse circumstances; and (2) that the observed relationships are due primarily, if not exclusively, to liquidity considerations and are not at all dependent on differences in equipment durability (defined in terms of useful life). Such behavior clearly agrees with at least the more relevant implications of recent theoretical and empirical emphasis on the importance of available liquidity in business investment decisions.

As for matters of tax policy, the results suggest that, to at least a limited extent, deflationary trends or incipient stagnation can be combated by grants of accelerated amortization. Furthermore, the cyclical pattern in the results indicates that the liquidity restraint may have been so inoperative in the 1946–1948 inflation that introduction of accelerated amortization at that time would have intensified the inflation less than is generally acknowledged. Whether or not this would be the case in all inflations, of course, is a *completely uncertain and different matter*. If it were true, however, a case could be made that a policy of more rapid depreciation stabilizes rather than destabilizes private investment outlay. On the other hand, it would also mean that the long-run impact of the policy is essentially limited to the amount that it increases investment during depressed or stable periods, slightly weakening the secular arguments presented by a few of the more ardent proponents of the policy. These remarks rest, however, on a number of uncertain conjectures about the future and must be regarded as more in the nature of hypotheses for further testing than established fact. Furthermore, the question of the overall advisability of a policy of accelerated amortization remains unanswered. Specifically, the evidence indicates only that such a policy should have some effectiveness and not that it is necessarily the most effective or best method for attaining the ends of secular growth and greater cyclical stability.

Chapter VIII

Profit and Acceleration Variables over the Business Cycle

INTRODUCTION: THE CYCLICAL PATTERN 1946–1950

The cyclical changes in overall economic conditions during the years 1946 through 1950 provide a unique opportunity to evaluate the relative roles of accelerator and liquidity hypotheses of investment behavior. These years break into two cyclically differentiated periods: (1) from the end of hostilities to mid–1948, a time of inflation and catching up with unsatiated demands accrued during the war; and (2) from mid–1948 to mid–1950, years of relative stability and transition from what had been essentially a seller market economy to what was slowly to become more a buyer market economy. The transition dates cannot always be rigidly specified and vary from industry to industry, but the break in pattern is sufficiently universal and demarcable to allow testing whether investment behavior at the micro level is influenced by a distinct change in overall business conditions. More explicitly, 1946 and particularly 1947 can be reasonably characterized as full throttle expansion years. On the other hand, 1948 was both prosperous and at the same time a year of transition with the first half continuing the upward trends of 1947 for most industries and the second half setting the stage for what has been generally known as the inventory recession of 1949. Of all the years in the study, moreover, 1949 best represents conditions of general recession. Like 1948, 1950 is again a mixed year differing, however, in underlying sequence since the first half continued to feel many lingering recession effects while the second half experienced a sharp war-engendered inflation.

Knowledge of these changes in cyclical phase will be employed in this chapter as the observed results are analyzed from three standpoints: (1) the effect of changing economic conditions on liquidity as a factor conditioning investment; (2) the workings of the accelerator or trade position variables at different stages of the cycle; and (3) an analysis of the interrelationships between liquidity and accelerator influences over the course of the 1946–1950 business cycle. It will be found that there is a pronounced difference in the implications of the various hypotheses at different stages of the cycle. To briefly anticipate, three primary conclusions emerge: (1) that the liquidity variables appear to be much more influential when overall economic conditions are either stable or deflationary; (2) that a capacity formulation of the accelerator provides a reasonably good explanation of investment when the economy is under strong inflationary pressures and expanding rapidly; and (3) that, of the many possible subsidiary conditions that might determine a firm's sensitivity or insensitivity to capacity pressures, liquidity considerations appear to be the most important.

THE LIQUIDITY VARIABLES

The final models contain two liquidity flow variables, depreciation expense and profits, and one liquidity stock variable, net quick liquidity. Among those who stress the importance of financial considerations, three conflicting opinions have been expressed about what the relationship between liquidity and investment might be over the course of the business cycle. In the first of these views, the liquidity restraint is held to be inoperative in times of recession but effective under prosperous conditions; that is, in a recession investment outlays are curtailed far short of available funds while during an upswing burgeoning optimism overtaxes the available liquidity. The second view just reverses this cyclical relationship, in the belief that money becomes scarce in a downturn because of restricted profit inflows and tougher credit requirements and, conversely, plentiful in a boom because of opposite conditions. Finally, a third group holds that the credit restraint is always operative, with the supply

TABLE 13

PARTIAL CORRELATIONS BETWEEN PROFITS AND INVESTMENT

Industry	Average Sample Size+	1946	1947	1948	1949	1950
Pulp and Paper	44	.239	-.019	.669**	.404**	.041
Light Chemicals	27	.184	.027	.124	-.013	.237
Heavy Chemicals	42	.039	.188	.346*	.027	.394*
Petroleum	31	.457*	.166	.335	.594**	.194
Rubber	13	-.572	-.298	.909**	.856**	.021
Heavy Steel	48	.028	-.066	.039	.237	.020
Metal Products	54	.245	.367*	.400**	.298*	.358**
Other Machinery	66	.135	.139	.149	.370**	.048
Light Electrical Machinery	18	-.355	.112	-.161	-.134	.194
Heavy Electrical Machinery	20	.246	.083	.000	.130	-.137
Vehicles and Suppliers	41	-.030	.200	.008	-.225	.221
Consumer Durables	28	-.483	-.064	.541**	.705**	.409**
Machine Tools	23	.253	.522*	-.140	.050	.296
Basic Textiles	18	-.195	-.428	.000	.501	.342
Other Textiles	18	-.085	.172	.249	.516	.544
Average Partial Correlation		.097	.073	.217	.266	.210

+Average of observations in the annual sample industries.
*Significant at the 5 per cent level.
**Significant at the 1 per cent level.

and demand curves for funds shifting together in synchronization over the course of the cycle.

On the basis of results shown in Tables 11, 13, and 14, the second view would appear to have the greatest empirical validity. The importance of both depreciation expense and profits rose markedly in 1949 and 1950, indicating that the liquidity restraint in at least the 1946–1950 cycle, with all its particular characteristics, became much more operative after pent-up, excess liquidity was dissipated and profits were squeezed by recession and stabilizing, or even declining, prices. (Some background data on profit, liquidity changes in the years 1946 through 1950 will be found in Table 18.) Not only was this behavior apparent in the overall figures, but to a striking degree the pattern is repeated in almost every individual industry. Only in the case of machine tools is this cyclical relationship substantially reversed, with earlier years showing a greater correlation between investment and profits than later years. Since the

TABLE 14

ANNUAL AVERAGES OF PARTIAL CORRELATIONS BETWEEN INVESTMENT AND LIQUIDITY STOCK AND FLOW VARIABLES

Year	Profits	Depreciation Expense*	Sales	Net Quick Liquidity*
1946	.007	.083	.076	.012
1947	.073	.066	.056	.130
1948	.217	.093	.206	-.043
1949	.266	.259	.255	-.084
1950	.210	.280	.181	.003

*Values associated with the profit model.

machine tool industry, relative to the other industries, faced the greatest market saturation in the initial postwar years, this behavior is fully compatible with the view that liquidity considerations receive greatest attention when business is less than booming. Heavy electrical machinery, moreover, illustrates the same point in a somewhat different fashion: for this secularly expanding industry, which was little affected by the 1949 downturn, profits were never of real importance at any time during the period.

When the time patterns in the behavior of the profit variable are contrasted with those for depreciation expense, the only important difference is the somewhat better performance of profits in 1948, as shown in Table 14. Actually, the discrepancy between the 1948 values is so small that it could occur by chance about 20 per cent of the time even if the true correlations were really identical. However, a plausible explanation of the observed difference can be made by noting that: (1) profits possess an expectational element absent in the depreciation variable and (2) the tightening of competitive conditions in the second half of 1948 could have resulted in more consideration being given to future possibilities than had been the case in the immediately previous years of unsatiated and rapidly expanding markets.

The behavior of the liquidity stock variable, net quick liquidity, contrasts sharply with that for the two flow variables, since 1947 is clearly the stock variable's best year; indeed, it is the only year in which the correlation between net quick liquidity and investment is not effectively zero.[1] Even in 1947, the average value is so small and the underlying industry results so inconsistent that little importance should be attached to this observation. It is sufficient to note that the variable has little consistent influence upon investment and that which is discernible does not correspond with the observed behavior of the two liquidity flow variables, profits and depreciation expense.

The sales variable obviously behaves much the same as profits, and distinguishing statistically between these two in the annual data is extremely difficult. It is interesting, however, that the average value for the profits partial correlations is somewhat better than that for absolute sales in every year except 1946. This suggests that while absolute sales is primarily a measure of the same factors as profits, namely liquidity and expectations, it is also a measure of some of the accelerator influences since, as we shall see, the capacity variable's absolute performance is substantially superior to that of the sales variable in 1946 and 1947. The absolute sales variable therefore appears to be something of a hy-

[1] Many explanations of this ineffectiveness are possible. Two of the more plausible are: (1) that net liquidity stock is the kind of variable which can be easily controlled or adjusted to desired levels at managerial discretion; and (2) that our measure does not adequately gauge the really pertinent aspects of a firm's liquidity position.

brid, measuring both accelerator and liquidity concepts and on the whole doing an inferior job in both instances.

THE ACCELERATION VARIABLES

Literature on the accelerator stresses those conditions or assumptions (about unincluded but influential variables)

TABLE 15

PARTIAL CORRELATIONS BETWEEN CHANGE IN SALES AND INVESTMENT [+]

Industry	Average Sample Size[++]	1946	1947	1948	1949	1950
Pulp and Paper	44	.131	-.106	.065	.010	-.173
Light Chemicals	27	.101	-.487	.224	.029	.060
Heavy Chemicals	42	.055	-.449	-.164	-.162	-.088
Petroleum	31	.254	.351	.362	-.259	-.498
Rubber	13	.628*	-.329	.096	-.259	.272
Heavy Steel	48	-.287	.420**	-.047	-.073	.285
Metal Products	54	-.195	.076	.051	-.168	.439**
Other Machinery	66	-.186	-.042	-.216	-.077	-.020
Light Electrical Machinery	18	.152	-.193	-.048	.142	-.153
Heavy Electrical Machinery	20	-.612	.027	-.182	.326	.126
Vehicles and Suppliers	41	.050	-.163	-.093	.434**	-.202
Consumer Durables	28	.603**	.187	.130	.064	.391
Machine Tools	23	-.157	-.339	-.224	.014	.348
Basic Textiles	18	.008	.104	-.367	-.040	.472
Other Textiles	18	-.100	.005	.060	.050	-.098

[+] Values associated with the profit model.
[++] Average of observations in the annual sample industries.
*Significant at the 5 per cent level.
**Significant at the 1 per cent level.

which have to be fulfilled if the hypothesized functional relationship between a change in sales and investment is to be observed in actuality. When all these qualifications are taken into consideration, a reasonably precise statement of the original and conventional acceleration hypothesis of investment would seem to be as follows: Investment will increase when sales undergo a non-temporary increase if existing capacity is already fully utilized and if sufficient funds are available to finance the acquisition of the new capital goods.

This basic hypothesis was significantly altered in the models, since a measure of capacity requirements was in-

TABLE 16

PARTIAL CORRELATIONS BETWEEN CAPACITY UTILIZATION AND INVESTMENT [+]

Industry	Average Sample Size[++]	1946	1947	1948	1949	1950
Pulp and Paper	44	.309	.399*	.076	.112	-.308
Light Chemicals	27	.439	.642**	.385	.286	-.108
Heavy Chemicals	42	.784**	.573**	.374*	.549**	.186
Petroleum	31	.286	.007	.242	.000	.218
Rubber	13	.718*	.720*	-.164	-.445	-.259
Heavy Steel	48	.482**	.484**	.438**	.000	-.117
Metal Products	54	.342*	.574**	-.145	.178	-.045
Other Machinery	66	.506**	.378**	.302*	.063	.172
Light Electrical Machinery	18	.624	.541*	.293	.008	-.176
Heavy Electrical Machinery	20	-.106	.699**	.257	-.056	.520*
Vehicles and Suppliers	41	.399*	.179	.016	-.139	.137
Consumer Durables	28	.610*	.302	-.180	-.269	.132
Machine Tools	23	.570*	.423	.279	.952**	-.027
Basic Textiles	18	.718*	.651*	.551	-.647*	.675**
Other Textiles	18	.096	.702*	-.544*	-.349	-.373
Average Partial Correlation for Profits Model		.476	.452	.173	.119	.049
Average Partial Correlation for Sales Model		.361	.478	.189	.010	.096

[+] Values associated with the profit model.

[++] Average of observations in the annual sample industries.

* Significant at the 5 per cent level.

** Significant at the 1 per cent level.

cluded along with the change in sales variable. To the extent that the capacity variable really does reflect needed levels of capital stocks, the models measure: (1) the relationship between investment and changes in sales given that capacity needs and availability are constant rather than fully utilized, and (2) the relationship between investment and capacity utilization given that changes in sales are constant.

When altered in this fashion, a change in sales becomes a measure of expectations and changing liquidity flows as well as an indication of technical need for greater capacity. And, once the traditional formulation has thus been broken, there is no reason why the function should not be reversible. In other words, if the measure of capacity requirements is valid, there is no reason why changes in sales should not be as effective a variable in situations that do not meet the classical accelerator assumptions as in situations that do. That this actually seems to be the case can be seen from Table 15, which lists the profit model partial correlations between investment and change in sales. The change in sales variable is clearly at its worst in 1947 when the accelerator assumptions were well met and at its best in 1950 when the assumptions were poorly met.

These mediocre and rather patternless results for sales changes contrast sharply with those shown in Table 16 for the capacity variable, which explains investment very well in the early years, 1946 and 1947, and then abruptly collapses, usually in 1949 but sometimes in 1948.[2] The capacity variable thus behaves just as one might expect an accelerator variable to behave, yielding good results when the accelerator assumptions are best met and poor results when these

[2] The superiority of the capacity variable in 1946 and 1947 could be explained as due to a mathematical identity if two assumptions were simultaneously satisfied: (1) that all firms reached their peak capacity utilization ratios (sales over gross fixed assets) in these years; and (2) that the pattern of minor mergers, land acquisitions, and particularly capital retirements was similar for all firms so that the change in gross fixed assets becomes closely correlated with investment. Actually, a careful scrutiny of the data indicates that the peak ratios were usually evenly divided between 1947 and 1948 in most industries and, even in the instances where this pattern was violated, the correlations usually did not reach peak values in the year or years the maximum ratios were numerically most prevalent. About the only exceptions, that is, where the correlations between investment and capacity might be overstated because of this factor, are machine tools in 1946 and basic iron and steel in 1948. As for the second assumption, relative equality of retirements, land acquisitions, and minor mergers, this was always violated to some extent throughout this period, so that the change in gross fixed assets was, at best, a poor approximation of investment.

assumptions are less well satisfied. Thus, even when a more explicit measure of capacity is substituted for the change in sales variable, the accelerator is still only effective when the underlying assumptions are adequately fulfilled.[3] At least one of the 1946–47 correlations is significant for every industry except petroleum, and several of the values which are not significant fall barely below the 5 per cent significance level. In fact, the only values which would not be significant at 10 per cent in these two early years are those for petroleum, the automotive industry in 1947, heavy electrical machinery in 1946, and other textiles in 1946. Furthermore, if the 1946 and 1947 values were averaged (weighting appropriately for differences in sample size) and then assessed for significance, only petroleum and heavy electrical machinery would have values for which the null hypothesis of no correlation in these years could not be rejected at the 1 per cent level or less.

The situation shifts rather dramatically in 1948 and thereafter, as most of the capacity-investment correlations effectively drop to zero or, in a few cases, to correlations which are significantly negative, with the overall yearly averages fully reflecting this behavior. Just as in the case of profits and depreciation expense, 1948 is a year of transition with the 1948 average value being approximately midway between those for 1947 and 1949. In addition, the individual industry results for 1948 are very heterogeneous, with the break in correlation patterns occurring in some industries in 1949, rather than 1948. Regardless of when it is made, the shift in behavior had almost universally occurred by 1949 and generally continued into 1950.

In sum, the modified accelerator concept represented by the capacity variable provides a good explanation of investment in the early years when, as shown in Table 18, the underlying assumptions were more nearly satisfied. Apparently, in the postwar years a capacity concept provided a reasonably adequate explanation of investment as long as all

---

[3] This result is not dependent on the fact that the two variables are included in the same model, since the same time patterns are discernible in the zero order correlations of each variable with investment.

the usual accelerator assumptions or enabling conditions were met; once these conditions were not satisfied, however, the enabling factors themselves, particularly liquidity, assumed a dominant role in conditioning the investment decision.

The heterogeneity of the relationships over time is also revealing as to the direction of causation between the variables. For example, if high investment rates caused greater sales and profits rather than vice versa, it would be hard to explain why the relationship should not have persisted throughout the period and why, as shown in the next section, a change in the significance of the relationship was generally accompanied by a reduced liquidity position. Similarly, if certain modifications in physical durability of a firm's capital goods are assumed to follow from high investment levels, it could be argued that greater investment causes more rapid depreciation. Such an explanation is again difficult to reconcile, however, with the break in the time pattern of the relationships since a purely technical influence should not be sensitive to changing cyclical and liquidity conditions. Furthermore, the fact that the rise in importance of both depreciation expense and profit variables coincide tends to strengthen the view that the profit-investment relationship is founded on liquidity rather than expectational considerations. Specifically, the depreciation variable combines both technical and liquidity influences and the profit variable encompasses both expectations and liquidity; the fact that the two behave very similarly suggests that it is the common liquidity element that underlies the observed behavior patterns. In short, the time and industry relationships between the correlations is most readily explained if causation is said to run from profits, depreciation, and sales to investment and if the underlying motivation is imputed primarily to a firm's financial considerations.

CAPACITY AND PROFIT VARIABLES IN 1948

It remains to investigate whether certain changes in underlying conditions were more responsible than others for the observed shift in investment behavior accompanying the

1948–49 transition. Explicitly, the following question is posed: Are some of the basic accelerator assumptions more necessary than others for the capacity utilization-investment relationship to be effective? Or from a different aspect: In what situation is "the profit principle" most likely to supersede a capacity type accelerator in importance?

Because of their extreme heterogeneity, the results for the year of transition, 1948, present an excellent opportunity to analyze the relative importance of these different influences. This can be seen by looking at Tables 13 and 16. For example, a few industries, like pulp and paper and consumer durables, registered significant partial correlations between investment and profits in 1948, anticipating the general 1949 turn in this direction. On the other hand, such industries as basic textiles, heavy chemicals, and basic iron and steel enjoyed a lagged transition with the 1948 partial correlations between investment and capacity still significantly high. Since the objective is to determine whether any particular factors were more important than others in creating this heterogeneous pattern, an attempt will be made to discover relationships between the level of these observed industry correlations and changes in the average values of the various liquidity, capacity, and sales position measures for the industries.[4]

The industries were first ranked according to the change in the probability between 1947 and 1948 that the true correlation between capacity and investment was greater than zero; the greater the positive change in probability, the lower the rank. In short, the industries were ranked according to how well the capacity variable did in 1948 compared with its 1947 performance; the better 1948 is relative to 1947, the higher the rank.[5] Exactly the same procedure was applied to the profit-investment partial correlations, so

[4] In essence, clues will be sought about which omitted multiplicative forms might have been worth including in the models.

[5] To correct for differences in the industry sample sizes, the changes in correlation values were deflated by the standard errors corresponding to the distribution of correlations drawn from a normal universe with zero correlation for that sample size.

the industries were also ranked according to how well the profit variable did in 1948 compared with 1947.

There are thus two sets of industry ranks, one based on capacity correlations and one on profit correlations, whose ordering is to be explained. Each of these two "dependent ranks" was next related to six possible "explanatory ranks" based upon measures of the various possible enabling conditions.[6] These were: (1) the 1948 mean values for the capacity utilization variable; (2) the change from the beginning of 1946 to the beginning of 1948 in the mean values of the age variable, which provides a rough index of the amount of modernization completed by the end of 1947; (3) the percentage change from 1947 to 1948 in the mean net quick liquidity; (4) the percentage change from 1947 to 1948 in the mean profit rate; (5) the percentage change from 1947 to 1948 in the mean sales turnover rate, that is, the ratio of absolute sales to gross fixed assets; and (6) the percentage of firms in the industry experiencing a positive increase in sales in 1948. All except (1), (2), and (6) (mean capacity utilization, modernization, and percentage of positive sales) were again expressed as year-to-year changes in order to eliminate inter-industry differences. For (1), (2), and (6) such manipulations were unnecessary because their values were already in percentage form. Highest rankings were given to values that *a priori* would be related to the largest increases in accelerator-investment correlations; for example, least modernization received rank 1, most modernization rank 15. This means that the rank order coefficient based on inversions should be positive between the explanatory ranks and the capacity ranks and, conversely, negative between explanatory and profit ranks. The results are presented in Table 17.

Obviously, the strongest relationship between demise of the accelerator and any of the explanatory variables exists

[6] An alternative method for handling this analysis would be to stratify the sample on these factors. The main difficulty with this procedure is that it either means fragmenting the sample into groups too small for effective analysis or abandoning the industry groupings and thus losing control over the capital intensity influences.

TABLE 17

RANK ORDER CORRELATIONS BETWEEN SELECTED LIQUIDITY, CAPACITY, AND SALES POSITION MEASURES AND PROFIT AND CAPACITY VARIABLE PERFORMANCE, 1948

Explanatory Measures	Rank Order Correlations With changes in capacity partials	With changes in profit partials
1. Mean Capacity Utilization, 1948	.105	.219
2. Per cent Change in Mean Age, 1946-48	.105	-.086
3. Per cent Change in Mean Net Quick Liquidity, 1947-48	.048	-.200
4. a. Per cent Change in Mean Profit Rate (zero order), 1947-48	.486**	-.243
b. With Mean Influence of (1), (2), (3), (5), and (6) Held Constant	.462+	-.362+
5. Per cent Change in Mean Sales Turnover, 1947-48	.067	.028
6. Per cent of Firms with Increase in Sales, 1948	.153	.074

**Significant at the 1 per cent level.

+For reasons explained by Maurice Kendall, <u>Rank Correlation Methods</u> (London, 1948), pp. 103-104, partial rank order correlations cannot be readily tested for significance with methods now available.

for changes in the mean profit rate, this rank order correlation being the only one that is significantly different from zero.[7] Furthermore, this same variable does the best job of explaining changes in the profit-investment relationship, recording the largest negative value when ranked against

[7] This, of course, does not mean that the other variables might not have had an influence in many particular instances. It merely implies that in the *generality of cases* a significant relationship was found only for changes in the profit rate.

TABLE 18
LIQUIDITY, CAPACITY, AND SALES CONDITIONS, 1946-50 *

Year	Liquidity - Median Net Quick liquidity	Liquidity - Median profit rate	Capacity - Median age	Capacity - Median utilisation†	Sales - Median sales increase	Sales - Per cent positive sales increase
1946	.378	.145	.556	.860	.011††	52.7
1947	.258	.221	.500	1.329	.681	90.8
1948	.224	.201	.460	1.343	.259	75.9
1949	.199	.128	.433	.831	-.224	29.3
1950	.319	.189	.434	.905	.334	82.9

*Based upon the data for firms in the sample. All values, except the percentage of positive sales changes, were weighted (deflated) by gross fixed assets.

†These figures are based upon the capacity variable after deflation, that is, it represents the median firm's present sales to fixed asset ratio divided by the peak such ratio in the years 1946 to 1949. Values can exceed unity because the peak ratio was computed using unlagged gross fixed assets as the deflator while the current ratio had lagged gross fixed assets in the denominator. The economic rational for this is that the stock existing at the end of the year better represents what is desired or considered normal relative to sales in a rising market while the stock as of the first of the year better represents productive capacity available to meet the expanding demand.

††The 1945 sales figures were still inflated by war contracts, so that the average change from 1945 to 1946 was lowered by the many firms adjusting downward from heavy overtime war work loads. In short, a more valid comparison might have been to contrast 1946 sales with those for the last peacetime year, 1941, allowing for price changes. Capacity utilization in 1946 was also biased downward, moreover, because of the heavy representation in the sample of the more capital-intensive durable goods industries which took longer to get back into peacetime production after the war.

profit changes.[8] In general, the signs of the coefficients were as expected; however, changes in mean capacity utilization ranked positively with losses of profit correlation — in fact, rather substantially so. Equally significant is the manner in which absolute sales turnover ranks are effectively uncorrelated with either profit or change in sales ranks. As a

[8] Explicitly, this value of —.243 would appear by chance about 10 per cent of the time if the two ranks of fifteen items each were ordered by a random process.

result, the partial rank order correlation[9] between percentage change in mean profit and the effectiveness of the profit variable (with the mean influence of all the other explanatory variables eliminated)[10] is definitely larger than the simple correlation, −0.362 as compared with −0.243.

These results suggest that ample liquidity is prerequisite to even the capacity accelerator's effectiveness. Of course, profits measure expectations as well as liquidity. It is therefore significant that other variables which gauge expectations, like absolute sales and changes in sales, do poorly and that the time pattern in the profit variable closely follows that of depreciation expense, which is a measure of liquidity and not of expectations. Furthermore, increases in the importance of profits are relatively closely related (−.200) to deterioration in the stock of net quick liquidity. It appears, therefore, that where profits inflows were still substantial the accelerator remained operative in 1948. On the other hand, the profit rate became the better variable for explaining investment in those instances where the liquidity stock had fallen or the profit rate itself was down.[11]

COSTS, PROFITS, AND THE LEVEL OF OUTPUT IN THE LONG AND SHORT RUN

One of the more intricate problems of investment theory hinges on the relative importance of different causal factors in the long and short run. The availability of correlation and regression results based on both annual and five-year averaged data provides an excellent opportunity to investigate whether these differences do exist and to test various hypotheses about the possible sources of such differences.

It has already been observed that profits and output (sales) are, as a rule, statistically very closely related to

[9] For a discussion of partial rank order correlation, see Maurice G. Kendall, *Rank Correlation Methods* (London, 1948), pp. 99–104.

[10] This was achieved by summing all the ranks (1), (2), (3), (5), and (6), ranking these sums, and then eliminating the influence of this rank by partial rank order correlation.

[11] This suggests a multiplicative model with profit times change in sales and profit times net quick liquidity as cross-product terms. An alternative would be to define the investment function differently at different mean profit rate, liquidity stock levels.

one another. This entanglement strongly suggests that marginal costs and prices are constant within relevant ranges of output since, when this is the case, profits in the short run will be a linear function of output. Under such conditions, it can therefore be reasonably argued that while profits may be the proximate cause of investment, their dependence on the output level really means that output ultimately determines investment levels.

This line of reasoning must be viewed, however, with some caution. In the short run there can be noticeable divergences from a strict linear relation between profits and output, particularly for firms observed at one specific point of time. Initial cost positions of firms will always differ to some extent and thereby affect operating profit. And as one moves from operating profit to net profit after various charges have been deducted (for example, interest, taxes), divergences are likely to be even more frequent. In other words, on a cross section, some independent variation between profits and sales is likely to be observed, particularly between net profits and the level of output. Consequently, the distinct influences of each may be subject to measurement and comparison. However, abrupt changes in output will undoubtedly bring in their wake abrupt changes in profits in the same direction. Thus, evaluations and distinctions that will be made in this section should *not* be taken to imply that massive independent variation would yield similar results since the distinctions will be drawn on the basis of relatively small variations.

Actually, the long- and short-run performances of the profit and sales variables are differentiable only at very low levels of significance, for example, 15 and 20 per cent. However, there is a discernible tendency for the long- and short-run importance of the two variables to be completely reversed. Specifically, profits shows a slight superiority over sales in the short run while sales is the better averaged data variable. Equally as important, the capacity variable which was so capricious in its annual behavior, generally does well in the averaged data regressions.

On a year-by-year basis profits were observed to be generally superior to sales in their ability to explain investment. The only exception occurred in 1946. While the absolute magnitude of the difference between the averaged partial correlations for each year was never over .07, a paired comparison of each and every year, industry result would show that the profit values are greater than those for sales at about a 15 per cent significance level.[12] Similarly, the capacity requirements variable was by far the most important independent variable in 1946 and 1947 but thereafter ceased to be of much significance. Thus, in the short-run data, and particularly after the cessation of the more extreme postwar seller markets, profits was superior to sales, and to a lesser extent relative capacity as an explanatory variable for investment.

When the long-run or averaged data results are examined, however, the comparative importance of sales and profits is reversed. Sales turns out to be the more powerful explanatory variable with its partial correlation with investment on the average exceeding that of profits with investment by 0.110. An industry breakdown of these results is shown in Table 19, along with the capacity, investment partial correlations. On a paired comparison test, the sales correlations are now significantly greater than the profits correlations at somewhere between the 15 and 20 per cent points. While neither this nor the previous 15 per cent levels are particularly significant in and of themselves, it should be remembered that these contrary results were obtained from different analyses of the same body of underlying data. In other words, these are not separate tests of the *same* null hypothesis of no difference between sales and profits correlations based on *different* samples but instead are *different* analyses of the *same* sample.

Equally as interesting, the capacity variable which performed so unevenly on the annual data turns out to have one

[12] The observations were first transformed into Fisher's logarithmic "z" values and the difference normalized by dividing each variable by the standard deviation of the difference. This will make the distribution of transformed values more normal than the original distribution and will also compensate for the effects of differences in degrees of freedom among the different regressions.

of the strongest partial correlations with investment in the averaged data. This is all the more significant since this is one variable which, because of normalization in terms of a firm's own peak performance, should be relatively uninfluenced by autocorrelation and therefore perform as well

TABLE 19

AVERAGED DATA PARTIAL CORRELATIONS OF INVESTMENT WITH PROFITS, SALES, AND RELATIVE CAPACITY

Industry	Profits	Sales	Capacity[a]
Pulp and Paper	.247	.190	.292*
Light Chemicals	.023	.294	.297
Heavy Chemicals	-.137	.526**	.452**
Petroleum	.566**	.342*	.177
Rubber	.789**	.729**	.135
Heavy Steel	.529**	.735**	.176
Metal Products	.211	.309*	.062
Other Machinery	.169	.211	.280*
Light Electrical Machinery	.239	.349	.478*
Heavy Electrical Machinery	.075	.113	-.163
Vehicles and Suppliers	.565**	.409**	.755**
Consumer Durables	.112	.547**	.463**
Machine Tools	.140	.547*	.730**
Basic Textiles	.538	.654**	.516*
Other Textiles	.336	.101	.262

*Significant at the 5 per cent level.

**Significant at the 1 per cent level.

[a] Values associated with the profit model.

with annual as with averaged data. Furthermore, there seems to be little relationship between this variable's relative performance in the annual and the averaged regressions, ruling out the possibility that the capacity, investment correlation in the averaged data is simply a measure of the industry's relative prosperity during the 1946 to 1950 period. Indeed, the second highest value is recorded by the machine tool industry which enjoyed the least postwar prosperity.

Apparently there is a strong desire to maintain a relatively constant or stable capital output ratio in the long run. Such a tendency is discernible in the short run, on the other hand, only when productive facilities are rather fully utilized and the necessary financing is readily obtainable. Otherwise, short-run investment policy seems to be dominated by financial considerations, particularly the availability of internal funds.

SUMMARY

A sharp break in the observed behavior of the variables that accompanied the economic transition of 1948 and 1949 permitted tests of the cyclical importance of several investment theories. In the immediate postwar years, 1946 and 1947, when demand was expanding rapidly and liquidity was plentiful, a capacity formulation of the accelerator had by far the closest relationship with investment. On the other hand, in 1948 and 1949, when economic conditions stabilized or declined in several lines of activity, the two liquidity flow variables, profits and depreciation expense, provided the best explanation of investment outlay. The liquidity stock variable and change in sales had, by contrast, little effective relationship with investment at any time during the 1946 to 1950 period.

A rise in the importance of the liquidity flow variables and a decline in the effectiveness of the capacity accelerator were almost always concomitant happenings in any given industry grouping. The transition from what might be called an accelerator to a liquidity model began for many industries in 1948 and was virtually universal by 1949. The heterogeneous nature of the different industry results in the transition year 1948 presented an opportunity to specify more explicitly the underlying characteristics of the transition. It was found that both decreased importance of the accelerator and increased importance of profits in explaining investment were accompanied by a drop in the mean profit rate for an industry. In fact, this was the only observed relationship of any importance between changes in the profit and capacity partials with investment and changes in mean levels of various explanatory variables. Of all the basic assumptions, plentiful liquidity seemed most essential to the effectiveness of the accelerator and once liquidity became somewhat pinched, the availability of funds became a crucially important determinant of investment outlay in and of itself.

In the long run, on the other hand, investment outlay seemed to be less sensitive to financial considerations and more closely conditioned by the kind of technological relationships between capital and output central to acceleration theories. Specifically, the relative importance of the sales and profits variables was just reversed in the results obtained from the annual and averaged data models, profits being more important in the former and sales more important in the latter. Furthermore, the capacity variable evidenced a relatively high relationship with investment on the averaged data for almost all industries, without regard to differing levels of postwar prosperity in the different industries.

Chapter IX

Financial Patterns, Dividend Policy and Trade Position Motivation

INTRODUCTION

For obvious reasons, the investment decision is inextricably intertwined with the problems of business financing. In particular, many businessmen feel that a scarcity of funds has often restrained their capital expenditures to a level below that which they would otherwise have undertaken. At a formal level this observation could be viewed as too obvious to deserve mention. Yet when credit-rationing is a factor of some importance, it can happen that the supply and demand for funds as a function of interest rates will not possess a simultaneous solution. A shortage of funds, in such an instance, will be manifested as simply an excess demand for funds. For this reason, among others, several liquidity variables were included in the regression models used in this study — explicitly, profits, depreciation expense, and net quick liquidity. These are the monetary magnitudes most closely related to current operations. Analysis of these variables in previous chapters has shown that the investment decision seems to be influenced by liquidity flows in times of recession but not in prosperity.

In this chapter those fund sources that are less directly

dependent upon current operation levels will be considered. Specifically, an analysis will be made of the changes over time in the use of external funds as financial sources.[1] In addition, the influence of dividend policy will be considered by studying the simple correlations between investment and the dividend to net income ratio. Attention will be focused on two questions:[2] (1) Given the manufacturing sector's well-known preference for internal funds, are external sources mainly used by producers in rapidly expanding or highly competitive industries in which the need for funds may be relatively more urgent? and (2) What pattern, if any, is there between the percentage of profits retained in surplus and the investment expenditure?

A SUMMARY OF FINANCIAL PATTERNS IN THE MANUFACTURING SECTOR, 1946–1950

The general financial characteristics which distinguish manufacturing from other corporate sectors have been outlined in previous studies.[3] Manufacturing firms have shown, above all else, a markedly greater aversion to outside financing of either the debt or equity variety. Only 10 per cent of postwar financial needs were met by new debt and equity issues as shown in Table 20, which presents sources and uses of funds for manufacturing corporations in the years 1946 through 1950. The overall percentage for all corporations, including the low manufacturing figure, was 17 per cent. This aversion to outside money particularly applied to

---

[1] The term "external funds" will be confined to long-term external sources only.

[2] One common hypothesis about business financing, namely, that small firms have greater difficulties getting outside funds than large firms, has been deliberately omitted and held over to Chapter X when a general comparison is made of small and large firm behavior in the years 1946–1950.

[3] Loughlin F. McHugh, "Financing Small Business in the Postwar Period," *Survey of Current Business,* XXXI (November 1951), 17–24; Loughlin F. McHugh and Leonard G. Rosenberg, "Financial Experience of Large and Medium Size Manufacturing Firms, 1927–51," *Survey of Current Business,* XXXII (November 1952), 7–13; Daniel H. Brill, "Financing of Capital Formation," in *Problems of Capital Formation* edited by Franco Modigliani, National Bureau of Economic Research Studies in Income and Wealth, Volume 19, 1957; and in numerous papers, or parts of papers presented at the National Bureau of Economic Research Conference on Business Finance, 1952.

equity; manufacturing firms raised only about 3 per cent of postwar needs from this source, perhaps reflecting a reaction to the low bond and high dividend yields in the years since 1946.

TABLE 20

SOURCES AND USES OF MANUFACTURING CORPORATE FUNDS 1946–50 *

Uses	$ Billions	Per Cent of Total
Plant and Equipment	36.2	58.3
Inventories	15.2	24.7
Receivables	6.7	10.8
Cash	3.6	5.8
U. S. Government Securities	1.0	1.6
Other	-.4	-.6
Total	62.3	100.6
Retained Earnings	32.8	51.4
Depreciation	13.9	22.4
Payables (Trade)	5.2	8.2
Federal Tax Liabilities	2.8	4.4
Other Current Liabilities	1.7	2.7
Bank Loans	1.4	2.2
Mortgage Loans	-.1	-.1
Net New Issues	6.2	9.7
Total	63.9	100.9

Discrepancy equals -1.6

*From Loughlin F. McHugh, "Financing Small Business in the Postwar Period," Survey of Current Business, XXXI (November 1951), 17.

Another side of the same phenomenon is revealed by the consistent tendency for manufacturing firms to pay out a lower percentage of net earnings in dividends. As a result, over one-half of the postwar expansion in manufacturing could be financed out of retained earnings. In addition, de-

TABLE 21

RELATION OF STOCK ISSUES TO TOTAL AMOUNT OF NEW CAPITAL ISSUES BY INDUSTRY GROUPS, 1925–50 FOR INDUSTRIAL AND MISCELLANEOUS CORPORATIONS

Year	Total New Issues $ Millions	Stocks as Per Cent of Total
1925	2224	30.3
1926	2342	26.4
1927	2645	21.0
1928	3117	50.5
1929	3939	66.5
Total 1925-29	14,267	
Average 1925-29	2,853	
1935	245	27.3
1936	811	43.3
1937	840	47.7
1946	2602	51.3
1947	2553	37.1
1948	2784	18.8
1949	1914	12.7
1950	1247*	32.1
Total 1946-50	11,100	
Average 1946-50	2,220	

*First ten months only.

SOURCE: Loughlin F. McHugh, "Financing Small Business in the Postwar Period, Survey of Current Business, XXXI (November 1951), 15.

preciation charges accounted for 22 per cent more of total needs so that approximately 74 per cent of the overall total was met with funds accruing from current operations. Thus the unparalleled peacetime expansion in manufacturing capacity carried out in the years 1946 through 1950 involved minimum contact with the money markets.

While such financial conservatism has always been a characteristic of manufacturing, the postwar experience displayed exceptional reliance on internal funds even for this sector. As a consequence manufacturing's relative interest and debt burden was significantly lower at the end of 1949 than it was at the end of the last period of rapid peacetime

TABLE 22

AGGREGATE FUND SOURCE ANALYSIS BY INDUSTRY GROUP [+]

Industry	(1) Bonds: end 1946 $Millions	(2) Bonds: end 1950 $Millions	(3) Per Cent Change: Bonds	(4) Stocks: end 1946 $Millions	(5) Stocks: end 1950 $Millions	(6) Per Cent Change: Stocks	(7) Per Cent Change: Stocks and Bonds
Pulp and Paper	128	249	96	704	843	20	31
Light Chemicals	89	103	15	414	493	19	19
Heavy Chemicals	258	399	55	1486	2038	37	40
Petroleum	1369	2365	73	5097	6094	20	31
Rubber	159	301	90	410	390	-5	21
Heavy Steel	576	717	24	2822	3146	12	14
Metal Products	81	136	68	671	719	7	14
Other Machinery	122	241	97	1086	1403	29	36
Light Electrical Machinery	97	223	129	228	288	26	57
Heavy Electrical Machinery	293	85	-71	548	580	6	-21
Vehicles and Suppliers	225	195	-14	1413	1643	16	12
Consumer Durables	19	36	100	145	167	15	25
Machine Tools	8	15	85	96	98	2	9
Basic Textiles	32	82	161	420	488	16	26
Other Textiles	11	32	179	159	181	14	25
Clothing	5	18	276	39	53	36	62
Radio and Television	38	88	130	139	194	40	71

[+] Based on all firms in sample.

expansion in the late 'twenties.[4] Table 21 illustrates this trend toward internal finance; the total value of new capital issues averaged 600 million dollars less per year in the recent prosperity than in the twenties despite the much higher

[4] As a crude indication, the interest payment to sales ratio fell from 1 per cent in 1929 to .35 per cent in 1949, U. S. Treasury Department, Bureau of Internal Revenue, *Statistics of Income,* 1929 (Washington, 1931), p. 344 and *ibid.,* vol. 2, 1949 (Washington, 1953), p. 82.

price level and the greater extent of manufacturing operations in the more recent period. Exemplifying the same tendency was a downward trend in the percentage of net income paid out in dividends by manufacturing firms.[5]

All these financial patterns were substantially duplicated, moreover, in the component industries of manufacturing so that manufacturing, which is so heterogeneous in most respects, was essentially homogeneous in its financial behavior. This is illustrated by the data of Table 22, which presents a source analysis of long-term debt and equity issues by the different industry groups used in this study. The clothing and radio and television industries have been reincluded since aggregate figures were used and a shortage in degrees of freedom is therefore no longer a handicap. Despite the fact that all but two industries, machine tools and heavy steel, experienced more than a 100 per cent expansion in the value of gross fixed assets in the period 1946–1950, not a single industry doubled the total value of its outstanding long-term debt and equity issues. A 71.3 per cent expansion by radio and television is the highest recorded performance, but this is also the industry that had the greatest expansion of assets in the postwar period. Indeed, all but three industries expanded outstanding long-term debt and equity less than 40 per cent and frequently substantially less. Similarly, the overall pattern of preference for debt to equity as a source of outside money is sustained by the individual behavior of all but three industries — heavy electrical machinery, vehicles and suppliers, and light chemicals.[6] Since the figures represent percentage changes computed on an end of 1946 base, the fact that industry-by-industry values

---

[5] Using Brill's figures, "Financing of Capital Formation" (Table 5), for all corporations, the average per cent dividend payout was 65 per cent for the 1922–1929 period and only 30 per cent in 1946–1952. Comparable ratios for dividend payments as a per cent of gross profit before taxes are 43 per cent and 15 per cent respectively.

[6] The difference is not too pronounced in the case of light chemicals, and the other two exceptions are readily explained by the fact that these are industries dominated by corporate giants who obtain equity money relatively cheaply. In fact, if General Electric is removed from the heavy electrical group and General Motors from vehicles and suppliers, these two industries also exemplify the general preference for debt over equity.

for long-term debt and equity expansion are substantially less than those for asset growth means that the general tendency toward even greater financial conservatism was also common to all constituent parts of manufacturing since equal percentage increases would be necessary to sustain the "status quo." Consequently, retained earnings and depreciation expenses must have been primary sources for each individual industry as well as the aggregate of manufacturing. The aversion or inability to secure outside funds noted in so many individual field interviews and questionnaire responses is certainly not contradicted by these figures. The existence of previously accumulated cash reserves and high inflationary levels of internally available funds apparently enabled most firms to expand at a rapid rate according to preferred financial arrangements.

INDUSTRY CHARACTERISTICS ASSOCIATED WITH THE USE OF OUTSIDE FUNDS

The great preference of manufacturing corporations for internal funds is certainly an economic regularity of some stability and importance. Such an observation immediately raises, however, an obvious further question. What explains the deviations from strict reliance on internal funds that do occur? Clearly, outside sources are still used by manufacturing corporations, albeit in limited amounts, and any satisfactory theory of corporation financial behavior must explain these "exceptions." Therefore, it is necessary to determine what the special situations or circumstances are that overcome such a strong aversion to outside financing.

One obvious possibility is that a need to "tap outside money" will arise in industrial sectors experiencing unusually rapid growth. Such growth could be due to the development of a revolutionary new product. Or it could be derived from a sudden surge in the demand for an established product which is in temporarily scarce supply because, say, of a wartime moratorium on production. Similarly, an upward surge in the business cycle could generate relatively greater pressures on the productive capacity of the more durable consumer and producer good sectors since the cyclical swings in the demand for these products is likely to exceed that of the non-durables.

To test the relationship between growth and the use of outside financing, a measure of growth is obviously needed. This is a difficult matter since such a measure must not reflect inter-industry differences that have no relation to differential growth rates. For example, gross investment and the change in gross fixed assets are unsatisfactory because they fail to account for between industry differences in the obsolescence and capital consumption rates.

One reason that a measure of growth that cuts across industry classifications is needed is the curious circumstance that identifying the use of external money sources as a function of growth is easier at the aggregate industry level than at the firm level of observation. This, of course, is the converse of the usual situation in which the greater the disaggregation, the easier it is to identify direction of causation. For an individual firm, however, access to outside funds could as logically determine growth as vice versa. On the other hand, for an entire industry, it is difficult to imagine that inter-industry differences in the availability of outside funds *cause* different growth rates. In other words, for an entire industry it seems likely that growth prospects determine both the necessity to use and the ability to obtain outside financing.

With these considerations in mind, the average net investment rate and the change in the mean age variable (that is, the change in the ratio of depreciation reserves to gross fixed assets) have been used as measures of industry growth. Both measures are shown for all seventeen industry groups in Table 23.

The net investment values are merely gross investment less depreciation expenses and thus, to the extent that depreciation represents actual capital consumption and obsolescence, this figure is a better indicator of real growth than gross investment. Furthermore, whether or not depreciation expenses do reflect capital consumption, the net investment figure is clearly a better gauge of possible money needs since depreciation expenses are invariably a source of funds as long as net profits are positive. In other words, the net investment figure at least represents the amount of plant and equipment outlay that must be financed out of retained earnings, a reduction in liquid assets, or external sources.

TABLE 23

A COMPARISON OF INDUSTRY GROWTH AND MODERNIZATION RATES

Industry	(1) Average Net Investment Rate 1946-50	(2) Change in Mean Age Index
Pulp and Paper	.167	.114
Light Chemicals	.149	.072
Heavy Chemicals	.101	.107
Petroleum	.094	.079
Rubber	.126	.033
Heavy Steel	.079	.042
Metal Products	.109	.034
Other Machinery	.093	.079
Light Electrical Machinery	.121	.085
Heavy Electrical Machinery	.150	.105
Vehicles and Suppliers	.120	.091
Consumer Durables	.155	.057
Machine Tools	.073	.070
Basic Textiles	.102	.085
Other Textiles	.106	.146
Clothing	.087	.125
Radio and Television	.250	.098

The change in age measure is obviously related to net investment[7] but avoids some of the more serious difficulties involved in that concept.[8] In general, an index of growth defined by the ratio of net investment to capital stock in a

[7] The rank order correlation between the two measures equals .26.
[8] For one thing, effects of price changes are alleviated if the new equipment is subject to roughly the same depreciation policies as the old. (See Chapter IV.)

base period will differ from the change in age index. (Equivalence will occur, however, in the rather limited case where net investment is zero, depreciation expenses equal actual capital retirements, and capital losses are nil.) The change in age index serves present purposes better than a net investment measure because it varies directly with gross investment and capital retirements and inversely with depreciation expense and capital losses while the net investment ratio varies only with gross investment directly and depreciation expense inversely.[9]

These properties are, perhaps, at least partially responsible for the much better explanation that the change in age variable provides of the inter-industry differences in the use of outside funds as contrasted with net investment. Specifically, the rank order correlation between the ranks based on the change in age measure and those based on the increase in outstanding debt and equity, as reported in Table 22, equals slightly more than 0.30 which is just significant, on a one-tailed test, at the 5 per cent level. On the other hand, the rank order correlation between the net investment ranks and the use of outside funds is a bare 0.06. A somewhat different approach to the relationship between use of outside money and growth was also attempted. In this instance, the median dividend payout ratio within industries was found for every year. These were then averaged across the years 1947–1949 for each industry to obtain an average figure that was not distorted by extreme values, since its constituent items were medians. The results are presented in Table 24. These "typical" dividend payouts were then rank correlated with the average investment rate for the particular industry during the postwar period, giving rank one to the industry with the highest payout and also the industry with the highest net investment rate. The result was a simple rank correlation coefficient of −0.38, which

---

[9] Capital retirement is here equated to the value of retired equipment which is already written off the books; a capital loss is construed to mean any residual value of such equipment, that is, original cost which has not been written off.

TABLE 24

MEDIAN DIVIDEND-PROFIT RATIO BY INDUSTRY AND YEAR

Industry	1945	1946	1947	1948	1949	Average 1946-1949*
Pulp and Paper	63.5	37.2	29.6	36.2	45.6	37.2
Light Chemicals	63.0	48.2	49.9	45.7	57.9	50.4
Heavy Chemicals	73.4	50.8	49.8	51.5	54.6	51.7
Petroleum	43.9	41.9	30.9	25.2	39.6	34.4
Rubber	47.9	32.4	37.6	41.8	52.2	41.0
Heavy Steel	67.2	54.2	40.6	31.3	42.0	42.0
Metal Products	59.9	45.5	37.2	43.8	50.9	44.4
Other Machinery	65.6	53.4	39.3	37.0	49.0	44.7
Light Electrical Machinery	65.9	50.7	43.8	42.4	47.8	46.2
Heavy Electrical Machinery	57.5	42.2	28.5	38.8	50.3	40.0
Vehicles and Suppliers	49.8	45.2	33.9	38.3	40.3	39.4
Consumer Durables	52.8	45.3	31.4	35.3	45.4	39.4
Machine Tools	58.6	48.1	56.3	51.1	62.5	54.5
Basic Textiles	40.2	24.6	30.1	37.5	64.1	39.1
Other Textiles	64.9	49.2	47.3	39.7	53.4	47.4
Clothing	58.0	33.0	45.0	36.0	52.0	41.5
Radio and Television	33.0	49.0	32.0	22.0	34.0	34.3
Average (all industries)	56.8	44.2	39.0	38.4	49.5	42.8

*Because of the exceptional circumstances governing dividend policy at the end of the war, the 1945 median was excluded from the averages.

on a one-tailed test is just significant at the 1 per cent level.[10] While only a partial explanation, it seems that growth influences the dividend payout and use of outside funds in an important way.

Such limited evidence leads to a reasonably certain but tentative conclusion that growth influences the extent to which external financing is used; apparently, some relation-

[10] It was thought that possibly market concentration and rivalry would affect the dividend payout rate. However, all rank correlations of the dividend payout rate with concentration indexes, monopoly ranks and the change in the age of equipment index proved to be essentially zero.

ship exists but this relationship provides far less than a total explanation of inter-industry differences in the use of outside money. Obviously, other factors must influence this process.

In the discussion in Chapter II on institutional, economic, and historical foundations of producers' attitudes toward internal funds, it was suggested that the use of outside financing might be much more extensive in industries subject to greater market competition or rivalry. Such a hypothesis could be tested by comparing an industry's use of outside money with an index of competition and rivalry. The usual index is based on some measure of an industry's concentration computed in terms of such values as sales, shipments, value added, or asset ownership. Strictly speaking, these concentration indices are merely proxy measures of monopoly concentration which ideally would be gauged by the degree of market interdependence in each industry and be based upon immensely detailed studies of individual market sectors. A primary difficulty of previous concentration measures has been the absence of the detailed information needed to compute indices on a sufficiently disaggregative level to correspond to realistic market definitions. This situation has recently been corrected by the publication of specific indices of concentration (based primarily on value of shipments) for over 500 individual industries.[11] These small industry indices have been aggregated for present purposes into the seventeen large industry groups of this study. This was done by weighting each "sub-industry's" concentration index by the value of its shipments. The final value of the concentration index, as reported in Table 25, is therefore a weighted average of the concentration indices for each of the constituent market areas of the large industry group. As a consequence, the final index is essentially free of any particular market bias that would result if concentration was measured with reference to the large industry group as a single entity. For example, the percentage of

[11] U. S., Congress, House, Committee on the Judiciary, *Hearings, Study of Monopoly Power,* 81st Cong., 1st Sess., 1949, Serial No. 14, Part 2-B (Washington, 1950), 1437–1457.

total automobile industry shipments accounted for by the first four firms is *not* that attributable to final fabricators alone, as it would be if the component market distinctions were ignored, but is instead the average percentage of shipments accounted for by the first four firms in the various

TABLE 25

CONCENTRATION INDICES BY INDUSTRY

Industry	Percentage of Total Value Shipments Accounted for by Top Eight Firms in Constituent Market Sectors
Pulp and Paper	29
Light Chemicals	53
Heavy Chemicals	68
Petroleum	59
Rubber	72
Heavy Steel	62
Metal Products	34
Other Machinery	46
Light Electrical Machinery	52
Heavy Electrical Machinery	63
Vehicles and Suppliers	40
Consumer Durables	17
Machine Tools	30
Basic Textiles	77
Other Textiles	31
Clothing	40
Radio and Television	39

kinds of parts, truck, and accessories production as well as final fabrication.

Appropriate consideration of the heterogeneous market character of large industrial groupings does not eliminate, of course, all the difficulties involved in measuring and defining competition or even market concentration. Above all, there is still the problem of reducing the concentration data for a given industry to one specific index or measure. To measure quantitative concentration some sort of area above the Lorenz curve is usually evaluated. The real question, of course, is just which area. For example, should it be all the area above the curve? Or all the area above the curve but below the 45-degree line? Or all above the first four firms? Or all above the first eight? Or all above the first 10 per cent of the total number of firms? The list could be extended almost indefinitely.[12] Whatever measure is selected, it obviously makes little difference to an ordinal interpretation if the Lorenz curves of the different industrial groupings never cross over one another. That is, in such a case, the industries would be in the same rank order irrespective of the particular point chosen to determine the rankings; industry ranks based on the first four firms would be the same as those based on the first eight, twenty, or fifty. Rosenbluth has already shown[13] that there is no apparent crossover of the Lorenz curve for the largest four firms since industry ranks are essentially equivalent whether based on the first two, three, or four companies. Using Cellar Committee data, the same appears to be true for industry ranks based on the top eight, twenty, and fifty companies.[14] It is apparently, therefore, a matter of small consequence which of the many candidate measures is actually used.

Thus, while admittedly arbitrary, the choice made here of measuring concentration in terms of the first eight firms also should be quite inconsequential in its influence on the ultimate results. The actual concentration indices are shown in Table 25. The simple product moment correlation of −0.853 between top-eight concentration and the percentage change in use of outside funds in Table 22 indicates that competitive conditions do force greater reliance on external

[12] An excellent discussion of the technical characteristics of some of the principal alternatives will be found in Dwight B. Yntema, "Measures of the Inequality in the Personal Distribution of Wealth or Income," *Journal of the American Statistical Association,* XXVIII (December 1933), 423–433.

[13] Gideon Rosenbluth, "Measures of Concentration," in *Business Concentration and Price Policy,* Conference of Universities — National Bureau Committee for Economic Research, 1954 (Princeton, 1955), 57–95.

[14] The rank order correlations for the seventeen industries of this study are .9 or better in all cases.

financing. However, the result may be more apparent than real since virtually all of the observed correlation is due to the extreme values associated with the heavy electrical, radio and television, and clothing industries. With these three industries removed, the correlation is effectively reduced to nothing. Another method of establishing the same point is to consider the rank order correlation between the two series since rank order measures are insensitive to the degree of difference between the constituent items in the series, that is, all differences between proximate observations are reduced to equality by ranking. This rank order correlation is a very nominal —0.15.

The somewhat negative nature of the results may, of course, be due to the inadequacies of the concentration index as a measure of competition. Specifically, concentration and firm size are not the only dimensions of monopolistic behavior in an industry; such other matters as regional dispersion of markets, product specialization, the degree of managerial autonomy for subordinates in a large corporation, and the intangible differences in corporation ambitions will clearly condition the extent of price competition and other forms of trade rivalry within a given industry. The importance of these factors has long been recognized and recent efforts to derive indices of competition have included an evaluation of their importance.[15] Unfortunately, the industry groupings of these previous studies are so much broader than those used in this investigation that the results are of little use for present purposes. Furthermore, the results pertain to an earlier historical period which may or may not be like the prewar period under investigation here.

A fresh attempt has therefore been made to derive roughly equivalent results for the industry groups and time period of this study. The approach was to use the simple expedient of independently asking three persons knowledgeable in the field to rank the seventeen industries by degree

---

[15] See Clair Wilcox, *Competition and Monopoly in American Industry*, Temporary National Economic Committee, Monograph No. 21 (Washington, 1940) and G. Warren Nutter, *The Extent of Enterprise Monopoly in the United States, 1899–1939* (Chicago, 1951).

of competitiveness. Competition was broadly defined to include all kinds of rivalry for market share and position as well as price competition. In other words, the measure of competitive behavior was linked to an evaluation of the "norms" of firm theory when modified to include monopo-

TABLE 26

A RANKING OF THE INDUSTRIES ACCORDING TO MARKET SHARE RIVALRY

Industry	Expert #1	Expert #2	Expert #3	Consensus
Pulp and Paper	13	14	9	11
Light Chemicals	5	2	5	4
Heavy Chemicals	14	13	13	13
Petroleum	12	15	12	12
Rubber	16	12	15	15.5
Heavy Steel	17	17	17	17
Metal Products	9	9	11	9
Other Machinery	10	10	10	10
Light Electrical Machinery	8	8	7	8
Heavy Electrical Machinery	15	11	16	15.5
Vehicles and Suppliers	11	16	14	14
Consumer Durables	6	6	6	6
Machine Tools	7	7	8	7
Basic Textiles	1	3	1	1
Other Textiles	3	4	2	3
Clothing	2	1	4	2
Radio and Television	4	5	6	5

Note: The consensus represents a ranking based on the sum of the first three columns.

listic competition. An entrepreneur or an industry thus was considered more or less "competitive" according to how many and to what extent any of the classical forms of rivalry are evidenced. Price concessions, product improvement, advertising outlay, cost reduction, etc., all became relevant variables in this evaluation.

The results of this ranking operation are shown in Table 26. The last column represents the mean rank, that is, a ranking according to the sum of the first three columns. Despite the potential ambiguity of the term "market rivalry," the rankings show a notable homogeneity. There is a particularly strong tendency toward agreement on industries belonging at either extreme of the competitive spectrum. Undoubtedly, this partly reflects the homogeneous background of those participating; all three individuals were participants in the Merrill Foundation study of competitive behavior being conducted under the supervision of Professor Mason. The ranks must reflect the established consensus that has emerged from the many discussions of that group on the extent and location of competition in the American economy. It is also interesting to note the relationship between these more "subjective" or inclusive ranks and those based solely on concentration. In general, the results are similar, the rank order correlation between the consensus of the experts and the concentration ranks being 0.54. The discrepancies, moreover, occur where they might be logically expected, for example, in pulp and paper which has relatively low concentration but is given a low competitive rank on the qualitative scale because of the strong tendency toward regional concentration of markets in this industry.

This slight alteration in the character of the competition measure has little effect, however, on the empirical results when use of outside funds is explained in terms of competitive pressures. The rank order correlation between the concensus of industry rankings for this new competition measure and percentage change in use of outside funds is only slightly better than that previously recorded for the concentration ranks: −0.18 as compared with −0.15.

In short, competitive factors apparently do not explain the use of outside funds as well as the growth factor. If the competition hypothesis has any validity at all, it is more as an explanation of the extreme values than of intermediate and minor differences in financial behavior. This, of course, might still be a fact of considerable importance. To summarize, the extent to which outside financing is used in different industries appears to be a multi-faceted phenomenon that is only partially explained by the two most obvious influences, growth and competitive pressures.[16]

THE RELATIONSHIP BETWEEN THE DIVIDEND PAYOUT AND INVESTMENT

By far the most outstanding characteristic of the zero order correlations between investment and the dividend to profit ratio is the heterogeneous nature of the results. When the frequency distributions for the various simple correlations were plotted by the technique described in Chapter IV, the values for most variables clung about some one clearly distinguishable central tendency and tapered off more or less normally on either side. With the dividend variable, however, the distribution was not only bimodal but the two modes were of different signs, as can be seen from Figure 1, in which the histogram of that distribution is reproduced.[17] Clearly, the more prominent of the two modes and the greater bulk of the distribution are above negative values. This agrees with the *a priori* expectation that the greater percentage of profits paid out in dividends, the fewer internal funds available for financing investment. However, a very substantial proportion of the results are positive. This is not immediately explicable since there is no reason for the pattern of intercorrelations with other potential independent variables to correct this tendency in the partials. Indeed, the most pronounced of the intercorrelations would work in just the opposite direction.[18]

The question thus arises of whether there is any pattern in the appearance of the positive correlations. As a first

---

[16] For completeness, it is worth noting that the two competition measures are positively (although slightly) related to the growth measures so the partial correlation between use of outside funds and either growth or market competition would deviate but slightly from the simple correlations.

[17] This is the distribution obtained by using unweighted results. The picture is not fundamentally changed if the results are weighted by either gross fixed assets or number of observations.

[18] For example, because of managerial rigidities in dividend policies, the dividend to profit ratio goes down when the profit rate goes up, but investment also goes up when profits go up, intensifying the negative tendency in the dividend to investment simple correlations.

FIGURE 1
DISTRIBUTION OF SIMPLE CORRELATIONS BETWEEN INVESTMENT AND THE DIVIDEND TO PROFIT RATIO

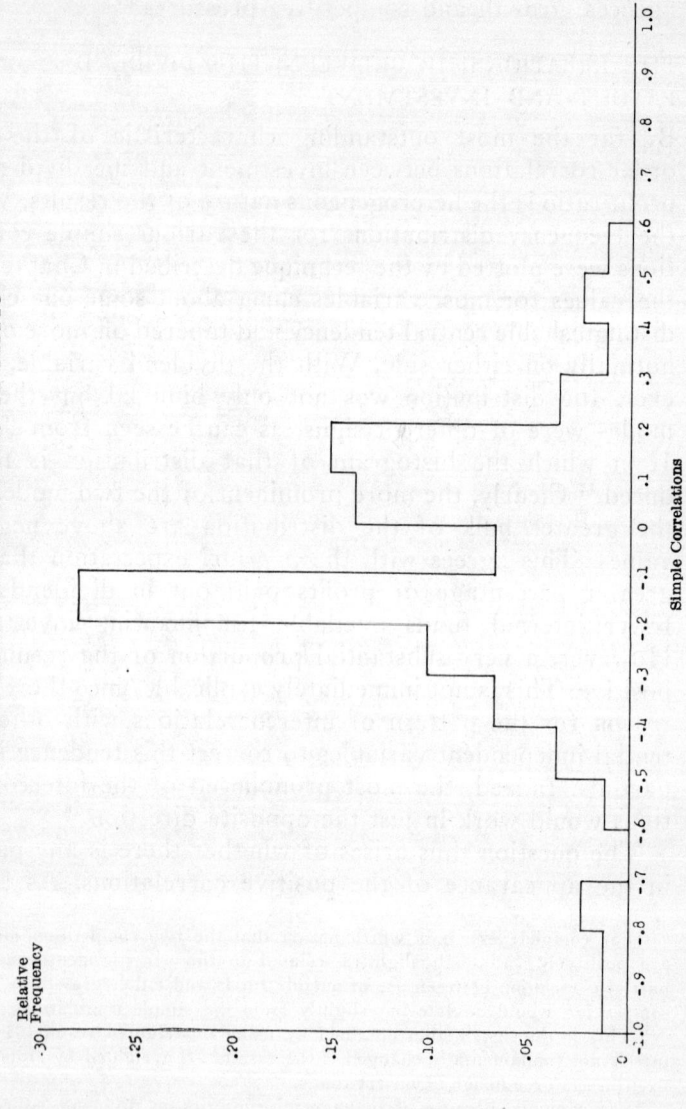

FINANCIAL PATTERNS

step, a scrutiny of the industry results by years presented in Table 27 certainly reveals little yearly emphasis except for the fact that 1946 has the fewest positive values — three. The other years range narrowly between six for 1949 and eight for both 1947 and 1948.

Nor is there any startlingly suggestive pattern in the industry-by-industry results. Machine tools, however, is the

TABLE 27
SIMPLE CORRELATIONS BETWEEN INVESTMENT AND THE DIVIDEND TO PROFIT RATIO

Industry	1946	1947	1948	1949	1950
Pulp and Paper	-.116	.106	.171	..280	-.076
Light Chemicals	-.247	-.196	-.138	-.150	.059
Heavy Chemicals	-.203	.256	.123	-.065	-.120
Petroleum	-.133	-.123	.513	-.181	.146
Rubber	-.272	-.366	-.502	-.328	.088
Heavy Steel	-.432	.028	-.108	-.103	-.714
Metal Products	.075	-.306	-.152	.259	-.070
Other Machinery	-.817	.142	-.189	-.190	.032
Light Electrical Machinery	-.916	-.138	.065	-.107	.440
Heavy Electrical Machinery	-.385	-.157	.134	.196	-.255
Vehicles and Suppliers	.089	-.145	-.022	.335	-.309
Consumer Durables	-.089	.049	-.210	-.130	-.364
Machine Tools	-.189	-.116	-.227	-.123	-.163
Basic Textiles	.149	.021	-.472	-.402	.043
Other Textiles	-.120	-.013	.129	.078	-.175
Clothing	-.263	.035	.144	-.233	.185
Radio and Television	-.234	.162	.452	.200	-.787

only industry which records no positive values; rubber, heavy steel, light chemicals, and consumer durables perform in very similar fashion with only one positive correlation each, and these so slightly positive as to be easily within the realm of pure chance. Looking back at Table 27, all these negative value industries are also seen to be more stagnant, less market share competitive, than average. Moreover, the greatest number and most substantial of the positive values occur in such rapidly growing industries as pulp and paper, clothing, and radio and television. To test whether this result is more than mere chance, a three by two contingency table is set up in Table 28 enumerating the actual and expected number of plus and minus correlations for the top six, middle five,

TABLE 28

A CONTINGENCY TABLE OF POSITIVE AND NEGATIVE CORRELATIONS BETWEEN DIVIDEND PAYOUT AND INVESTMENT OBSERVED FOR TOP SIX, MIDDLE FIVE, AND LOWEST SIX INDUSTRIES ON CHANGE IN AGE INDEX

	Number of Negative Correlations	Number of Negative Correlations	Total
1. Top Six Industries on Age Index	14 (18.8)	16 (11.2)	30
2. Middle Five Industries on Age Index	22 (15.6)	3 (9.4)	25
3. Bottom Six Industries on Age Index	17 (18.8)	13 (11.2)	30
TOTALS	53	32	85

Chi-square = 10.19

For two degrees of freedom Chi-square is 9.210 at the 1 per cent significance level.

Note: The parentheses enclose the expected number for each box.

and lowest six industries on the change in age scale of Table 23. When a Chi-square test is applied, a value of 10.19 results, which would occur by chance with a probability of less than 1 per cent. While these are highly significant results, this outcome would be slightly more satisfying if the pattern of change were a little more consistent between groups; specifically, top six and middle five firms account for the great bulk of discrepancies.

Still, the results clearly suggest that in secularly expanding industries, where the need for outside funds is likely to be great, the firm which maintains a good money market relationship by paying higher dividends thereby enables itself to obtain the funds to invest and expand rapidly. If one also assumes that a larger dividend is more likely to raise the price of a "growth stock," the relationship becomes even more plausible. In other words, higher dividend payments are more likely to be rewarding in a dynamic than in a stagnant industrial sector because of: (1) a greater need to obtain outside funds in growing industries with unsettled trade position ambitions; and (2) the greater effect upon stock price such payments may have when the long-term outlook is expansionary.

SUMMARY

In the 1946 to 1950 period, manufacturing firms in general displayed a strong reluctance to finance needs from external sources; this was true not only for the manufacturing sector as a whole but for most component industries as well. When external sources were used in the postwar period, long-term debt was very strongly preferred to equity.

In addition, the use of external financing in different industries was found to be at least slightly related to the presence of competition and growth. Competition seemed to be particularly effective in explaining the extreme cases of extensive or very slight utilization of outside funds. The correlations between percentage expansion in outside funds and growth and competition were very limited, however, and provide only a partial explanation of the use of outside funds.

The simple correlations between dividends and investment were chiefly marked by extreme heterogeneity in the results. Two substantial clusters in the correlations were observed: one negative as expected from *ex ante* considerations and another positive which was not expected. It was found that the positive results were associated with the industries recording a large change in the mean value of the age variable and vice versa. The tentative explanation advanced for this behavior was that firms in growing industries not only needed outside funds and consequently good relations with the money market more than did stagnant industries but also stood the best possibility of deriving appropriate benefits from a more generous dividend policy.

In sum, the picture is one of extreme financial conservatism departed from only with reluctance and then, primarily, in industries that are growing rapidly or are subject to some sort of competitive pressure.

Chapter X

The Liquidity Restraint and the Internal Growth Rates of Small and Large Firms

INTRODUCTION

Long-standing American worries about the possibility of growing economic centralization received new impetus in recent years. These anxieties stemmed from a variety of sources connected with war and postwar conditions. For example, many felt that large firms received preference in war contracts or liquidation of government industrial holdings at the end of World War II. Furthermore, anxiety arose because of the higher corporate tax rates that were inaugurated during the war, since, it is argued, small firms place greater reliance on internal funds for investment needs, in part because of less access to long-term capital markets.[1] Objective measurement of whether such developments have fostered increased market concentration is, however, exceedingly difficult. Not only do discussants often disagree on interpretation of observed results but also on what constitutes a proper measure of such a multi-dimensional problem.[2]

[1] These points have already been discussed at length in Chapter VII.
[2] This is well illustrated by the discussion which followed publication of Morris Adelman's work, "The Measurement of Industrial Concentration," *Review of Economics and Statistics,* XXXIII (November 1951), 269–296, measuring war and postwar concentration in terms of broad aggregates, e.g.,

The disagreements have resulted in an unfortunate tendency to overlook the remarkable unanimity in the basic findings of most recent investigations.[3] For example, there is substantial agreement that recent events have done little to increase the market power of the very largest firms. In fact, the recent merger movements, as contrasted with those at the turn of the century and in the 1920's, involved mostly small and medium sized rather than the very largest firms. Furthermore, there is good evidence that as a means of expansion internal growth is more important than external [4] — although primary emphasis of previous studies has been upon the politically more volatile issue of external growth by merger or acquisition.

This relative neglect of empirical measurement of internal growth rates constitutes the main *raison d'être* for this chapter. A comparison will be made of small and large firm investment rates in the 1946 to 1950 period for the industry groups included in this study. Moreover, the average internal growth rates for the five-year period will be compared with those just for the year 1949 to evaluate the impact of recession upon large and small firm growth. Finally, because the financial aspect is frequently considered to be the primary handicap to small firm internal expansion, the reliance upon different financial forms will be inspected for the different size groups. Explicitly, the following hypothesis will be tested: that small firms rely more on internal funds and

---

see the discussion by Corwin D. Edwards, George W. Stocking, Edwin B. George, and Adolph A. Berle, Jr., "Four Comments on 'The Measurement of Industrial Concentration,'" *Review of Economics and Statistics,* XXXIV (May 1952), 156–174.

[3] This is based on the authors' scrutiny of what they consider to be four recent and excellent studies on the subject, those by Adelman, "The Measurement of Industrial Concentration"; J. Keith Butters and John Lintner, "Effect of Mergers on Industrial Concentration, 1940–47," *Review of Economics and Statistics,* XXXII (February 1950), 30–48; Gertrude G. Schroeder, *The Growth of Major Steel Companies, 1900–1950* (Baltimore, 1953); and J. Fred Weston, *The Role of Mergers in the Growth of Large Firms* (Berkeley and Los Angeles, 1953).

[4] Internal growth is defined as that achieved when a firm invests funds in the creation of new plant facilities while external growth represents the acquisition of control over the facilities of already existing firms through merger or similar devices.

short-term bank debt than do large firms. This will be checked both by considering different financial patterns and also by looking at the partial correlations between investment and the various liquidity variables to see whether the small firms evidence greater or less sensitivity to financial constraints.

In general, this investigation shows there is little reason to dispute previous findings that small firms grow internally every bit as fast as large firms. However, there are also good reasons for believing that this result may be a fortuitous consequence of the extreme prosperity and easy money policies of the period. Similarly, the evidence on relative ease of access to outside funds is mixed: overall the small firms seem to have done as well as the large firms. On the other hand, where access to outside funds would seem to really count, that is, in rapidly growing industries, the small firms have used or been able to obtain substantially less outside money than their large competitors. Furthermore, there is fairly clear evidence that small firm investment plans are more sensitive to levels of liquidity flow and less sensitive to capacity utilization than those of the large firms.

CONCEPTS AND DEFINITIONS

Before proceeding, it is obviously necessary to define certain terms. Small and large, for example, are extremely uncertain and relative concepts since a firm that is large in one industry may be small in another. Consequently, size categories have been defined differently in different industries. The general procedure has been to modify the size classes[5] used in the correlation models only when necessary to obtain a more representative number of firms in a size group. This procedure permits maximum comparability with the parametric results obtained from the correlations. For the most part "small" will still mean zero to 4.9 million dollars of gross fixed assets since this category is well represented in most industries. The lower boundary for large firms, on the other

---

[5] The six size groups, in million dollars of gross fixed assets held in 1945, described earlier, are: (1) 0 to 4.9; (2) 5.0 to 14.9; (3) 15.0 to 29.9; (4) 30.0 to 74.9; (5) 75.0 to 299.9; (6) 300.0 and up.

162   THE INVESTMENT DECISION

hand, will fluctuate widely as can be seen from Table 29 in which the definitions of small and large used with the different industry groups are recorded.

Radio and television producers previously excluded because of insufficient degrees of freedom when running the

TABLE 29

DEFINITIONS OF SMALL AND LARGE FIRM USED WITH DIFFERENT INDUSTRY GROUPS

Industry	Small Firms $ Millions gross fixed assets	Large Firms $ Millions gross fixed assets
Pulp and Paper	0- 4.9	30.0 and up
Light Chemicals	0- 4.9	15.0 and up
Heavy Chemicals	0- 4.9	75.0 and up
Petroleum	0-14.9	75.0 and up
Rubber	0- 4.9	75.0 and up
Heavy Steel	0- 4.9	75.0 and up
Metal Products	0- 4.9	30.0 and up
Other Machinery	0- 4.9	30.0 and up
Light Electrical Machinery	0- 4.9	15.0 and up
Heavy Electrical Machinery	0- 4.9	75.0 and up
Parts Suppliers	0- 4.9	15.0 and up
Vehicle Manufacturers	0-74.9	75.0 and up
Consumer Durables	0- 4.9	5.0 and up
Machine Tools	0- 4.9	5.0 and up
Basic Textiles	0- 4.9	30.0 and up
Other Textiles	0- 4.9	15.0 and up
Radio and Television	0- 4.9	15.0 and up
All Industries	0- 4.9	75.0 and up

correlations have been reintroduced into the sample since this deficiency is not too important for present purposes. The automotive industry has been separated into parts suppliers and vehicle manufacturers. This separation, considered marginally desirable at other stages, was avoided until now because of the substantial reduction in degrees of freedom resulting from such a step. Failure to make the distinction at this point, however, would be serious since most large parts suppliers are smaller than the smallest vehicle manufacturers. Use of the term "and up" in the large definitions means only that for that particular industry all firms above the specified size have been categorized as large and not that the industry has firms ranging up to the highest size categories. For example, the largest machine tool producer has less than 30 million in gross fixed assets.

Gross fixed assets was used as the criterion of size.[6] Internal growth will be measured by the ratio of investment in both new and used equipment to lagged gross fixed assets. The term "used" does not include physical assets acquired by merger so that the ratio constitutes a fairly pure measure of internal growth and involves no acquisitions which could be categorized as external. Average internal growth for a firm over the five-year period 1946 to 1950 was computed by taking the simple arithmetic mean of the values for the five years.

A COMPARISON OF SMALL AND LARGE
FIRM INVESTMENT RATES

To obtain a measure of relative growth by small and large firms for the period from 1946 to 1950 the firm averages were themselves arithmetically averaged within size groups; the initial results are presented by industry group in Table 30. The small firms had strikingly more rapid average expansion rates than the large. Only in the case of three industries — the two autos and other machinery — is the relationship reversed; furthermore, only in the automotive group is the expansion by the large firms substantially more rapid. Indeed, if the chances of getting a higher average for small firms were really 50–50 in all industries, such a pattern of

---

[6] What constitutes the best measure of size and growth has been a matter of some disagreement: Weston, *The Role of Mergers in the Growth of Large Firms*, feels that sales is clearly superior; Schroeder, *The Growth of Major Steel Companies, 1900–1950*, prefers gross fixed assets; Butters and Lintner, "Effect of Mergers on Industrial Concentration, 1940–47," doubt that it makes much difference.

results would happen less than 2 times out of 1,000 purely by chance.

Averaging, of course, means that very rapidly growing firms are heavily weighted and, for obvious reasons, it is much easier for a small firm to execute a 100 per cent ex-

TABLE 30

ARITHMETIC AVERAGE 1946 TO 1950 GROWTH RATES FOR SMALL AND LARGE FIRMS

Industry	Small Firms per cent	Large Firms per cent
Pulp and Paper	.225	.148
Light Chemicals	.201	.180
Heavy Chemicals	.175	.168
Petroleum	.194	.117
Rubber	.150	.112
Heavy Steel	.161	.092
Metal Products	.172	.153
Other Machinery	.146	.150
Light Electrical Machinery	.186	.167
Heavy Electrical Machinery	.187	.150
Parts Suppliers	.194	.256
Vehicle Manufacturers	.135	.225
Consumer Durables	.223	.181
Machine Tools	.159	.081
Basic Textiles	.147	.093
Other Textiles	.159	.125
Radio and Television	.330	.175
All Industries (weighted average)	.192	.126

pansion than a corporate giant. One reason therefore that the smaller firms might record much higher group averages is that there are more extreme values, that is, very high expansion rates, in the smaller firm distributions. In fact, one interesting characteristic of the large firm groups is a tendency for the observations to be very closely bunched although the large firms in heavy chemicals and the two textiles are important exceptions.

This pattern clearly suggests that the median would be a more useful measure of central tendency than the arithmetic mean. Table 31 presents these median values. In most

TABLE 31

MEDIAN 1946 TO 1950 GROWTH RATES FOR SMALL AND LARGE FIRMS BY INDUSTRY GROUP

Industry	Small Firms per cent	Large Firms per cent
Pulp and Paper	.209	.132
Light Chemicals	.181	.186
Heavy Chemicals	.158	.158
Petroleum	.149	.119
Rubber	.091	.116
Heavy Steel	.092	.084
Metal Products	.199	.116
Other Machinery	.137	.149
Light Electrical Machinery	.216	.199
Heavy Electrical Machinery	.188	.149
Parts Suppliers	.166	.199
Vehicle Manufacturers	.125	.225
Consumer Durables	.195	.138
Machine Tools	.137	.078
Basic Textiles	.094	.087
Other Textiles	.137	.149
Radio and Television	.288	.175
All Industries (weighted average)	.166	.121

cases, the small firms as a group still grow at faster rates than the large firms even when the median is the measure. The overall edge is reduced, however, and the results are actually reversed in three industries — rubber, light chemicals, and other textiles. The rapid internal growth and prog-

TABLE 32

MEDIAN GROWTH RATES, 1949, FOR SMALL AND LARGE FIRMS

Industry	Small	Per Cent Decline from Overall Median	Large	Per Cent Decline from Overall Median
Pulp and Paper	.131	-.37	.088	-.33
Light Chemicals	.083	-.54	.149	-.20
Heavy Chemicals	.015	-.91	.076	-.52
Petroleum	.205	.38	.174	.46
Rubber	.056	-.38	.065	-.44
Heavy Steel	.048	-.48	.088	.05
Metal Products	.076	-.62	.085	-.27
Other Machinery	.063	-.54	.076	-.49
Light Electrical Machinery	.187	-.13	.115	-.42
Heavy Electrical Machinery	.089	-.52	.085	-.43
Parts Suppliers	.098	-.41	.080	-.60
Vehicle Manufacturers	.095	-.24	.150	-.33
Consumer Durables	.048	-.75	.068	-.51
Machine Tools	.064	-.53	.037	-.53
Basic Textiles	.160	.70	.111	.28
Other Textiles	.165	.20	.108	-.28
Radio and Television	.099	-.66	.171	-.02
All Industries (weighted average)	.081	-.51	.093	-.23

ress of the small firms in these years remain, though, as reasonably well-established facts.[7]

But in 1949, the one year of recession, small firms did not fare so well; their median growth rates in 10 of 17 instances fell beneath those of their bigger brethren in the same industry. Such a pattern could appear by chance about 30 per cent of the time if the odds of small firms exceed-

---

[7] On a paired comparison basis, the computed t statistics of 2.497 for differences between means and 1.441 for differences between medians of large and small firms are significant at the 2 per cent and 15 per cent level respectively.

ing large, or vice versa, were actually equal. The figures are presented in Table 32. Even more important, the small firms suffered larger percentage declines from the overall five-year median growth rates. For the entire sample the small firm median growth was off by 51 per cent as compared with 23 per cent for the large firms.

The explanation for the small firm difficulties in 1949 is not hard to find: the smaller producer is apparently more pervious to the adverse effects of recession than his larger colleague.[8] This is well illustrated by the relative sales losses sustained by the two size groups. The median decline in sales as a percentage of gross fixed assets for all firms, small and large, was —.111. Of 218 small firms, 127 were beneath this median value while only 16 of 51 large firms fell below. Using Chi-square to test the hypothesis that there is no significant difference in the sales experience between the two groups, a value is obtained which is more than twice that which would occur by chance 1/1000 of the time.

The moral is quite obvious and agrees with an observation made sometime ago by Butters and Lintner:[9] specifically, nothing helps the small firm so much as a liberal fiscal policy, good times, and general economic growth. The overall economic character of the postwar years fully met these conditions and small firms prospered accordingly, more than holding their own insofar as internal growth is concerned. Then, in the only year of general recession, this overall pattern was substantially reversed.

This point can be further elaborated by considering the few exceptions to the rule in 1949. In six industries — rubber, light electrical machinery, vehicle manufacturers and their suppliers, and the two textiles — the larger firms registered either greater percentage declines in growth rates or smaller percentage gains. Three of these six, the vehicle manufacturers and suppliers, and light electrical machin-

---

[8] On this point, see Irwin Friend and Jean Bronfenbrenner's comments on why small firms fell so much further beneath projected investment levels than large firms ("Business Investment Programs and Their Realization," *Survey of Current Business*, XXX (December 1950), 11–22).

[9] Butters and Lintner, "Effect of Mergers on Industrial Concentration, 1940–47."

ery, were industries that felt little impact from the 1949 recession. Textiles, on the other hand, suffered as much in 1949 as any industry in the non-durable sector of the economy. The perversity might have been due to the southward migration going on at the time; perhaps the smaller textile firms were more able to move because of fewer fixed northern commitments and more flexible management. In rubber, the difference is not sustantial and the large firms still retained about the same advantage enjoyed throughout the period. The cyclical reactions of these industries are broadly portrayed by sales behavior shown in Table 33. Thus, with

TABLE 33

QUARTERLY RATIOS OF 1949 TO 1948 SALES

Industry	First Quarter	Second Quarter	Third Quarter	Fourth Quarter
All manufacturing corporations	.985	.944	.923	.891
Rubber	.951	.928	.915	.901
Electrical	.955	.964	.935	.941
Vehicles	1.152	1.244	1.229	.887
Textile Mill Products	.789	.763	.883	1.013

Source: Federal Trade Commission and Securities and Exchange Commission, *Quarterly Financial Report, United States Manufacturing Corporations*, 1948 and 1949.

the exception of the textile group, the point remains that areas where small firms did best in 1949 were also the areas which did not feel the downturn so extensively.

THE LIQUIDITY AND FINANCIAL FACTOR

The greater susceptibility of small firm investment plans to depression influences might also be explained in terms of those special characteristics of the financial markets which affect small firm access to outside funds. *Ceteris paribus*, the same downward adjustment in sales and demand should have least immediate effect on the long-range plans of those firms that are most able to secure external funds to supplement any temporary deficiencies in current liquidity inflows. To the extent, then, that long-term outside money can be obtained more easily and cheaply by large than by small firms, the large firm should be less inclined to alter plant and investment plans in the face of temporary adversity. In short, not only would small firms suffer a greater proportional market loss in recession but they would also be more vulnerable to such losses if they must rely more on internal financing.

This poses the following explicit questions: Did small firms place greater reliance than large firms on internal and short-term sources of funds in the postwar period? Note the time period to which the question refers; all the well-documented complaints and studies of small firm financial difficulties in the thirties will be accepted as substantial and *prima facie* evidence that an affirmative answer was warranted in those years. Furthermore, to focus attention upon the very core of the problem, analysis will be confined to comparisons of the relative use by large and small corporations of what are commonly called "net new issues," that is, total new long-term bond and equity issues less retirements.[10]

Koch and Schmidt have already documented the situation as it existed in general terms at the end of 1946, the point at which the present investigation begins.[11] They noted that the larger (over 10 million in total assets) corporations at

---

[10] Unfortunately, it was impossible with available data to make an accurate appraisal of equity issued by one firm in exchange for the equity of another firm resulting from a merger action. This means that net is here defined with relation to the individual firm unit. Accepting the characterization reported earlier that recent merger movements involved small firms relatively more than large firms, this means that the percentage of small firm net new issues to end of 1946 outstanding issues may be biased slightly upward and the results must be correspondingly interpreted with caution.

[11] Albert R. Koch and Charles H. Schmidt, "Financial Position of Manufacturing and Trade in Relation to Size and Profitability, 1946," *Federal Reserve Bulletin,* XXXIII (September 1947), 1091–1102. In this and succeeding analyses of financial patterns the period from the end of 1946 to end of 1950 is used rather than the usual end of 1945 to end of 1950 period employed throughout the rest of the study. The primary reason for this change was that end of 1945 balance sheet data still reflected too many extraneous war influences.

that time were differentiated financially from small firms (under one million) in three respects: (1) the larger firms had in 1946 experienced a greater percentage increase in bank debt; (2) a larger ratio of long-term to short-term debt characterized large firm borrowings; (3) the larger firms had slightly better current ratios. In a later report Schmidt indicates that the same pattern existed in the first quarters of 1947, 1948, and 1949 as well.[12] A major difficulty with the Koch and Schmidt findings is that no stratification by industry group is performed.[13] Thus their results may reflect industry biases if certain industries have proportionally more small firms and also use short-term debt more extensively.

This deficiency has been rectified in the subsequent analysis of this chapter, but unfortunately the sample does not contain as many small firms as the Koch-Schmidt sample. Explicitly, the definitions of small and large set forth in Table 29 have been used and the ratio was computed of net new issues for the years 1947 through 1950 inclusive to the issues outstanding at the end of 1946 for all large and all small firms within each industry. In addition, the ratios of big firm net new issues to total net new issues in the industry and of big firm investment outlay 1947–1950 to total industry outlay 1947–1950 were computed. These latter figures permit a comparison of the relative need for funds between small and large firms. The results are presented in Table 34.

If small firms must rely more on internal and short-term sources than large firms, the net new issue growth ratios should be larger for the big firms than for the small firms. In other words, if large firms both expanded outside issues proportionally more and relied to a greater extent, either by choice or ability, on net new issues to finance postwar expansion, one can infer that the large firm was characteristically less reliant on those other sources of funds, internal

---

[12] Charles H. Schmidt, "Analyzing the Effects of Business Size on Sources and Uses of Funds," in *Conference on Research in Business Finance,* Universities-National Bureau Committee for Economic Research (New York, 1952), pp. 35–62.

[13] Koch and Schmidt, "Financial Position of Manufacturing and Trade," distinguish only the non-durable from the durable sector.

short-term, and trade debt, which are more cyclically volatile. Actually, this does not seem to be the case since the net new issue growth ratios are about the same for the small and large firms in the same industry. In fact, in petroleum, vehicle manufacturers, and machine tools the small firms expanded their long-term debt and equity holdings sub-

TABLE 34

LARGE AND SMALL FIRM USE OF OUTSIDE FUNDS COMPARED WITH GROWTH RATES

	Per Cent Change in Outstanding Issues 1946-50		Big Firm Per Cent Share in:	
Industry	Small	Large	Net New Issues 1947-50	Total Industry Investment 1947-50
Pulp and Paper	33.4	39.6	81.2	80.6
Light Chemicals	19.0	15.1	56.6	70.4
Heavy Chemicals	-4.8	47.2	69.6	73.1
Petroleum	77.1	27.8	88.0	95.4
Rubber	23.2	19.0	77.7	82.6
Heavy Steel	21.4	13.0	80.6	87.9
Metal Products	12.8	10.2	45.4	61.6
Other Machinery	14.8	42.0	56.4	54.1
Light Electrical Machinery	45.2	61.2	80.3	84.3
Heavy Electrical Machinery	40.8	-25.8	-107.8[+]	92.4
Parts Suppliers	47.3	12.0	30.2	68.1
Vehicle Manufacturers	25.9	4.8	42.7	82.2
Consumer Durables	21.4	27.5	55.8	44.1
Machine Tools	20.4	-4.6	-23.6	56.2
Basic Textiles	-8.7	16.7	22.0	22.3
Other Textiles	26.4	24.4	68.8	57.8
Radio and Television	72.2	56.4	66.3	61.8
All Industries	37.4	22.1		

[+] This is entirely due to the action of one firm, General Electric, which paid off by 1950 a $200 million debt issue floated in 1946. At the same time, General Electric floated no new equity issues.

stantially more percentagewise than the large firms. Only in the case of heavy chemicals, basic textiles, and other machinery is the observed relationship consonant with the view that the smaller firms had less access to outside funds. The same conclusion is borne out by a comparison of the relative shares of large firm participation in net new issues and investment outlay. The striking aspect of these ratios is how closely the two series correspond: big firms dominated the money markets in almost direct correspondence to their domination of investment growth.[14] Thus, insofar as the sample goes, the smaller firms, in aggregate, apparently did not rely on cyclically sensitive money sources in the postwar period. Any generalization of such a conclusion must, however, be carefully limited since there are several extraneous influences operating to make the small firm ratios larger than they would otherwise be. For example, as already pointed out, if equity issues exchanged at the time of a merger were netted out, the small firm percentages might drop more than the large firm values. Furthermore, the small firm group undoubtedly contains a higher percentage of young corporations. In light of evidence presented by Evans and Bridge that new firms tend to place greater reliance on equity sources than older establishments, it appears likely that the small firm ratios are probably for still another reason overstated.[15] And of course, it must be remembered that the sample does not include many of the very smallest firms.

Furthermore, the data deal with a particular period characterized by unusual prosperity and liberal monetary management. Thus while small firms may have been able to expand long-term debt and equity relatively as much as large

[14] Table 36 also makes evident how thoroughly large firms do dominate several industries in the absolute sense. Thus one might easily be led to substantial agreement with the view that big firms did not gain much in the postwar period mainly because they had already grown so much in the past.
[15] G. Heberton Evans, "Comment on Historical Series on Sources and Uses," *Conference on Research in Business Finance,* Universities-National Bureau Committee for Economic Research (New York, 1952), pp. 28–34 and Lawrence Bridge, "The Financing of Investment by New Firms," in *Conference on Research in Business Finance,* Universities-National Bureau Committee for Economic Research (New York, 1952), pp. 65–74.

firms when the period 1947–1950 is taken as a whole, it does not necessarily follow that small firms had equal access to those sources in 1949, the year of recession. It is possible that small firm ability to obtain outside money is cyclically sensitive in the same way that their sales and profits have already been observed to be. Testing for this possibility is extremely difficult — for the usual reason that control over relevant variables is virtually impossible. For example, a smaller increment or larger reduction of outstanding long-term debt and equity in times of recession may be as much a sign of financial strength as of inability to obtain outside funds.

Despite these hazards, an attempt to measure whether small and large firm financial practices differed under the recession conditions of 1949 seems useful. In order to proceed with the analysis, it will be assumed that secular forces in operation during the postwar period were definitely expansionary since under such conditions alone can it be inferred that the direction of causation runs from scarcity of funds to reduced plant and equipment outlay.[16] The value of net new issues made in 1949 was computed for the small and large firm group in each industry; this figure was then taken as a percentage of the 1949–1950 total for the group.[17] The percentage is thus a rough measure of just how much of the expansion in long-term debt and equity was left to the other, non-recession years; the lower the percentage, the more debt and equity expansion was retarded by the 1949 experience. A figure of 25 per cent represents a sort of break-even point since in such a case the 1949 expansion contributed its proportional share, one-quarter of the total four-year growth. Therefore if the percentage is more than 25, the industry group more than "held its own in 1949," and vice versa. Consequently, to be in agreement with the hypothesis that small firms find outside financing more difficult in recession than large firms, the percentages for the

---

[16] Only in the case of machine tools would exception, then only minor, to this premise seem warranted.

[17] If T equals total net new issues 1947–1950 and Y equals 1949 net new issues, then the percentage equals Y/T.

large firms should be greater than those for the small firms in the same industry and should more often fall near or above the 25 per cent value. Furthermore, particular stress should be put upon those results associated with the industries in which the upward secular tendencies were strongest. The results are presented in Table 35.

The evidence is extremely mixed, particularly when

TABLE 35

A COMPARISON OF 1949 NET NEW ISSUES WITH TOTAL NET NEW ISSUES FOR SMALL AND LARGE FIRMS BY INDUSTRY GROUP

Industry	SMALL FIRMS Total 1947-50 New New Issues $Millions	SMALL FIRMS 1949 Net New Issues $Millions	LARGE FIRMS Total 1947-50 Net New Issues $Millions	LARGE FIRMS 1949 Net New Issues $Millions	1949 PER CENT SHARE IN 1946-50 EXTERNAL FUND GROWTH Small Firms	1949 PER CENT SHARE IN 1946-50 EXTERNAL FUND GROWTH Large Firms
Pulp and Paper	21	2	202	17	9	12
Light Chemicals	15	3	˙53	24	21	45
Heavy Chemicals	-4	-1	481	2	--	1
Petroleum	26	3	1754	485	12	28
Rubber	6	0	95	-10	6	10
Heavy Steel	11	4	373	55	38	15
Metal Products	11	9	47	18	78	39
Other Machinery	17	10	245	56	60	19
Light Electrical Machinery	18	2	149	1	8	1
Heavy Electrical Machinery*	41	-4	-190	-57	-10	--
Parts Suppliers	40	5	29	-5	13	-16
Vehicle Manufacturers	60	2	45	40	4	88
Consumer Durables	18	-13	23	4	-71	20
Machine Tools	11	2	-2	0	21	--
Basic Textiles	-9	36	26	0	--	0
Other Textiles	26	9	29	0	32	0
Radio and Television	72	4	69	13	6	18
All (Total)	440	76	3615	645	17	18

*This is entirely due to the action of one firm, General Electric, which paid off by 1950 a $200 million debt issue floated in 1946. At the same time, General Electric floated no new equity issues.

viewed in an overall sense, since both small and large firms in the sample did 83 per cent of their total long-term debt and equity expansion in the non-recession years 1947, 1948, and 1950, or, in other words, did 17 per cent of their expansion in 1949. The large firms did better in 1949 in seven industries, the small firms in eight industries, while two industries — machine tools and heavy electrical machinery — cannot be interpreted because of special peculiarities. Though the costs of obtaining the funds may have been different for the two groups,[18] there again seems to be little doubt that small firms as a group obtained their proportional share of outside funds even in the recession year of 1949.[19]

When attention is confined to the growth industries, however, the picture is somewhat altered. Looking back at Table 35, the top six growth industries as measured by the change in age index are, in order: radio and television, pulp and paper, heavy chemicals, heavy electrical machinery, other textiles, and vehicle manufacturers. Of these six industries, the large firms in 1949 expanded long-term debt and equity more than the small firms in four instances: radio and television, pulp and paper, heavy chemicals, and vehicle manufacturers. Furthermore, a glance back at Table 35 indicates that in two of these four instances the 1949 experience reverses the situation existing for the whole period, that is, the small radio and television and vehicle manufacturers expanded long-term debt and equity more than the large firms when the whole period is taken into account.[20] Only in the case of other textiles did the small firms do better in the growth industries; heavy electrical machinery,

---

[18] Costs have been ignored here since the small firm complaints have been primarily directed against the unavailablity of long-term and equity money rather than to the terms of this availability.

[19] We do not know, of course, how much more money could have been obtained by the two groups if urgent needs had arisen. Perhaps the small firms managed to keep pace only by taking much fuller advantage of their opportunities. Still, the point remains that they did keep pace.

[20] Perhaps reflecting the inadequacy of the growth measure, two other industries generally considered to be growth industries in the postwar period — light chemicals and petroleum — also experienced this reversal in pattern with the small firms doing better for the whole period but worse in the one year, 1949.

for reasons pointed out before, remains a special case unto itself. It is therefore possible that the small firms kept pace in the overall figures for 1949 mainly because they led in those industries where the big firms had no desire to obtain outside money since internal sources sufficed. Where the desire to obtain outside funds might be expected to be strongest, the growth industries, the small firms were held back in 1949 even though they usually kept pace, or more than kept pace, for the whole 1946–1950 period.

A COMPARISON OF SMALL AND LARGE FIRM CORRELATION ESTIMATES

There is thus little evidence, insofar as the overall figures go, that small firms had poorer access to external funds than large firms but this does not mean that small firm investment outlay might not be more sensitive to profit inflow than that for large firms. For one thing, a small firm's ability to acquire outside funds may be more dependent upon a good profit showing. Furthermore, there are several reasons why the highly aggregative data used in the preceding section might be misleading. Actually, when a comparison is made of the relative importance of the different independent variables in the small and large firm models, the small firms are clearly more sensitive to the liquidity variables while the large firms are more capacity-accelerator prone.

Regressions by size groups, it will be recalled, were confined to the averaged data and to the models which set up investment as a function of either sales or profits, depreciation expense, capacity requirements, age of equipment at the end of 1945, and liquidity stock at the end of 1945. Due to capital intensity heterogeneity within the size groups most of the results could be expected to be biased downward.[21] The exceptions to this rule would be the capacity variable which should not be affected since it is based upon a comparison internal to each firm and the depreciation expense variable in which all the biases are upward. Partial correlation results are presented in Table 36 for the two size groups

[21] See Chapter V.

of particular interest in the present instance, those firms under 4.9 and over 75.0[22] million of gross fixed assets at the end of 1945. All results are reported except those for age and liquidity which were effectively zero in every case and therefore omitted. To adjust for differences in degrees of

TABLE 36

PARTIAL CORRELATIONS FOR DIFFERENT SIZE GROUPS BETWEEN INVESTMENT AND FOUR EXPLANATORY VARIABLES

Independent Variable	Partial Correlations Unadjusted for Sample Size		Partial Correlations Adjusted for Sample Size	
	Small[a]	Large[b]	Small[a]	Large[b]
Profits	.386**	.427*	.380	.370
Sales	.454**	.351	.451	.275
Depreciation Expense In Profit Model	.188*	.248	.165	.145
Depreciation Expense In Sales Model	.137*	.232	.120	.090
Capacity in Profit Model	.155*	.492**	.146	.452
Capacity in Sales Model	.056	.351**	.020	.270

*Significant at the 5 per cent level.

**Significant at the 1 per cent level.

[a] Under 4.9 million dollars gross fixed assets at the end of 1945.

[b] 75.0 million dollars and up gross fixed assets at the end of 1945.

freedom, the figures in the last two columns have been translated into unbiased point estimates of the correlations.

Primary interest centers on the comparison between size categories of the liquidity inflow and accelerator variables'

---

[22] Results for the over 75.0 million category were found by averaging the results for the 74.9 to 299.9 and 300.0 and up categories which were estimated separately. In every instance the results were virtually equivalent and certainly sufficiently homogeneous to permit averaging.

correlations with investment. If external financing was as easy for small as for large firms, the relationship between liquidity inflows and investment could be expected to be the same for the different size categories. Furthermore, with equal ease of access to outside funds, high capacity ultilization should be as conducive to increased investment outlay in the one case as the other; as pointed out in Chapter VIII, acceleration variables were most effective when unhampered by shortages of liquidity. Thus some significance must be attached to the two liquidity inflow variables, profits and depreciation expense, being more influential with small than large firms at the same time the capacity variable is best with the large firms. Explicitly, profits, measuring expectations as well as liquidity, is important in both cases but fares somewhat better, 1 per cent rather than 5 per cent significance, in the small size group. Depreciation expense, free from the expectations aspect, is a somewhat purer liquidity measure and its substantially greater significance for the small firms thus takes on special importance, assuming that the upward bias due to the technical factor of capital intensity heterogeneity is approximately equivalent in the two size groups. The pronounced reversal of these relationships for the capacity variable is even more striking. Therefore, the tentative implication is that large firms tend to invest somewhat more in accord with capacity requirements and less with reference to internal availability of funds while small firms find the liquidity restraint not only important but apparently important enough to defer acceleration induced expansion of productive output.[23]

SUMMARY

The findings of this chapter, particularly those dealing with business financing, have been primarily characterized by

---

[23] These results also have a certain significance for the investigation of Chapter VII. If the conclusion is correct that large firms operate in an environment in which the liquidity restraint is less crucial, this means that a policy of accelerated amortization may help the established small firm more than the large since it makes available to the smaller firm funds that it would not otherwise be able to obtain.

their heterogeneous character. The most evident conclusion, by far, was that small firms tend to grow at internal rates every bit as fast, if not faster, than large firms as long as the general economic climate is one of prosperity and easy availability of necessary funds. This was illustrated, in the first place, by the small firms generally growing at a more rapid rate in the period 1946–1950 than their larger competitors; furthermore, in 1949, the one year of recession, the overall pattern was sharply reversed as the large firms fared substantially better than the small firms.

In similar fashion, the small firms, in aggregate, also expanded their long-term debt and equity issues proportionately more than the large firms in the period 1946–1950. Whether or not small firms found it more difficult than big firms to procure outside funds in 1949 was very difficult to determine since there was conflicting evidence. Overall the small firms did about as well as the big firms; however, there was some evidence that this was because small firms did much better in those industries where the secular growth rate was less and the large firms could comfortably finance expansion needs out of internally available funds; in addition, the small firms recorded their worst relative performances in those growing industries where contact with outside money would seem most helpful and essential.

Finally, when the correlation models were applied to the data for the different size groups, the small firms evidenced a greater sensitivity to the liquidity flow variables, profits and depreciation expense, than did the large firms; conversely, the large firms were much more responsive than the small firms to the capacity variable. Taken together with the findings of Chapter IX, this suggested that the small firms might be somewhat more subject to liquidity restraints than large firms. This is reconcilable with the previous findings on the relative use of long-term debt and equity if it is assumed that small firm access to outside funds is much more dependent upon good profit performance.

All in all, the impediments to small firm progress and growth may be somewhat greater than those facing their large colleagues but they do not appear to be prohibitive. Certainly, in the immediate postwar period with its particular economic climate, small entrepreneurs were at least able to more or less maintain their relative position.

Chapter XI

Some Marginalist Hypotheses

INTRODUCTION

Had this study been exclusively limited to cross-section information, there would have been meager prospect of testing hypotheses or examining relationships concerning important variables which vary principally over time rather than within a given time period. For example, such important marginalist price variables as interest rates, stock prices, and the relative price of labor can be effectively studied only by using time series. In this chapter, an investigation will be made of these variables, which requires that brief consideration be given to the statistical problems peculiar to time series analysis.

The main technique to be used in exploring the behavior of the marginalist variables will be to combine certain estimates of parameters obtained from cross sections with time series estimates. For reasons more fully explained later on, only the profit and sales regression coefficients from cross-section data were used. The conclusions obtained are not much different from those reached by earlier investigators using similar variables. As in previous studies, interest rates proved to be of negligible significance. In accordance with Tinbergen's findings about the influence of stock prices, the results presented below indicate that these may well be important dynamic determinants of investment behavior.[1]

---

[1] Jan Tinbergen, *Statistical Testing of Business Cycle Theories* (Geneva, 1938). Also see appendix to Chapter II.

Finally, preliminary examination of the data revealed that the relative cost of capital and labor, although undoubtedly of some importance in the long run, did not significantly influence the behavior of investment in its year-to-year changes.

STATISTICAL PROBLEMS IN COMBINING
CROSS-SECTION AND TIME SERIES ESTIMATES

It should be recalled from Chapter V that it was thought advisable to use regression rather than correlation models to test the time series hypotheses. In order to do so and, at the same time, exploit information accumulated from the studies of cross-section interrelationships, procedures developed by Marschak, Tobin, Stone, Durbin, and Wold were used.[2] Specifically, these contributions have devised a systematic rationale for the joint use of parameter estimates from outside or "extraneous" sources, on the one hand, and time series sample estimates, on the other. Heretofore, these techniques have been used exclusively in connection with consumer demand studies, although their applicability to a wider range of phenomena is quite possible. In Stone's notation, the objective is to estimate the parameters B_1 and B_2 in the following regression equation:

$$Y = B_1 X_1 + B_2 X_2.$$

The most straightforward procedure is to simultaneously estimate B_1 and B_2, using standard regression procedures. A second possible way to estimate, say B_2, would be to take an outside or extraneous estimate of B_1, multiply this estimate times its relevant time series and then subtract the product from the time series dependent variable, Y. In this simple

[2] Jacob Marschak, "On Combining Market and Budget Data in Demand Studies: A Suggestion," *Econometrica,* VII (October 1939), 332–335; James Tobin, "A Statistical Demand Function for Food in the U. S. A.," *Journal of the Royal Statistical Society,* Series A, CXIII (Part II 1950), 113–141; Richard Stone, *The Measurement of Consumers' Expenditure and Behavior in the United Kingdom 1920–1938; Volume I* (Cambridge, England, 1954); J. Durbin, "A Note on Regression when There Is Extraneous Information about One of the Coefficients," *Journal of the American Statistical Association,* XLVIII (December 1953), 799–808; and Herman Wold and Lars Jureen, *Demand Analysis* (New York, 1953).

example, the bivariate regression of the "reduced series" (i.e., $Y - B_1X_1$) on X_2 could then be estimated. This would yield an unbiased estimate of B_2, if, first of all, the estimate of B_1 was unbiased and, secondly, B_1 was uncorrelated with X_2. No categorical statement can be given that will tell which of the two procedures is the best in any given situation. Objections can and have been made to the use of extraneous estimators.[3] For example, the extraneous estimators estimated on different types of information may reflect basically different underlying behavior and therefore cannot appropriately be combined with time series estimates. This, of course, will be true sometimes; but there are no rules or laws which assert that this will invariably or even generally be so. However, it will frequently occur that the cross-section estimates reflect long-run behavior and in such circumstances will be overestimates of the parameters that would correctly reflect short-run behavior. The advantages of using an extraneous estimator are twofold. First, the estimate of B_2 will sometimes be more efficient when an extraneous estimator is used. This will be so when the variance of the extraneous estimator is less than that of the non-extraneous estimator and if the two variables, X_1 and X_2, are correlated. Because of multicollinearity it frequently turns out that the variances of jointly estimated parameters based on time series information will be very large so that if an extraneous estimate can be obtained from a non-collinear situation, it will frequently have a smaller variance than its jointly estimated counterpart. A second advantage arising from the use of an extraneous estimator is directly concerned with multicollinearity. As Stone points out, there will be no reduction in the variance of the estimated B_2 if X_1 and X_2 are uncorrelated. The same remark applies to the extraneous estimator B_1 if the correlation between X_1 and X_2 is perfect. "In the latter case the further analysis

[3] In particular see the review of Stone's book, *The Measurement of Consumers' Expenditure and Behavior in the United Kingdom 1920-1938; Volume I*, by Arnold C. Harberger, *Econometrica*, XXIII (April 1955), 217-218 and the review article by William C. Hood, "Empirical Studies of Demand," *The Canadian Journal of Economics and Political Science*, XXI (August 1955), 309-327, especially pp. 322-323.

using the extraneous estimator does nothing to reduce its sampling variance, but it does permit B_2 to be estimated despite the fact that X_1 and X_2 are perfectly correlated. Thus extraneous estimators are likely to be of great value in cases of multicollinearity." [4]

Statistical interpretation of the time series estimates obtained from combined time series–cross-section procedures is rather difficult. For reasons set forth in detail elsewhere,[5] it is believed by the present authors that the multiple correlation coefficient defined as follows:

$$R^2 = 1 - \frac{\Sigma(Y - \hat{b}_1 X_1 - b_2^* X_2 - b_3^* X_3 - \cdots - b_k^* X_k)^2}{\Sigma(Y)^2}$$

provides the most straightforward evaluation of the total goodness of fit of the regression equation. In this expression, all variables are measures from means and $\hat{b}_1$ has been estimated from a cross section, and there are k parameters fitted, $(k-1)$ of which (all the b^*'s) are estimated using time series. For alternative measures the reader is referred to Richard Stone and J. Durbin.[6] While the measure presented may most adequately describe the facts relevant to evaluating the regression equation, it should be re-emphasized that the hazards of combining annual time series of a short-run nature with longer run cross-section measures are so very great that the results should be viewed cautiously. For making such evaluations, the standard errors of the regression coefficients obtained from the normal equations in which the dependent variable is considered to be the reduced series $(Y - \hat{b}_1 X_1)$ will be presented.

Application of the combined technique in the present study ran into one immediate snag, namely that the cross-section parameters appeared to have a good deal of cyclical variability. This fact could easily result in correlation between the conditional error of the "reduced" dependent

[4] Stone, *The Measurement of Consumers' Expenditure and Behaviour*, p. 305.

[5] The authors', "How Extraneous Are Extraneous Estimators?", *Review of Economics and Statistics*, forthcoming.

[6] See references in footnote 2. The article cited in footnote 5 also discusses these measures.

variable series and the explanatory time series variables. The consequence, of course, will be biased parameter estimates unless the correlation can be eliminated. In order to reduce or eliminate bias from this source estimates obtained from the averaged data were used. Absence of bias in this model can be justified on the assumption that cyclical effects have been averaged out in the information from which the parameters were estimated and that therefore the error term of the "reduced" dependent variable time series will be independent of cyclical effects associated with the included time series variables.

THE MODELS

It was necessary to make several decisions about the manner in which the data should be used. At first it was decided to try absolute values of the variables, whose nature was indicated in Chapter IV. These regressions were obtained and appeared unsatisfactory on two counts. First, the first order autoregression slope coefficients of the residuals were so high that one could not reject the hypothesis that the residuals were uncorrelated. The second difficulty is the familiar one of multicollinearity. The intercorrelations among the independent variables were very marked so that the standard errors of estimated parameters with time series were relatively large. This reflected the large extent of common trend and cyclical effects among the independent variables. By contrast, the dependent investment variables, after removal of the profit or sales influences, were essentially free of trend influences and to a lesser extent, cyclical effects. To minimize this difficulty, the data were first differenced and the parameters re-estimated.[7] Since first differencing removes linear trend and, in this particular period, the effects due to the passage of time could be very well

---

[7] Guy H. Orcutt and D. Cochrane, "Application of Least Squares Regression to Relationships Containing Autocorrelated Error Terms," *Journal of the American Statistical Association*, XLIV (September 1949), 32–61, use sample data to indicate how certain autocorrelation relations in the regression error term can be eliminated by first differencing. Also see Stone, *The Measurement of Consumers' Expenditure and Behavior*, pp. 287–291 and pp. 306–308.

approximated by a linear function, trend was rather effectively eliminated by this operation.

THE PRESENT APPLICATION

Joint cross-section, time series models were used in conjunction with three of the seventeen industries in this study, rubber, pulp and paper, and textiles. For the same reason as before, their collinearity, profit and sales were not used in the same estimating equations. This results in a total of six regression equations of the following types:

$$\Delta I = a + b_1^* \Delta R + b_2^* \Delta E + \hat{b}_3 \Delta S$$

$$\Delta I = a + b_1^* \Delta R + b_2^* \Delta E + \hat{b}_4 \Delta P.$$

It should be observed that only one cross-section parameter has been used in each model, associated with either profits or sales.

For various reasons it seemed unsuitable to use the other cross-section parameters. In cross sections, disparities in depreciation expense rates were due to a variety of factors described in detail in Chapter VII. For time series applications, on the other hand, the disparities or rather year-to-year variations arise from altogether different sources. First, given straight-line depreciation policies, time series changes in depreciation expense occur because the capital stock has increased in the previous year, not as in the cross section because one firm might have a larger capital stock or different depreciation policies than another. Second, in the period of the cross-section analysis, depreciation was earned by almost all firms, that is, most corporations made sufficient returns on operations not only to recoup book charges but also to record a positive profit as well. With the time series, on the other hand, during several of the deep depression years of the thirties many firms failed to earn depreciation. Third, depreciation behavior of time series is predominately trend and as such can be accounted for in a variety of other ways. The age variable was not used because it proved impossible to obtain estimates of the gross capital stock for enough years into the past to yield reliable estimates. This is unfortunate, because testing the echo effect requires such time series. Similarly, the unavailability of capital stock figures meant that the capacity variable could not be used in time series; in addition, distinctions between sales and capacity variables on time series would be very slight indeed. The liquidity stock variable was eliminated because it proved to be so completely ineffectual in the cross sections previously reported as well as in previous attempts by others to measure the influence of liquidity stock on investment.[8] For similar reasons, the simple accelerator, that is, the change in sales, was not included.

The third time series variable, relative cost of labor, was not used, since from the simple correlations and intercorrelations it became clear that it was not a statistically strong variable. The basic hypothesis can be stated very simply: that investment behavior, after the influence of either profits or sales has been eliminated, will primarily be influenced by stock prices and interest rates.

EMPIRICAL RESULTS

In Table 37 which summarizes the results of the computations, it is immediately seen that all but one of the multiple correlations differ significantly from zero. The situation is quite the reverse, however, when one looks at the standard errors of the regression coefficients for the interest rate variable. In no case does the regression coefficient approach twice the value of its standard error. Hence the refinement of computing t statistics will be passed by. In almost all cases, however, with the exception of the sales model for the textile and rubber industries, the stock price variable is significant at the 5 to 8 per cent level for a two-tailed test. Furthermore, in all cases, it has the correct *a priori* sign, which is positive. Contrarily, the sign of the interest rate variable is almost always opposite to what might be expected.

The principal conclusion would therefore be that stock prices, a variable ignored in most investment studies since

[8] These results are commented on in Chapters II and VIII.

those by Tinbergen, may well prove to be a useful variable in investment studies. It is the only marginalist variable that stands up to the scrutiny of the preceding analysis.

The exact sense in which it is a "useful" variable, however, should be examined further. It is unlikely that the relatively influential relationship between stock prices and investment is due to the fact that firms respond immediately

TABLE 37

COMBINED CROSS-SECTION, TIME SERIES REGRESSIONS

	REGRESSION COEFFICIENTS: PROFIT MODEL			
	Cross-Section Estimate	Time Series Estimates		Multiple Correlation
Industry	Δ Profit	Δ Interest Rate	Δ Stock Price	
Textiles	.0948 (.0509)	.5057 (.3237)	.1010 (.0566)	.983**
Pulp and Paper	.1538 (.1427)	.2916 (.3462)	.0515 (.0234)	.963**
Rubber	.4555 (.2563)	.2520 (.0572)	.0408 (.0093)	.762**

	REGRESSION COEFFICIENTS: SALES MODEL			
	Cross-Section Estimate	Time Series Estimates		Multiple Correlation
Industry	Δ Sales	Δ Interest Rate	Δ Stock Price	
Textiles	.0165 (.0183)	.2050 (.3677)	.0693 (.0643)	.979**
Pulp and Paper	.0157 (.0108)	.1714 (.3456)	.0432 (.0234)	.964**
Rubber	.0545 (.0235)	-.3128 (.3265)	-.0509 (.0355)	.495

**Significant at the 1 per cent level.

Note: Standard errors are shown in parentheses.

to changes in their market share values by new security issues. Rather, it is more likely that the stock market is a good reflection of business anticipations. Insofar as this latter interpretation is correct, it is relevant to the investment decision-making process in one or both of two ways. First, the stock market may observe the same information as that observed by the business firm and both react accordingly in the formation of their expectations. A second possibility is that the business firm observes the stock market behavior and to some extent takes this activity into account in making its own investment plans. From the data available it is very difficult to determine the causal structure, if indeed any really exists.

SUMMARY

In this chapter three hypotheses originating directly from marginalist theories were tested by using time series data in conjunction with certain cross-section parameter estimates. From preliminary investigation, it was clear that the relative cost of labor was not, as might easily have been anticipated, a useful short-run explanatory variable for investment.

While it must be emphasized that the results obtained from combined cross-section–time series analyses must be interpreted with the greatest reserve, the empirical findings do not seem so far out of line with previous findings and other knowledge as to be totally unacceptable. As with most previous regression analyses of investment behavior, it was found that interest rates do not exert an important influence on the rate of investment. It appears, however, that in a statistical sense, stock prices do exert an influence on the rate of investment.

The observed outcome about stock prices is subject to two interpretations, the first holding that stock prices and investment are influenced in common by similar economic phenomena, while the second interpretation stresses the causal relation between stock market actions and investment expectations. The data were insufficient to permit a clear-cut choice between these alternative explanations of the observed relationship.

Chapter XII

A Residual Funds Theory of Investment

THE PRINCIPAL FINDINGS

The empirical work contained in the preceding chapters suggests a variety of conclusions but all converge in their emphasis upon the importance of internal liquidity. Such conclusions are most apparent in the correlation patterns on depreciation and the profit and acceleration variables over the cycle. The chapter on large and small firms again strongly suggests that the liquidity aspects of investment behavior are of substantial importance, particularly for the smaller firm, although they are certainly not negligible for larger firms as well. Referring to the appendix of Chapter II, it is obvious that the profit principle and other liquidity manifestations have proven to be a powerful although by no means exclusively the best explanation of investment behavior in previous studies.

In more specific terms, three broad categories of investment hypotheses were tested in this study — those associated with the accelerator, profit expectations and liquidity, and trade position motivation — and some support was found for each. The technical accelerator, for instance, worked very well in 1946 and 1947 when almost every industry faced a seller's market, had good prospects, and ample liquidity — the presence of the latter being particularly important. On the other hand, the availability of liquidity became the paramount consideration in 1949. By contrast, the years 1948 and 1950 evidenced a mixture of acceleration and liquidity reactions. In 1948 technical acceleration continued to dominate in those industries with high liquidity inflows but, for those deficient in this respect, liquidity and anticipations became ascendant. In 1950 there were limited signs of acceleration influences on the investment decision at the same time that liquidity continued to be the prime consideration in most instances.

Furthermore, the investment decision was found to be influenced by factors other than those associated with the dynamics of the business cycle. Size, for example, seemed to condition a firm's sensitivity to variations in liquidity inflows, small firms being more responsive to depreciation expense and profit levels than large firms. Contrarily, the large firm was much more prone to adjust investment in response to technical pressures on capacity, a condition which perhaps reflects differing terms of small and large firm access to outside funds — although little quantitative evidence of such differences was discovered. In the same vein, firms in growing industries were more likely to need and use outside funds and were more likely to benefit, probably by way of increased equity values, from more generous dividend policies. At the same time, firms experiencing most rapid growth were also the ones with the lowest dividend payout rate.

It is interesting, moreover, to compare annual and averaged data results for particular variables. For example, sales and profits have a tight linear relationship with each other in the annual data, probably because of approximately linear cost functions in conjunction with narrow price variations over most ranges of output encountered by the firms entering the sample. The independent variation that did exist between the two suggests that profits rather than sales is the more important short-run determinant of the rate of gross investment. When the averaged or long-run data were surveyed, however, the relative importance of profits was substantially diminished and sales and capacity pressures rose to the fore. Another strongly evidenced long-run tendency related to what might best be called a "senility effect"; this simply indicated that firms which once fall behind in the competitive race, by failing to maintain as modern a plant as their competitors, usually remain behind.

Finally, the only economic hypotheses about investment behavior for which little direct confirmation could be found were those relating to the influences of various price variables. While there was some evidence that a good market for corporate equities tended to increase investment outlay, this result has to be interpreted cautiously because of the close interrelationship between increases in stock prices and improvements in sales levels; both of these, of course, are in turn closely related to the presence of generally buoyant attitudes about the future prospects of the economy.

COSTS, PRICE POLICY, MARKET STRUCTURE, AND INVESTMENT

Virtually all of the preceding discussion can be reduced to two salient points: The investment decision is subject to a multiplicity of influences and evidences different behavior under different environmental circumstances and in different time periods. The most suggestive of these differences is the clear tendency for liquidity and financial considerations to dominate the investment decision in the short run while, in the long run, outlays on plant and equipment seem geared to maintenance of some relation between output and the capital stock.

Any interpretation or attempt to integrate these observed differences into a cohesive theoretical structure must necessarily begin by noting that the available empirical evidence indicates that the marginal cost functions in manufacturing are approximately linear at constant factor prices. Also within a narrowly defined region of output, marginal costs tend to increase very sharply when the plant is working the maximum number of hours possible while still allowing time for maintenance. Such a level of output is generally termed the capacity region or point.[1] Similarly, there is considerable

[1] On cost functions, see Theodore O. Yntema, *An Analysis of Steel Prices, Volume and Costs Controlling Limitations on Price Reductions: Pamphlet No. 6* in *United States Steel Corporation T. N. E. C. Papers,* 3 vols. (New York, 1940), I, 223–302 and Conference on Price Research, *Price Behavior and Cost Policy,* ed. Edward S. Mason (New York, 1943); Joe S. Bain,

evidence, although less strong than that for short-run cost behavior, that industrial firms set prices on the basis of a percentage markup on average variable costs. Of course, the margin varies from product to product and through time as market conditions change.[2]

With this cost structure, firms that go beyond the designated capacity point will ordinarily work with a higher proportion of inefficient equipment than usual and will also have to pay higher factor prices. This will occur either through overtime or extra pay for night shifts or through deteriorating quality of labor inputs. Efforts to maintain conventional markups beyond this point would lead to higher and higher prices as total cost becomes more heavily weighted with high cost factors. In effect this results in a rising supply schedule (and total cost curve) beyond the designated capacity point or region for firms pricing on a "cost plus" basis.

What are the implications of these cost and price relationships for investment? To begin, in a non-inflationary situation an increase in demand which pushed firms beyond the minimum cost capacity point would lead firms to price themselves out of the market if they adhered to strict

---

"Economies of Scale, Concentration and Entry," *American Economic Review*, XLIV (March 1954), 15–39; Joel Dean, *Statistical Determination of Cost with Special Reference to Marginal Costs*, Studies in Business Administration, Vol. VII, No. 1 (Chicago, 1936); Dean, *Statistical Cost Functions of a Hosiery Mill*, Studies in Business Administration, Vol. XI, No. 4 (Chicago, 1941); Dean, *The Relation of Cost to Output for a Leather Belt Shop*, National Bureau of Economic Research (New York, 1941); Dean, "Department Store Cost Functions" in *Studies in Mathematical Economics and Econometrics*, ed. Oscar Lange et al. (Chicago, 1942); and Caleb A. Smith, "The Cost-Output Relation for the U. S. Steel Corporation," *The Review of Economic Statistics*, XXIV (November 1942), 166–176. A useful discussion of capacity is contained in Hans Brems, "A Discontinuous Cost Function," *American Economic Review*, XLII (September 1952), 577–586.

[2] Development of these points may be found in Richard B. Heflebower, "Full Costs, Cost Changes, and Prices," in *Business Concentration and Price Policy*, A Conference of the Universities-National Bureau Committee for Economic Research (Princeton, New Jersey, 1955), pp. 361–392 and Richard Ruggles, "The Nature of Price Flexibility and the Determinants of Relative Price Changes in the Economy," in *Business Concentration and Price Policy*, A Conference of the Universities-National Bureau Committee for Economic Research (Princeton, New Jersey, 1955), pp. 441–495.

markup pricing. The alternatives are twofold. One possibility is to reduce the markup, maintain the same price and thereby squeeze profits. The other course would be to expand plant and equipment so that the firm could once again operate in the minimum average variable cost range. For similar reasons, in an oligopolistic situation where demand is large relative to the given capital stock and rivals are also operating beyond the capacity region, the incentives would be strong both to increase price and expand capital stock.

But, while higher prices or other rationing devices may be used as temporary methods of equilibrating a market, from the long-run point of view the more important incentive will be to expand plant and equipment and act roughly in conformance with accelerator postulated behavior. The short-run profit maximizer who raised prices would do so at the long-run cost of his relative market share. It therefore would follow that the maintenance of a fairly stable capital output[3] ratio will, particularly in oligopolistic markets, be the most profitable long-run behavior. Thus, although short-run variations in investment may not have a tight relation to changes in output, it is likely that because of pricing and cost considerations, the accelerator will come into its own over longer periods of time. At the very least, such an investment theory agrees with the facts of modern economic behavior better than that suggested by conventional price theory.[4]

[3] A stable capital-output ratio would be desirable only if firms were operating under conditions of constant returns to scale. Suitable modification can be made for other cases, which have not been considered here in order to simplify the presentation. It seems reasonable, however, to suppose that sharply increasing or decreasing returns to scale are very unlikely for a well-established firm.

[4] Indeed, recent thinking on oligopolistic price theory has tended to the view that industrial markets are equated primarily by quantity movements — both long- and short-run — rather than price movements, as emphasized by post-Marshallian price theorists. Failure to rely primarily on quantity adjustments implies willingness to be priced out of the market or, equally, acceptance of an increasingly smaller share of the market. Where demand exceeds supply, market disequilibrium is manifested in long waiting lists on the order books, not by rapidly adjusting prices except where arbitragers or gray-marketeers can break into well-established channels of distribution. The *ex-ante* theory of price formulation developed by Scandinavian economists, particularly in Sweden, is based on the same sort of reasoning used

While business motivation in an oligopoly situation will obviously be somewhat more complex than outlined here, these considerations do provide a plausible and realistic explanation of observed behavior with respect to long-run profitability and capacity considerations. Furthermore, empirical results of both this and other studies have found that changes in output explain investment less well than the level of output. Bearing in mind the nature of the average variable cost function assumed in the analysis, it is clear that the price-cost relation changes gradually beyond the capacity region so that the incentive to invest beyond this region is also likely to increase gradually. Should demand fall again, the cost of immediately eliminating a capacity discrepancy would be the presence of excess capital earning no return. Thus gradual elimination of the gap, by investing in proportion to the size of the discrepancy, as internal finance becomes available, can be viewed as a policy of prudence and one that would indicate adjustment to the level of output rather than the change in output.

DIVIDENDS, INVENTORIES, AND INVESTMENT
IN RELATION TO SHORT-RUN FINANCIAL
REQUIREMENTS

While the previous analysis provides a plausible explanation of why accelerator and output variables have a closer long-run relationship with investment than the profit level, it does not explain why the converse holds true in the short run. Basically, this short-run superiority of profits would seem to depend on the relative flexibility of marginal investment needs as compared with the rigidity of cash requirements for the other major demands for funds, inventories, and dividends.

Indeed, as previously pointed out, J. Lintner[5] has found

---

here, although the Swedish reliance on inventory fluctuations may overstate the extent to which markets are equilibrated on the buying side of the market in the short-run. Their emphasis on the importance of quantity adjustments, however, is wholly correct for industrial markets.

[5] "The Determinants of Corporate Savings," in *Savings in the Modern Economy (A Symposium)* (Minneapolis, 1953), pp. 251–253, edited by Walter W. Heller, Francis M. Boddy, and Carl L. Nelson; and "Distribution

that current dividend distributions are primarily determined by last year's dividends and current profits. The net effect of other factors, insofar as they are not systematically reflected by current profits and lagged dividends, is "small and random." Furthermore, time series data for dividends are highly autocorrelated so that fluctuations of the more volatile net income fall with amplified force on retained earnings. This may be seen either from a casual inspection of the data or by comparing variations of changes in net corporate retained earnings with changes in dividends. The standard deviation of the former is 2.80 billion dollars while that of year-to-year changes in dividends is 0.62 billion dollars. Their respective coefficients of variation are 6.70 and 3.91.[6] However measured, dividends show much less variation in annual changes than do profits. The high autocorrelation of dividends becomes even more plausible when it is remembered that when output and net income are high, management arguments to retain earnings for expansion purposes are strongest while the contrary holds true in the reverse situation. Thus, where influence over demand and prices is, to a large extent, beyond the firm's control, there will be a large increase in retained earnings but only a moderate increase in the dividend when higher levels of output and net income are realized.[7]

The second major claim on funds, inventories, presents a much more complicated picture, especially in the light of asymmetric responses to intended and unintended changes in

---

of Incomes of Corporations among Dividends, Retained Earnings and Taxes," *American Economic Review*, XLVI (May 1956), 97–113.

[6] Data from undeflated national income statistics in *Survey of Current Business*, XXXIII (July 1953), for the years 1929 to 1951, excluding the war years of 1942–1945.

[7] The relative volatility of profit levels can also be used as the basis of an alternative, purely statistical explanation of the profit variable's poorer long-run correlations: namely, that net profits are less autocorrelated than sales so that averaging increases sales correlations more than it does the profit values. However, if this interpretation is adopted, relative capacity's superior averaged data performance remains unexplained since this variable should be the least autocorrelated of all those in the models. Consequently, because it explains a wider range of observed phenomena, the previous, purely economic rationale for differences in long- and short-run investment behavior seems entirely suitable.

stocks. When unintended accumulation of inventories occurs, the consequence is likely to be a thin cash position with a resultant squeeze of fixed capital investment. On the other hand, voluntary inventory changes will be competitive with fixed capital acquisitions in many circumstances. When a positive change in sales occurs, inventory additions will provide a claim on funds competing with fixed capital additions for expansion and replacement requirements. It is most probable that inventories will, because of technical scheduling problems, have precedence over many marginal capital expenditures. On the other hand, when inventories have been built up to desired quantities for a specified high level of output, the demand for capital equipment is likely to continue in strength while inventory requirements will drop off in relative importance.

During periods of falling activity, it would appear likely that involuntary accumulation is short-lived; certainly the cases in which annual data show additions to inventories when output is falling are decidedly rare. Where decumulation of inventories occurs voluntarily because of a drop in output, it is an important source of funds which arises at a time when the demand for investment is likely to be weak. At such times, competition for funds for either fixed or working capital will be less pressing. Unanticipated inventory decumulation is also likely to be short-lived and, occurring during an upswing, would be a temporary source of funds probably destined for immediate reinvestment in working capital and would thus be relatively independent of fixed capital investment.

As for the rate of fixed capital investment, the above considerations suggest that the finance available from currently generated funds will permit a rate of accumulation of fixed capital, in the short run, consonant with the residual quantity of finance remaining after these prior claims have been met. The major flows of current funds are net retained income and depreciation expense. With usual straight-line methods of depreciation, the latter is primarily a constant proportion of the original dollar cost of the existing capital stock for a given firm and largely independent of current levels of output or capacity utilization.[8] Profits present an entirely different picture. Unless average variable costs and prices manifest large departures from constancy in usual ranges of operation, an infrequent occurrence in most manufacturing operations, it follows that profits will be a positive linear function of the level of output for a given stock of capital. Since profits show marked variations over time, it immediately follows that the residual claimant on funds, marginal investment requirements, will conform closely to variations in profits.

DEBT, EQUITY, AND THE INVESTMENT PROCESS

The question must inevitably arise of just how the equity and money markets relate to the real investment picture. It should not be inferred from the previous analysis that it establishes a theoretical framework in which the capital markets do not exist. This is very far from the case. What is asserted is only that insofar as short-run investment behavior is concerned, capital markets are of lesser importance than internal funds. The importance of long-term external funds arises from the fact that during an investment boom there will be, in a large variety of circumstances, a lagged reaction in the supply of funds from the capital markets and the demand for funds by the industrial sector. Access to the capital market will be sought on occasion and at irregular intervals, particularly during prosperous periods. These irregular intervals will be largely determined by several factors. For example, the extent of lucrative opportunities foregone by not borrowing and the strength of the internal equity position that a firm has achieved through the retention of earnings are of major importance. With a strong equity base, borrowing is cheaper and more feasible. Firms may thus go to the capital market at irregular and discrete intervals to achieve a desired long-run capitalization structure. Administrative procedures, the importance of the action, and the long period of time required to float a security issue will prevent, however, frequent reliance on

[8] The only exception would be instances in which a current level of output was insufficient to earn a return in excess of current out-of-pocket costs.

new issues so that occasional use of outside funds is fully compatible with short-run (that is, year-to-year) behavior that is largely determined by the level of current liquidity inflows. To repeat, it is very possible for firms to go to the capital market and yet maintain a close short-run relationship between retained profits and additions to fixed capital stocks.

There are also a number of important credit sources in addition to the conventionally spotlighted bond or stock markets. Among these, the most important is probably trade credit. As can be seen by looking at the aggregate figures, trade credit supplied approximately 20 per cent of the total increase in manufacturing short-term funds in the postwar years 1946 to 1950 and covered 8.2 per cent of total money requirements.[9]

Another but less direct source of funds is consumer credit which has played such an important role in the postwar period. Although not shown on the books, it is clear that these "tied" funds are, through the very act of tying, a financial source for industrial firms. The consumer credit agency granting the loan is, of course, the proximate source and the consumer is really a financial intermediary. The importance of this sort of credit for the automobile industry need only be mentioned, while in other industries, particularly other consumer durables, it is also of substantial importance.

In all these ways, financial markets are of great importance in establishing the monetary milieu in which the firm operates. Therefore, the monetary picture can be of crucial importance even though these factors are frequently not so directly obvious as to enter into the firm's immediate calculations. Furthermore, short-term funds can and have acted to an important extent as a substitute for longer-term funds and this has created the one-sided impression that the long-term capital markets are perhaps less important than they really are. Although short-term credits are often quasi-automatic, it behooves no one to minimize the importance of the credit markets. To say this is not to say that the firm

[9] See Table 20, Chapter IX.

will program its investment activities explicitly considering each source of funds as a good substitute for every other source since to do so in a world of large discrete differences would be foolish.

A THEORETICAL MODEL

The preceding discussion can be reduced to a theoretical model that is readily set up in the framework of conventional price theory. Consider a firm with a short-run marginal cost curve that is approximately flat and linear up to the capacity restraint point at which a sharp rise occurs.[10] Furthermore, the long-run marginal cost curve is assumed to be flat and linear. In other words, it is assumed that if a firm is already at the low point of its long-run average cost curve for a single plant, it can make necessary duplications in plant without any great diseconomies. In addition, it is assumed that the firm is faced with a price-quantity demand curve. Formally, demand curves could include an income variable but, from the point of view of the firm, income is an autonomous influence which can be viewed as a shift variable in the price-quantity relation, which is the firm's immediate concern. Thus, when the demand curve shifts, it will be assumed that there is no change in the slope of the demand curve.[11] In long-run equilibrium, a reasonable assumption appears to be that, for the marginal firm, profits are zero while the intra-marginal firms in the industry will be paying positive dividends equal to the rent not appropriated by other fixed factors.[12] It is thus assumed that the intra-marginal firms are paying out all profits (in this case rent because in the usual framework of the theory of the

[10] There is no need to postulate complete horizontal linearity of the marginal cost function with a vertical segment appended to it. All that is necessary is that there be approximate flatness in the marginal cost curve and that there be a rise in the marginal cost curve which eventually becomes very steep.

[11] Specifically, the only essential assumption is that income and price affect quantity demanded in an additive, not multiplicative, fashion.

[12] As has been shown in Table 24, Chapter IX, this remark has empirical foundations in the fact that the most rapidly growing industries were also the industries with the lowest dividend payout rate.

firm it is assumed there are no excess profits in long-run equilibrium).

Any upward shift in the demand curve will, of course, upset this equilibrium. Where entry, even though difficult, is distinctly possible it behooves firms already in the industry to act on the assumption of quite high long-run demand elasticities. It is therefore to their advantage to increase output rather than permit new entrants to gather the benefits. In actual practice, the availability of expertise and awareness of the profitable possibilities will usually be concentrated in those firms already in the industry so that outsiders will be able to take advantage of the changed market situation only with a lag.[13] If existing firms do not expand, they may find an actual downward shift in their own demand curve because other firms (either new entrants or those already in the industry) have expanded, and weakened the unexpanded firm's market position. According to the traditional theory of price formation the short-run impact of the demand increase will be an increase in price. An obvious consequence is that the increase in price will also increase profits and the marginal efficiency of investment.

However, under the prevalent forms of market organization in the industrial sector, market equilibrium is not likely to be achieved by a full and instantaneous price adjustment. If, on the one hand, the market structure were monopolistic, or on the other, competitive or monopolistically competitive in the Chamberlinean sense,[14] the short-run adjustment would involve both price and quantity adjustments. In oligopolistic markets, however, there exists a powerful tendency to avoid short-run price adjustments. Once price adjustments are restricted, two major alternatives remain: (1) the short-run adjustment will be exclusively a quantity adjustment, as will be the case when prior to the shift in demand there existed excess capacity; and (2) if excess capacity is insufficient to satisfy the shift in demand there

[13] An excellent discussion on this matter can be found in Joe S. Bain, "Economies of Scale, Concentration and Entry," *American Economic Review* (March 1954) XLIV, 15–39.

[14] Edward H. Chamberlin, *The Theory of Monopolistic Competition*, 5th ed. (Cambridge, Mass., 1947), pp. 71–100.

will not be short-run market equilibrium but instead a virtual price increase manifested in waiting lines, queues, and other informal rationing devices. In effect, oligopolistic adjustments to short-run changes through price adjustments will be slight, and those that do occur seem more likely to be generated by cost rather than demand considerations.

As previously noted, the adjustment to a long-run equilibrium will require an increase in plant capacity. The firm will push out along its long-run marginal cost curve and in many circumstances this can be financed primarily from within the firm since increases in demand also create an increase in internally available funds. Specifically, with increased profits the firm has the two major options of either increasing dividends or using the earnings to finance internally the acquisition of new assets. As a rule, the firm will do both, gradually increasing dividends as the acquisition of additional assets lowers the marginal efficiency of investment, thereby reducing the incentive to retain funds within the firm. Moreover, the pressure from stockholders to increase dividends will become greater. At the end of this adjustment process, the firm will once again be back in a situation similar to that postulated initially. That is, it will be paying out all profits as dividends and will once more be at a long-run profit optimum.

The impact of technological advance upon investment will be, of course, quite different from the case described in which investment possibilities were created by an increase in demand. First of all, normal technological improvements will, in a rough sort of way, be taken care of by the depreciation expense item so that it can be assumed that finances will automatically be provided internally and therefore no outside funds will be required.[15]

However, when quite large technological alterations occur, the effects will be quite different and outside funds will

---

[15] Of course, some technological changes will lead to different factor combinations which in turn imply different forms of current financing. For instance, technological advance will tend to reduce financing through wage accruals.

be sought. Take for instance the case of an innovation the effect of which is to only reduce cost. Other things equal, firms in the industry will have to borrow on the capital markets in order to take advantage of the cost-reducing possibilities. This is the classical case usually considered in investment theory. Firms, however, have another alternative when in the long-run equilibrium described earlier: specifically, in some instances they will find it advantageous to reduce "100 per cent" dividend payout. Only if the increased profit prospects are very large need the firm seek outside money. Therefore the adjustment process could still be like that described for the demand shift case.

The extent to which external long-term funds will be sought during this period of adjustment will depend on several factors. Among the more important will be the size of the demand shift and the rate at which the shift continues. That is, if the increase in demand is large, the marginal efficiency of capital could become so high that the firm will go to outside sources in order to finance the extremely profitable investment opportunities. The market structure will also vitally affect the extent to which outside funds are sought. If the market is highly oligopolistic and entry is correspondingly unlikely, the speed with which a long-run adjustment must be made in order to maximize profits through time is less than that required when the market is more competitive. In a competitive market where there is greater freedom of entry, existing firms will be under pressure to go to the capital markets to exploit an increase in demand in order to preclude either entry of new firms or being "beaten out" by their existing competitors. In a less competitive atmosphere, firms can wait a longer period of time before expanding and permit the expansion to take place out of internal funds as these become available. In addition, profit margins will be higher in more tightly organized oligopolies than in competitive industries so that, *ceteris paribus,* the more oligopolistic the market, the less will be the need to go to outside funds because of higher profit margins. Finally, it is also obvious that capital intensity will be an important factor in determining the need for outside funds.[16]

SUMMARY

Previous pages have been devoted to the technical aspects of investigating, testing for, and reporting on possible regularities in the investment process. In general, a number of regularities have been noted but not universal stability. That is, industries in like economic situations do make similar investment decisions but the economic environment which creates or conditions these reactions is itself highly volatile and complex. As a consequence, no one of the principal existing theories of investment was found to be completely adequate or completely inadequate; the explanatory value of each has been critically dependent on numerous "other variables," quantifiable and non-quantifiable, which must almost necessarily be assumed as given and thereby eliminated from consideration at the stage of pure deduction. In short, there is a varying amount of empirical truth in each theory but nothing to justify any claim to unique superiority for any one theory above all other alternatives.

Consequently, an alternative theory, highly eclectic in nature, has been proposed in this concluding chapter. In this formulation the investment decision is explained within the framework of a modern industrial economy typified by oligopolistic markets, large corporations distinctly separated in management and ownership, and highly imperfect equity and monetary markets. Under such circumstances, the investment outlay on fixed and working capital seems, in the short run, most plausibly treated as a residual defined to be the difference between the total net flow of funds realized from current operations less the established or conventional

[16] In the same vein, current asset requirements could influence outside capital fund requirements. It is highly unlikely, however, that cash requirements, receivables financing, and inventories will absorb all of increased retained earnings arising from the postulated demand shift. In most manufacturing industries the proportion of total assets composed of working capital is a moderately small fraction. It therefore seems unlikely that marginal requirements for such purposes will be radically different from previous proportional levels.

dividend payments. This equality is, of course, only a first approximation; investment will often exceed or fall short of this residual. These excesses and deficiencies should be primarily related to changes in the sales picture since there is strong evidence that maintenance of some sort of relatively fixed relationship between capital and output is a desired long-run objective of most producers. Furthermore, the rapidity with which a change in demand is met by an increase in output and capital outlay will depend on many factors, the most important of which is probably the character of the market structure and the extent of competition for market share.

The proposed theory is thus compounded from many sources. The technological relationship central to the acceleration principle defines the long-run objectives of investment policy. Considerations of financial conservatism, dictated in large part by the motivational patterns that emerge in an economy whose ownership and control are separated, largely determine the timing and thus the short-run pattern by which these long-run objectives are attained. Finally, the profit motive, closely linked in a world of oligopolistic markets to long-run retention of market share and trade position, remains the central wellspring of entrepreneurial action.

Appendices

Appendices

Appendix A

The Sample: Industry and Firm Coverage

All firms and smaller component industries within our major industry categories are listed below. Roman numerals denote the major classifications which follow Securities and Exchange Commission two-digit manufacturing designations except where modified to attain greater capital homogeneity by the procedure outlined in Chapter III. Constituent industry groups within these larger manufacturing categories are listed under capital letter subheadings; these smaller industries are based upon the Standard Industrial Classification three-digit classes and will sometimes appear in more than one major industry group because the Securities and Exchange Commission's two-digit groupings sometimes cut across three-digit Standard Industrial Classifications. The reason for firms in the same smaller industry being placed in different large industry classes will usually be readily apparent, particularly since the individual firm constituency of the different industry groups is given in the arabic numeral subheadings. Numbers after a firm's name represent the last digit of years the firm was omitted from the sample, for example, American Baby Bumpers (6,8) would mean that American Baby Bumpers was not included in the sample in the years 1946 and 1948. When no numbers are listed, of course, the firm is in the sample every year. Reasons why firms were excluded were given in detail in Chapter III.

I. Pulp, Paper and Allied Products

    1. APW Products Co., Inc. (6,7)
    2. American Box Board Co. (7)
    3. American Seal-Kap Corp.
    4. American Writing Paper Co. of Delaware
    5. Camp Mfg. Co., Inc.
    6. Chesapeake Corp. of Va., The

APPENDIX A

7. Consolidated Paper Co.
8. Consolidated Water Power & Paper Co.
9. Container Corp. of America
10. Crystal Tissue Co. (6,7,8,9,0)
11. Dennison Mfg. Co.
12. Dixie Cup Co.
13. Dobeckmun Co., The (6,7,0)
14. Eastern Corp.
15. Eddy Paper Corp., The
16. Fabricon Products, Inc.
17. Fort Wayne Corrugated Paper Co. (7,0)
18. Gair Co., Inc., Robert
19. Gaylord Container Corp.
20. Glatfelter Co., P. H.
21. Hammermill Paper Co.
22. Hinde & Dauch Paper Co., The
23. Hollingsworth & Whitney Co.
24. Hudson Pulp & Paper Corp. (6,7,8,9,)
25. International Paper Co. (New York)
26. Keyes Fibre Co.
27. Lily-Tulip Cup Corp.
28. Mapes Consolidated Mfg. Co.
29. Marathon Corp.
30. Mead Corp., The
31. Morris Paper Mills
32. Nashua Gummed & Coated Paper Co.
33. National Container Corp.
34. Nekoosa-Edwards Paper Co. (7,0)
35. Oswego Falls Corp.
36. Puget Sound Pulp & Timber Co.
37. Rayonier Inc. (6,7)
38. River Basin Paper Co.
39. St. Regis Paper Co.
40. Scott Paper Co.
41. Seaboard Container Corp. (6,7)
42. Shellmar Products Corp.
43. Sonoco Products Co. (6,7,8,9)
44. Soundview Pulp Co.
45. Southern Advance Bag & Paper Co., Inc. (0)
46. Southland Paper Mills, Inc,
47. Standard Cap & Seal Corp. (6)
48. Stone Container Corp. (6,8,9,0)

APPENDIX A

49. Sutherland Paper Co.
50. Union Bag & Paper Corp.
51. United Wallpaper, Inc. (7)
52. Warren Co., S. D.
53. West Va. Pulp & Paper Co.
54. Kimberly-Clark Corp. (0)
55. Crown Zellerbach Corp. (6)
57. Champion Paper & Fibre Co., The
57. United Board & Carton Corp. (6)

II. Light Chemicals

   A. Cleaning, Polishing Preparations, and Household Disinfectants

      1. Purex Corp. Ltd. (6,0)
      2. Babbitt Inc., B. T.
      3. Clorox Chem. Co.
      4. Bon Ami Co., The
      5. F R Corp.
      6. Continental Car-Na-Var Corp. (6)

   B. Paints and Varnishes

      1. Glidden Co., The
      2. Reliance Varnish Co. (6,7,8,9,0)
      3. American Marietta Co.
      4. Ferro Corp. (6,7)
      5. Patterson-Sargent Co., The
      6. Valspar Corp., The
      7. General Paint Corp. (6)
      8. Grand Rapids Varnish Corp.
      9. Cook Paint & Varnish Co.
      10. Devoe & Raynolds Co., Inc.
      11. Pratt & Lambert Inc. (7)

   C. Drugs and Medicines

      1. Plough, Inc.
      2. Zonite Products Corp.
      3. Norwich Pharmacal Co., The (7)
      4. Allied Laboratories, Inc.
      5. Merck & Co., Inc.
      6. Abbott Laboratories
      7. Rexall Drugs, Inc.

8. Lambert Co., The
9. Sharp & Dohme, Inc. (0)
10. Sterling Drug, Inc.
11. American Home Products Corp.
12. Parke, Davis & Co.
13. Vick Chem. Co. (Delaware) (6)
14. Squibb & Sons, E. R. (6)

D. Toilet Preparations

1. Curtis Industries Inc., Helene (6,8,9,0)
2. Avon Products, Inc. (6,7,8,9,0)
3. Bristol-Myers Co.
4. Coty, Inc. (6)
5. Lehn & Fink Products Corp.
6. Rubinstein Inc., Helena (7)
7. Universal Laboratories, Inc. (6,7)
8. Bourjois, Inc. (6,7,8,9,0)

E. Soap

1. Wrisley Co., Allen B. (6)
2. Colgate-Palmolive-Peet Co.
3. Procter & Gamble Co., The (6)

F. Vegetable Oil

1. Drackett Co., The (6,7,8,9,0)
2. Archer-Daniels-Midland Co.
3. Chickasha Cotton Oil Co.
4. Central Soya Co., Inc. (7,8,9,0)
5. Spencer Kellogg & Sons, Inc.
6. El Dorado Oil Works (6,7,8,9,0)

III. Heavy Chemicals

A. Yarn Mills

1. Celanese Corp. of America
2. Hartford Rayon Corp.
3. Industrial Rayon Corp.
4. American Viscose Corp.
5. North American Rayon Corp. (9,0)

APPENDIX A

B. Potash
   1. American Potash & Chemical Corp.
   2. United States Potash Co.
   3. Potash Co. of America (6,7,8,9,0)

C. Fertilizers
   1. American Agricultural Chemical Co., The (6,1)

D. Vulcanized Fibre and Miscellaneous Fabricated Plastics Products
   1. National Vulcanized Fibre Co.
   2. Continental-Diamond Fibre Co.

E. Nonferrous Metals — Smelting and Refining
   1. Eagle-Picher Co., The

F. Chemicals
   1. Allied Chemical & Dye Corp.
   2. U. S. Industrial Chemical Inc.
   3. Liquid Carbonic Corp., The (6,7,8,9,0)
   4. Union Carbide & Carbon Corp.
   5. Monroe Chemical Co.
   6. National Aluminate Corp. (6)
   7. Victor Chemical Works (7,8,9)
   8. National Cylinder Gas Co.
   9. Nopco Chemical Co.
   10. Parker Rust Proof Co. (7)
   11. Catalin Corp. of America (6,7,8,9,0)
   12. Hooker Electrochemical Co. (6)
   13. Consolidated Chemical Industries, Inc.
   14. Novadel-Agene Corp. (6,7)
   15. California Ink Co., Inc., The
   16. Sun Chemical Corp.
   17. Newport Industries, Inc. (7)
   18. Interchemical Corp.
   19. Pfizer & Co., Inc., Chas.
   20. American Cyanamid Co.
   21. Air Reduction Co., Inc.
   22. Atlas Powder Co.
   23. Mathieson Chemical Corp.
   24. United Carbon Co.

25. Columbian Carbon Corp.
26. duPont de Nemours & Co., E. I.
27. Monsanto Chemical Co.
28. Hercules Powder Co.
29. Commercial Solvents Corp.
30. Publicker Industries, Inc.
31. Harshaw Chemical Co., The
32. Heyden Chemical Corp. (6)
33. Lithium Corp. of America, Inc. (6,7,8,9,0)
34. Park Chemical Co. (6,7)
35. Pennsylvania Salt Mfg. Co.
36. Durez Plastics & Chem., Inc.
37. Dow Chemical Co., The (6)
38. Lindsay Light & Chemical Co. (6,7,8,9,0)
39. Ohio-Apex, Inc. (6,7,8,9,0)
40. Koppers Co., Inc.
41. Dewey & Almy Chemical Co.

IV. Petroleum

1. Shell Oil Corp.
2. Texas Co., The
3. Standard Oil, The (Ohio)
4. Socony-Vacuum Oil Co., Inc.
5. Sun Oil Co.
6. Sinclair Oil Corp.
7. Continental Oil Co.
8. Standard Oil Co. (N. J.)
9. Phillips Petroleum Co.
10. Cities Service Co.
11. Pure Oil Co., The
12. Ohio Oil Co.
13. Atlantic Refining Co., The
14. Richfield Oil Corp.
15. Gulf Oil Corp.
16. Standard Oil Co. of California
17. Standard Oil Co. (Indiana)
18. Skelly Oil Co.
19. Tide Water Associated Oil Co.
20. Union Oil Co. of California
21. Ashland Oil & Refining Co.
22. Mid-Continent Petroleum Corp.
23. Lion Oil Co. (8)

APPENDIX A

24. Anderson-Prichard Oil Corp. (6,7,8,9,0)
25. Shamrock Oil & Gas Corp., The
26. Derby Oil Co., The
27. Deep Rock Oil Corp.
28. Panhandle Producing & Refining Co.
29. Quaker State Oil Refining Corp.
30. Crown Central Petroleum Corp.
31. Consumers Cooperative Association (6,7,8,9,0)
32. Cosden Petroleum Corp. (6)
33. Frontier Refining Co. (6,8)
34. Hancock Oil Co. of California, The
35. Kerr-McGee Oil Industries, Inc.
36. Mohawk Petroleum Corp.
37. Sunray Oil Corp. (6,7,8,9,0)
38. Wilcox Oil Co.

V. Rubber

   A. Tires and Tubes

      1. Goodyear Tire & Rubber Co., The
      2. U. S. Rubber Co.
      3. Seiberling Rubber Co.
      4. General Tire & Rubber Co., The
      5. Firestone Tire & Rubber Co., The
      6. Lee Rubber & Tire Corp.
      7. B. F. Goodrich Co., The
      8. Dayton Rubber Co.
      9. Mansfield Tire & Rubber Co., The
      10. Armstrong Rubber Co., The (7,8,9,0)

   B. Rubber Products — Miscellaneous

      1. Plymouth Rubber Co., Inc. (6,8,9,0)
      2. Hewitt Robins, Inc.
      3. Kleinert Rubber Co., I. B.
      4. Brown Rubber Co., Inc. (0)
      5. Baldwin Rubber Co.
      6. Midwest Rubber Reclaiming Co., (6,7)
      7. O'Sullivan Rubber Corp. (6,7,8)

   C. Asbestos and Allied Rubber Products

      1. Thermoid Co.

APPENDIX A

VI. Heavy Steel

   A. Pig Iron Producers
1. Woodward Iron Co.
2. Molybdenum Corp. of America
3. Sloss-Sheffield Steel & Iron Co.
3. Vanadium Corp. of America
5. Climax Molybdenum Co.
6. Pittsburgh Coke & Chem. Co.
7. Interlake Iron Corp.
8. Pittsburgh Metallurgical Co., Inc. (0)

   B. Steel Producers
1. Continental Steel Corp.
2. Detroit Steel Corp. (8,0)
3. Barium Steel Corp. (6,0)
4. Lukens Steel Co.
5. Youngstown Sheet & Tube Co., The
6. Allegheny Ludlum Steel Corp.
7. Inland Steel Co.
8. U. S. Steel Corp.
9. National Steel Corp.
10. Jones & Laughlin Steel Corp.
11. Sharon Steel Corp.
12. Wheeling Steel Corp.
13. Armco Steel Corp.
14. Bethlehem Steel Corp.
15. Crucible Steel Co. of America
16. Republic Steel Corp.
17. Pittsburgh Steel Co.
18. Alan Wood Steel Co.
19. Universal-Cyclops Steel Corp.
20. Copperweld Steel Co.
21. Follansbee Steel Corp.
22. Granite City Steel Co.
23. Jessop Steel Co. (0)
24. Colorado Fuel & Iron Corp., The
25. Newport Steel Corp. (6,8)
26. Carpenter Steel Co., The
27. Keystone Steel & Wire Co.
28. Rotary Electric Steel Co. (6,8,9)
29. Vanadium-Alloys Steel Co.

APPENDIX A

C. Rolling Mills without Steel-Making Facilities

    1. Eastern Stainless Steel Corp. (6)
    2. Thomas Steel Co.
    3. Washington Steel Corp. (6,7,8)
    4. Acme Steel Co.
    5. Superior Steel Corp.
    6. Bliss & Laughlin, Inc.

D. Iron and Steel Foundry Products

    1. Byers Co., A. M.
    2. U. S. Pipe and Foundry Co.
    3. Warren Foundry & Pipe Corp.
    4. Central Foundry Co., The
    5. Detroit Gray Iron Foundry Co.
    6. Duraloy Co. (6,7,8)
    7. Indiana Steel Products Co., The
    8. Pittsburgh Steel Foundry Corp.
    9. Scullin Steel Co.

E. Iron and Steel Forgings

    1. Moore Drop Forging Co.
    2. Midwest Piping & Supply Co., Inc.
    3. Transue & Williams Steel Forging Corp.
    4. Standard Forgings Corp.

F. Railroad Parts and Equipment

    1. National Malleable & Steel Castings Co.
    2. American Brake Shoe Co.
    3. Poor and Co. (6,7,8,9,0)
    4. Pittsburgh Forgings Co. (6,7,8,9,0)
    5. General Steel Castings Corp.

VII. Metal Products

A. Parts and Accessories

    1. Michigan Steel Tube Products Co. (6,7)
    2. Campbell, Wyant & Cannon Foundry Co.
    3. Standard Tube Co., The (7)
    4. Lakey Foundry & Machine Co.

APPENDIX A

B. Heating, Air Conditioning Equipment, and Plumbers' Supplies

1. American Radiator & Standard Sanitary Corp.
2. Crane Co.
3. Holland Furnace Co.
4. Richmond Radiator Co.
5. U. S. Radiator Corp.
6. Alliance Ware, Inc. (6,7,8,9,0)
7. Iron Fireman Mfg. Co. (6)
7. Ruud Mfg. Co. (7)
9. The National Radiator Co. (6)
10. Trane Co., The

C. Locks and Builders' Hardware

1. Yale & Towne Mfg. Co., The
2. Segal Lock & Hardware Co., Inc. (9)
3. McKinney Mfg. Co.

D. Building Material and Equipment — Miscellaneous

1. Detroit Steel Products Co.
2. General Bronze Corp. (7)
3. Kawneer Co., The
4. Southern States Iron Roofing Co. (6,7,8,9,0)
5. Martin-Parry Corp. (6)
6. Russell Co., The F. C. (6,7,0)

E. Rolling Mills without Steel-Making Facilities

1. Signode Steel Strapping Co.

F. Bolts, Nuts, and Rivets

1. Elastic Stop Nut Corp. of America
2. Lamson & Sessions Co., The
3. Pittsburgh Screw & Bolt Corp.
4. Aero Supply Mfg. Co., Inc.
5. American Screw Co. (6)
6. Buffalo-Eclipse Corp.
7. Serrick Corp., The
8. Chicago Rivet & Machine Co. (9,0)

G. Metal Stamping, Coating, and Plating

1. Hupp Corp. (7,8,9,0)
2. Mullins Mfg. Corp.

APPENDIX A

    3. Lansing Stamping Co. (6,7)
    4. National Stamping Co.
    5. Bingham-Herbrand Corp., The (6,7,8,9,0)

H. Steel-Wire, Springs, and Rope
    1. Associated Spring Corp. (6,7,8,9,0)
    2. Union Wire Rope Corp. (6,7)
    3. Macwhyte Co. (6,7,8)
    4. Nachman Corp.
    5. Reynolds Spring Co.
    6. Young Spring & Wire Corp., L. A.

I. Cleaning, Polishing Preparations, and Household Disinfectants
    1. Metal Textile Corp. (8)

J. Iron and Steel Forgings
    1. Belmont Iron Works (6,7,8,9)
    2. National Tank Co. (6,8)
    3. Rheem Mfg. Co. (6,7)
    4. United-Carr Fastener Corp.
    5. Atlas Tack Corp. (7,8)
    6. Black, Sivalls & Bryson, Inc. (6,7,8,9,0)
    7. Continental Copper & Steel Ind., Inc. (6,7,8,9,0)
    8. Van Dorn Iron Works Co., The

K. Nonferrous Metal Products
    1. Anaconda Wire & Cable Co.
    2. Metals Disintegrating Co., Inc. (6)
    3. Reading Tube Corp. (6,7,8,9,0)
    4. Akron Brass Mfg. Co., Inc.
    5. Beldon Mfg. Co.
    6. General Cable Corp.
    7. Rome Cable Corp.

L. General Industrial Machinery and Equipment
    1. American Chain and Cable Co.

M. Ball and Roller Bearings
    1. Timken Roller Bearing Co., The
    2. Hoover Ball & Bearing Co.
    3. Aetna Ball & Roller Bearing Co. (6,7,8,9,0)
    4. Bower Roller Bearing Co.

APPENDIX A

N. Electrical Supplies and Equipment
   1. Curtis Lighting Inc. (6,0)

O. Household Machines
   1. Clyde Porcelain Steel Corp. **(6,7)**

P. Household Utensils and Table Cutlery
   1. Ekco Products Co.
   2. National Pressure Cooker Co. (6,7,8,9,0)
   3. National Stamping Co.

Q. Metal Working Machinery
   1. Birdsboro Steel Foundry & Machinery Co.

R. Frames, Bodies and Wheels
   1. Smith Corp., A. O. (7)

S. Parts and Accessories — Motor Vehicles
   1. Hurd Lock & Mfg. Co.
   2. Hall Lamp Co., C. M. (0)
   3. Hayes Mfg. Corp. (6,7)
   4. Soss Mfg. Co.
   5. Standard Steel Spring Co. (6)
   6. American Forging & Socket Co.
   7. Peninsular Metal Products Corp.
   8. Standard Products Co., The

T. Metal and Glass Containers
   1. American Can Co.
   2. Continental Can Co., Inc.
   3. Crown Cork & Seal Co., Inc.
   4. National Can Corp.
   5. Pacific Can Co. (6,7)

U. Steel-Wire, Springs, and Rope
   1. National-Standard Co.

VIII. Other Machinery

A. Construction, Mining and Related Machinery
   1. Joy Mfg. Co. (6)
   2. Parkersburg Rig & Reel Co., The (6,7,8,9,0)

APPENDIX A

   3. National Supply Co., The
   4. Bucyrus-Erie Co.
   5. Reed Roller Bit Co. (6)
   6. LeTourneau Inc., R. G.
   7. Emsco Derrick & Equipment Co.
   8. Axelson Mfg. Co.
   9. Jaeger Machine Co., The (7)
   10. LaPlant Choate Mfg. Co., Inc. (6,7,8,9)
   11. Gar Wood Industries, Inc.
   12. Athey Products Corp.
   13. American Iron & Machine Works Co. (6)
   14. Adams Mfg. Co., J. D. (6,7,8,9,0)

B. Engines and Turbines

   1. Atlas Imperial Diesel Engine Co. (6,7,8,9,0)
   2. Briggs & Stratton Corp.
   3. Continental Motors Corp. (6)
   4. Cooper-Bessemer Corp., The
   5. Cummins Engine Co., Inc. (6,7)
   6. Le Roi Co.
   7. Hercules Motors Corp.
   8. Sterling Engine Co. (6,7,8,9,0)
   9. Outboard, Marine & Mfg. Co.
   10. Waukesha Motor Co.

C. Printing-Trades and Food Products Machinery

   1. Harris-Seybold Co.
   2. Lanston Monotype Machine Co.
   3. Gellman Mfg. Co.
   4. Meyer-Blanke Co.
   5. Intertype Corp.
   6. Merganthaler Linotype Co.
   7. Hoe & Co., R.
   8. Daystrom, Inc.
   9. Food Machinery Chemical Corp. (6,7,8,9,0)
   10. Hobart Mfg. Co., The (6,7,8,9,0)
   11. Cherry-Burrell Corp.

D. Special Industry Machinery

   1. American Laundry Mach. Co., The
   2. American Machinery & Foundry Co. (6)
   3. Continental Gin Co.

APPENDIX A

    4. Foster Wheeler Corp.
    5. Key Co.
    6. Lynch Corp.
    7. Saco-Lowell Shops (6,7,8,9,0)
    8. U. S. Hoffman Mach. Corp. (6,8)
    9. National Rubber Machinery Co.
  10. Reece Folding Machine Co., The (7)
  11. Super Mold Corp. of California (6)
  12. Yates-American Machine Co.
  13. Universal Winding Co. (1)

E. General Industrial Machinery and Equipment

    1. American Machine & Metals, Inc.
    2. Byron Jackson Co.
    3. Chain Belt Co.
    4. Chicago Pneumatic Tool Co.
    5. DeVilbiss Co., The
    6. Dresser Industries Co.
    7. Fairbanks, Morse & Co.
    8. Farquhar Co., A. B.
    9. Gardner-Denver Co.
  10. Harnischfeger Corp.
  11. Hein-Werner Corp.
  12. Independent Pneumatic Tool Co.
  13. Industrial Brownhoist Co.
  14. Ingersoll-Rand Co.
  15. Lamson Corp. of Del. (6,7,8,9,0)
  16. Link-Belt Co.
  17. Lunkenheimer Co., The (6,7)
  18. Oliver United Filters Inc.
  19. Walworth Co.
  20. Worthington Pump & Mach. Corp. (8)
  21. Air Products Inc. (6)
  22. Binks Mfg. Co. (8)
  23. Buffalo Forge Co.
  24. Dodge Mfg. Co. (6)
  25. Locke Steel Chain Co., The
  26. Mathews Conveyor Co. (6)
  27. Myers & Bro. Co., The F. E.
  28. Parker Appliance Co., The (6)
  29. Torrington Co., The (6,7,8,9,0)
  30. Towmotor Corp. (6,7,8,9,0)

APPENDIX A

F. Automobile Service Station Equipment

   1. Allen Electric & Equipment Co. (6,7,8,9,0)
   2. Wayne Pump Co., The
   3. Balcrank, Inc.
   4. Aro Equipment Corp., The
   5. Bowser, Inc. (6,7,8,9,0)
   6. Tokheim Oil Tank & Pump Co.

G. Agricultural Machinery and Tractors

   1. Case Co., J. I.
   2. Minneapolis Moline Co.
   3. Oliver Corp., The (9)
   4. Deere & Co.
   5. Caterpillar Tractor Co. (7)
   6. Allis-Chalmers Mfg. Co.
   7. International Harvester Co.
   8. Avery & Sons Co., B. F.
   9. Gleaner Harvester Corp.

H. Metal Working Machinery

   1. Federal Machine & Welder Co., The (6,8)
   2. Victor Equipment Co. (0)

I. Miscellaneous Machinery

   1. Otis Elevator Co.
   2. Elliott Co.
   3. Sterling Aluminum Products Inc.
   4. Federal-Mogul Corp.
   5. Stewart-Warner Corp.
   6. Acme Aluminum Alloys, Inc.
   7. Randall Co., The

IX. Light Electrical Goods and Machinery

   A. Batteries

   1. Elec. Storage Battery Co., The (8)
   2. General Dry Batteries Inc. (6,7,8,9,0)
   3. Globe-Union Inc. (6,7)
   4. Edison Inc., Thomas A. (6)
   5. National Battery Co. (1)

APPENDIX A

B. Radio, Television, and Electronic Parts & Equipment
   1. American Phenolic Corp.
   2. Cornell-Dubilier Elec. Corp. (6,7,8,9,0)
   3. International Resistance Co. (0)
   4. Muter Co. (8)
   5. Sprague Electric Co.
   6. Tung-Sol Electric, Inc.
   7. Aerovox Corp. (6,8,9,0)
   8. Clarostat Mfg. Co., Inc. (6)
   9. Dumont Electric Corp. (6,7,8,9,0)
   10. General Instrument Corp.
   11. National Union Radio Corp.
   12. Oak Mfg. Co.
   13. Potter Co., The

C. Office Machines and Equipment
   1. National Cash Register Co., The
   2. International Business Machines Corp.
   3. Burroughs Adding Machine Co.
   4. Marchant Calculating Machine Co. (6,7,8,9,0)
   5. Underwood Corp.
   6. Pitney-Bowes Inc. (6,7,8,9,0)
   7. Remington Rand, Inc.
   8. Felt & Tarrant Mfg. Co. (6)
   9. McBee Co. (6)
   10. Smith & Corona Typewriters Inc., L. C.
   11. Royal Typewriter Co., Inc. (6)
   12. Addressograph-Multigraph Corp.
   13. Clary Multiplier Corp. (6,7,8,9,0)

D. Railroad Parts and Equipment
   1. General Railway Signal Co.

E. Parts and Accessories — Motor Vehicles
   1. American Bosch Corp.
   2. Electric Auto-Lite Co., The
   3. Casco Products Corp., The (6)
   4. Kingston Products Corp. (6,7)

X. Automotive

A. General Industrial Machinery and Equipment
   1. Pierce Governor Co., Inc.

APPENDIX A

B. Automobiles
   1. Checker Cab Mfg. Corp. (6,7,8,9,0)
   2. Chrysler Corp. (8)
   3. General Motors Corp. (6)
   4. Hudson Motor Car Co.
   5. Kaiser-Frazer Corp. (6,7,8,9)
   6. Nash-Kelvinator Corp. (6)
   7. Packard Motor Car Co.
   8. Studebaker Corp., The (6,8)
   9. Willys-Overland Motors, Inc. (6)
   10. Crosley Motors, Inc. (6,7,8,9)

C. Commercial Cars and Trucks
   1. Autocar Co., The
   2. Diamond T Motor Car Co.
   3. Divco Corp. (6,7)
   4. Mack Trucks, Inc.
   5. Reo Motors Inc.
   6. Twin Coach Co. (6)
   7. White Motor Co., The
   8. Federal Motor Truck Co.
   9. Marmon-Herrington Co., Inc. (8)
   10. Meteor Motor Car Co., The
   11. Seagrave Corp., The
   12. Four Wheel Drive Auto Co., The (7)

D. Frames, Bodies, and Wheels
   1. Briggs Mfg. Co. (7)
   2. Budd Co., The
   3. Midland Steel Products Co., The
   4. Kelsey-Hayes Wheel Co. (7)
   5. Motor Wheel Corp. (6)
   6. Central Ohio Steel Products Co.

E. Pistons, Piston Rings, and Bushings
   1. Burd Piston Ring Co.
   2. Cleveland Graphite Bronze Co., The
   3. Detroit Aluminum & Brass Corp. (7,8,9,0)
   4. McQuay-Norris Mfg. Co. (0)
   5. Muskegon Piston Ring Co.
   6. Aluminum Industries, Inc.
   7. Perfect Circle Corp. (7,8,9,0)

F. Parts and Accessories
   1. Ainsworth Mfg. Corp. (6,9,0)
   2. American Metal Products Co. (7)
   3. Borg-Warner Corp. (6)
   4. Campbell Co., Inc., A. S. (6,7,8,9,0)
   5. Clark Equipment Co. (9)
   6. Detroit Harvester Co.
   7. Eaton Mfg. Co.
   8. Fedders-Quigan Corp. (8,9)
   9. Gabriel Co., The (6)
   10. Houdaille-Hershey Corp.
   11. Noblitt-Sparks Industries, Inc.
   12. Sheller Mfg. Corp. (6,7)
   13. Thompson Products Inc. (6)
   14. Universal Products Co., Inc.
   15. Chefford Master Mfg. Co., Inc.
   16. Dana Corp. (6)
   17. Gemmer Mfg. Co.
   18. Jacobs Co., F. L. (6)
   19. King-Seeley Corp.
   20. McCord Corp.
   21. Michigan Bumper Corp.
   22. Modine Mfg. Co.
   23. Monroe Auto Equip. Co. (6,7,8)
   24. Motor Products Corp.
   25. Ryerson & Haynes Inc.
   26. Schwitzer-Cummins Co. (6)
   27. United Specialties Co.
   28. Weatherhead Co., The
   29. Timkin-Detroit Axle Co., The
   30. U. S. Spring & Bumper Co. (6,7,8,9,0)

G. Trailers
   1. Fruehauf Trailer Co. (6,7)
   2. Trailmobile Co. (7,8,9)
   3. American Bantam Car Co. (0)
   4. Liberty Products Corp.

XI. Consumer Durables

A. Household Ranges and Stoves
   1. American Stove Co.
   2. Coleman Co., Inc., The

APPENDIX A

   3. Cribben & Sexton Co.
   4. Florence Stove Co. (6)
   5. Kalamazoo Stove & Furnace Co. (6)
   6. Roper Corp., George D. (6,7)
   7. Tappan Stove Co., The (6,7,8,9,0)
   8. Detroit-Michigan Stove Co.
   9. United Stove Co.

B. Heating, Air Conditioning Equipment, and Plumbers' Supplies

   1. Bell & Gossett Co. (6,7,8,9)
   2. U. S. Air Conditioning Corp. (6)
   3. York Corp.
   4. Carrier Corp.
   5. Hussmann Refrigerator Co. (0)
   6. Super-Cold Corp., The
   7. Utility Appliance Corp. (6,7)
   8. American Air Filter Co., Inc.

C. Household Machines

   1. Nineteen Hundred Corp. (9)
   2. The Hoover Co.
   3. Easy Washing Machine Corp.
   4. Air-Way Electric Appliance Corp. (8,9,0)
   5. Thor Corp.
   6. White Sewing Machine Corp.
   7. Maytag Co., The (8,9)
   8. Servel Inc.
   9. Automatic Washer Co.
   10. Bendix Home Appliances, Inc. (6,7,8,9,0)
   11. Ironrite Inc. (0)
   12. Seeger Refrigerator Co. (6,7,8,9,0)
   13. Eureka Williams Corp.

D. Household Appliances

   1. Chicago Elec. Mfg. Co. (8)
   2. Knapp-Monarch Co.
   3. McGraw Elec. Co. (9)
   4. Samson United Corp.
   5. Sunbeam Corp. (8)
   6. Gilbert Co., The A. C.

APPENDIX A

 E. Household Utensils and Table Cutlery
  1. Silex Co., The (6)

 F. Safety Razors
  1. American Safety Razor Corp.
  2. Gillette Safety Razor Co.
  3. International Safety Razor Corp. (8,9,0)

XII. Apparel
  1. Beau Brummell Ties, Inc. (6,7)
  2. Charis Corp. (6,7,8,9,0)
  3. Cluett, Peabody & Co., Inc.
  4. Curlee Clothing Co. (0)
  5. Elder Mfg. Co. (6)
  6. Fownes Bro. & Co., Inc.
  7. Gossard Co., The H. W.
  8. Hart Schaffner & Marx (6,7,8)
  9. Hat Corp. of America
  10. L'Aiglon Apparel Inc. (6,7,8,9,0)
  11. Manhattan Shirt Co., The (8)
  12. Oberman & Co.
  13. Phillips-Jones Corp.
  14. Reis & Co., Robert
  15. Reliance Mfg. Co.
  16. Society Brand Clothes Inc.
  17. Stein & Co., A. (6,7,8,9,0)
  18. Wentworth Mfg. Co.
  19. Yolande Corp.

XIII. Machine Tools
  1. Cincinnati Milling Machine Co.
  2. Superior Tool and Die Co.
  3. Hanson-Van Winkle-Munning Co. (8,9)
  4. Hydraulic Press Mfg. Co., The
  5. Allied Products, Corp.
  6. Union Twist Drill Co.
  7. Monarch Machine Tool Co., The
  8. McKay Machine Co., The (6,7,8,9)
  9. South Bend Lathe Works
  10. Sundstrand Machine Tool Co. (8,9)
  11. Udylite Corp., The (6)

APPENDIX A

12. Van Norman Co.
13. Warner & Swasey Co., The (7,8)
14. Clearing Mach. Corp. (6,7,8,9,0)
15. Gisholt Mach. Co.
16. Greenfield Tap & Die Corp. (6)
17. Kearney & Trecker Corp.
18. Black & Decker Mfg. Co., The
19. National Acme Co., The
20. Mesta Machine Co.
21. Bullard Co., The
22. Brown & Sharpe Mfg. Co.
23. Bliss Co., E. W. (0)
24. United Engineering & Foundry Co.
25. Seneca Falls Machine Co. (6,7,8,9)
26. Giddings & Lewis Mach. Tool Co.
27. Cross Co., The (7)
28. Mackintosh-Hemphill Co. (6,7)
29. Micromatic Hone Corp. (6)
30. Starrett Co., The L. S.
31. Avildsen Tools & Machines, Inc.
32. Ex-Cell-O Corp. (6,7,8,9,0)
33. New Britain Mach. Co., The (6,7,8,9,0)
34. Simonds Saw & Steel Co.

XIV. Heavy Electrical Machinery
1. Allis Co., The Louis (7)
2. Century Electric Co.
3. Clark Controller Co., The
4. Cutler-Hammer Inc. (8)
5. Emerson Electric Mfg. Co., The (0)
6. General Electric Co.
7. I-T-E Circuit Breaker Co. (6,7)
8. Joslyn Mfg. & Supply Co.
9. Kellogg Switchboard & Supply Co.
10. Kerite Co., The (6,7,8,9,0)
11. Leland Electric Co., The (6,7,8,9,0)
12. Master Elec. Co., The (6,7)
13. Ohio Brass Co., The (6,7,8,9,0)
14. Reliance Electric Engr. Co., The (7)
15. Sangame Electric Co.
16. Speer Carbon Co. (6)
17. Square D Co.

APPENDIX A

18. Wagner Electric Corp.
19. Westinghouse Electric Corp. (8)
20. Duro-Test Corp.
21. Electric Controller & Mfg. Co., The
22. Gamewell Co., The
23. Howell Electric Motors Co.
24. Hubbell, Inc., Harvey (9,0)
25. Jack & Heintz Inc.
26. Leece-Neville Co., The (6)
27. Noma Electric Corp. (6,7,8)
28. Pennsylvania Electric Switch Co.
29. Philadelphia Insulated Wire Co.

XV. Textiles

1. Riegel Textile Corp. (6)
2. Verney Corp. (6)
3. Blumenthal & Co., Inc., Sidney (8,9)
4. Cannon Mills Co.
5. Wyandotte Worsted Co. (6)
6. Collins & Aikman Corp.
7. American Woolen Co.
8. Stevens & Co. Inc., J. P. (6,7)
9. Pacific Mills
10. Kendall Co., The
11. Burlington Mills Corp.
12. Dwight Mfg. Co. (6)
13. Consolidated Textile Co., Inc.
14. Bates Mfg. Co.
15. Mount Vernon-Woodberry Mills, Inc.
16. Powdrell & Alexander, Inc.
17. Belding Heminway Co. Inc.
18. Reeves Bros., Inc. (6,1)
19. Century Ribbon Mills, Inc.
20. Beaunit Mills, Inc. (9,0)
21. Dan River Mills, Inc. (6,7,8,9,0)
22. Duplan Corp., The (0)
23. Lonsdale Co. (6,7,8,9,0)
24. Lowenstein & Sons, Inc., M.
25. Newmarket Mfg. Co.
26. Stroock & Co., Inc., S. (6,8)
27. Textron Incorporated (6)
28. National Mallinson Fabrics Corp. (6,7,8,9,0)

APPENDIX A

29. United Merchants & Mfgrs., Inc. (6,1)
30. Goodall-Sanford, Inc.

XVI. Other Textiles

    A. Carpets, Rugs, and Other Floor Coverings
1. Paulsboro Mfg. Co. (6,7)
2. Lees & Sons Co., James
3. Firth Carpet Co., The
4. Patchogue-Plymouth Mills Corp.
5. Smith & Sons Carpet Co., Alexander
6. Armstrong Cork Co.
7. Mohawk Carpet Mills Inc.
8. Bigelow-Sanford Carpet Co., Inc. (0)
9. Congoleum-Nairn Inc.
10. Artloom Carpet Co., Inc.
11. Carthage Mills Inc. (0)

    B. Hosiery
1. Gotham Hosiery Co., Inc.
2. Adams-Millis Corp.
3. Davenport Hosiery Mills, Inc.
4. Mojud Hosiery Co., Inc.
5. Van Raalte Co., Inc.
6. Phoenix Hosiery Co.
7. Real Silk Hosiery Mills, Inc.
8. Wayne Knitting Mills, Inc. (7,8)
9. Chadbourn Hosiery Mills, Inc.
10. Kayser & Co., Julius (6,7)

XVII. Radio and Television

1. Admiral Corp. (7,8,0)
2. Aircraft Radio Corp. (6,7,8,9,0)
3. Dumont Laboratories, Inc., Allen B. (6,7,8,9)
4. Emerson Radio & Phono. Corp. (6,7,0)
5. Hytron Radio & Electronics Corp. (7,8,9,0)
6. Motorola Inc. (6,7,8,9,0)
7. Philco Corp. (6)
8. Radio Corporation of America
9. Stromberg-Carlson Co.
10. Sylvania Elec. Prod., Inc. (6)
11. Hallicrafters Co., The

APPENDIX A

12. Lear, Inc.
13. Magnavox Co. (0)
14. Raytheon Mfg. Co. (8)
15. Reeves-Ely Laboratories, Inc.
16. Sentinel Radio Corp. (6)
17. Sparks-Withington Co., The (6)
18. Wells-Gardner & Co.
19. Zenith Radio Corp. (8,1)
20. Collins Radio Co. (6,7,8,9,0)

Appendix B

Cross-Section Correlation and Regression Estimates

This appendix reports all partial correlations, multiple correlations, and partial regression coefficients, the latter expressed both in standard units and in their regular form. Profit model results precede sales model results. The order of presentation is the following:

I. Annual Data
   A. Partial and Multiple Correlation Coefficients for the years 1946 through 1950.
   B. Partial Regression Coefficients in Standard Units for the years 1946 through 1950.
   C. Partial Regression Coefficients for the years 1946 through 1950.

II. Averaged Data
   A. Partial and Multiple Correlation Coefficients.
   B. Partial Regression Coefficients in Standard Units.
   C. Partial Regression Coefficients.

ANNUAL RESULTS — PROFIT MODEL
PARTIAL AND MULTIPLE CORRELATIONS

1946

Industry	Depreciation Expense	Age	Change in Sales	Capacity	Liquidity Stock	Profits	Multiple Correlations
Pulp and Paper	.0415	-.3633	.1312	.3094	.0509	.2390	.6221
Light Chemicals	-.0703	-.3578	.1005	.4393	.0577	.1849	.6364
Heavy Chemicals	-.0754	.3240	.0546	.7842	-.1288	.0387	.8474
Petroleum	-.2254	.0095	.2540	.2855	.0906	.4572	.6823
Rubber	-.4765	-.6856	.6277	.7183	.1988	-.5718	.8204
Heavy Steel	.0332	-.0742	-.2865	.4817	-.1849	.0283	.5625
Metal Products	.2665	-.2760	-.1952	.3421	-.0811	.2448	.6489
Other Machinery	.1407	-.4561	-.1863	.5060	.0173	.1353	.7305
Light Electrical Machinery	.1584	-.0542	.1523	.6237	.1860	-.3550	.8204
Heavy Electrical Machinery	.3924	-.2843	-.6124	-.1063	.3127	.2460	.7430
Vehicles and Suppliers	.1661	-.1473	.0504	.3988	-.1212	-.0302	.5376
Consumer Durables	.3479	-.2585	.6025	.6099	.3578	-.4827	.7880
Machine Tools	.3661	.3317	-.1572	.5701	-.3435	.2526	.7328
Basic Textiles	-.2811	.1446	.0084	.7176	.0435	-.1952	.8620
Other Textiles	-.1507	.0215	-.1000	.0964	.6124	-.0846	.7029

1947

Industry	Depreciation Expense	Age	Change in Sales	Capacity	Liquidity Stock	Profits	Multiple Correlations
Pulp and Paper	.0831	-.3087	-.1063	.3988	.2768	-.0192	.5745
Light Chemicals	.0530	-.4324	-.4868	.6419	.3406	.0267	.6928
Heavy Chemicals	-.1319	-.3808	-.4494	.5727	-.2502	.1881	.6878
Petroleum	-.1741	-.3332	.3507	.0071	.1897	.1658	.6620
Rubber	-.0849	-.4775	-.3286	.7204	-.2751	-.2977	.8944
Heavy Steel	-.0897	-.0947	.4195	.4837	-.0537	-.0660	.7287
Metal Products	-.1196	-.2598	.0756	.5736	-.1723	.3674	.6173
Other Machinery	.1404	-.3464	-.0424	.3782	.0927	.1389	.5300
Light Electrical Machinery	-.0469	-.4171	-.1926	.5413	.1658	.1118	.6507
Heavy Electrical Machinery	-.2069	-.1533	.0265	.6986	.1755	.0828	.7727
Vehicles and Suppliers	.1822	.0000	-.1631	.1794	.4159	.2000	.6240
Consumer Durables	.3051	-.0875	.1871	.3022	.3661	-.0636	.7162
Machine Tools	.3619	.3450	-.3391	.4231	-.4450	.5215	.8234
Basic Textiles	.4359	.0283	.1039	.6512	.2538	-.4278	.7642
Other Textiles	.0867	-.3564	.0045	.7021	.7477	.1721	.9055

APPENDIX B

ANNUAL RESULTS — PROFIT MODEL
PARTIAL AND MULTIPLE CORRELATIONS

1948

Industry	Depreciation Expense	Age	Change in Sales	Capacity	Liquidity Stock	Profits	Multiple Correlations
Pulp and Paper	-.0338	-.1503	.0654	.0764	-.0927	.6686	.6928
Light Chemicals	.2142	-.1670	.2241	.3847	.2371	.1237	.6512
Heavy Chemicals	.0217	-.1020	-.1640	.3742	-.1998	.3464	.5586
Petroleum	-.1924	.1786	.3619	.2421	.2030	.3347	.7218
Rubber	-.0751	.1345	.0961	-.1640	-.1192	.9089	.9333
Heavy Steel	-.0559	.2681	-.0473	.4382	-.1510	-.0394	.5568
Metal Products	.0436	.0300	.0510	-.1446	-.1229	.4000	.4930
Other Machinery	.0663	-.1241	-.2159	.3018	.0938	.1490	.3578
Light Electrical Machinery	.1543	-.1980	-.0475	.2928	.0955	-.1609	.4243
Heavy Electrical Machinery	.6641	-.7642	-.1817	.2565	.0000	-.0459	.7389
Vehicles and Suppliers	.2933	-.0417	-.0933	.0164	.1063	.0084	.3661
Consumer Durables	-.0326	-.2823	.1300	-.1803	-.4506	.5413	.7362
Machine Tools	.2768	.4099	-.2236	.2793	-.1404	.1670	.5459
Basic Textiles	.4912	.2625	-.3674	.5505	-.2163	.0000	.7711
Other Textiles	-.0365	-.2853	.0599	-.5441	.1503	.2492	.6870

1949

Industry	Depreciation Expense	Age	Change in Sales	Capacity	Liquidity Stock	Profits	Multiple Correlations
Pulp and Paper	.0939	-.1118	.0095	.1123	.3347	.4037	.7078
Light Chemicals	.5788	-.0130	.0285	.2862	.3035	-.0134	.6964
Heavy Chemicals	.4266	.0358	-.1619	.5486	-.1972	.0270	.7085
Petroleum	.1649	-.2546	-.2587	.0000	-.9050	.5941	.7029
Rubber	.7746	.3102	-.2588	-.4450	-.6768	.8562	.9685
Heavy Steel	-.0526	-.1296	-.0728	.0000	-.2821	.2373	.4013
Metal Products	.3782	-.0228	-.1679	.1778	.0658	.2982	.6099
Other Machinery	.1149	-.0910	-.0765	.0630	-.1166	.3701	.5357
Light Electrical Machinery	.2283	-.3302	.1421	.0084	.2175	-.1342	.3975
Heavy Electrical Machinery	.1703	-.0985	.3256	-.0558	.2650	.1296	.5413
Vehicles and Suppliers	.2872	.0700	.4336	-.1386	.3406	-.2247	.5119
Consumer Durables	.2897	-.3225	.0640	-.2685	-.0560	.7050	.8198
Machine Tools	.3167	-.0265	.0141	.3001	-.1338	.0498	.6515
Basic Textiles	.4630	.0000	-.0400	-.6465	-.1261	.5010	.7552
Other Textiles	.3749	-.2300	.0500	-.3493	-.1549	.5158	.7188

APPENDIX B

ANNUAL RESULTS — PROFIT MODEL
PARTIAL AND MULTIPLE CORRELATIONS
1950

Industry	Depreciation Expense	Age	Change in Sales	Capacity	Liquidity Stock	Profits	Multiple Correlations
Pulp and Paper	.2421	-.2280	-.1726	-.3084	.3962	.0414	.6716
Light Chemicals	.4631	-.0469	.0600	-.1077	-.1039	.2366	.5562
Heavy Chemicals	.2042	.0453	-.0875	.1855	-.2811	.3937	.5604
Petroleum	.3278	-.3834	-.4980	.2184	.1288	.1939	.7129
Rubber	.7477	.1225	.2720	-.2587	.0084	.0207	.8050
Heavy Steel	-.1058	.1049	.2850	-.1166	-.1682	.0203	.3860
Metal Products	.1470	.0045	.4393	-.0446	-.0931	.3578	.6790
Other Machinery	.3526	.0000	-.0200	.1720	-.0283	.0480	.4950
Light Electrical Machinery	.7273	.4301	-.1530	-.1761	-.2893	.1942	.8474
Heavy Electrical Machinery	.0000	-.4359	.1264	.5196	.3302	-.1371	.7407
Vehicles and Suppliers	.3362	-.0501	-.2017	.1368	.1323	.2207	.6017
Consumer Durables	.1304	-.3178	.3912	.1315	.1166	.4087	.7649
Machine Tools	.5119	.0937	.3479	-.0267	-.1288	.2960	.8130
Basic Textiles	.8075	.5639	.4722	.6753	.0964	.3421	.8896
Other Textiles	-.0123	-.2520	-.0977	-.3728	.1118	.5441	.9290

ANNUAL RESULTS — SALES MODEL
PARTIAL AND MULTIPLE CORRELATIONS
1946

Industry	Depreciation Expense	Age	Change in Sales	Capacity	Liquidity Stock	Sales	Multiple Correlations
Pulp and Paper	.0739	-.3406	.0581	.2881	.0161	.1706	.6075
Light Chemicals	-.0089	-.2135	.0593	.4013	.0253	.3391	.6753
Heavy Chemicals	-.1127	.2443	-.2170	.8062	-.8000	.3975	.8729
Petroleum	-.4453	.0860	.3873	.3022	.2612	.3847	.6516
Rubber	-.3782	-.4183	.0532	-.4439	-.1273	.0346	.6656
Heavy Steel	.1034	-.0173	-.1887	.3043	-.1700	.2045	.5869
Metal Products	.2379	-.2278	-.2234	.3391	-.0303	.1735	.6340
Other Machinery	.3142	-.5109	-.0534	.6066	.1688	-.2973	.7530
Light Electrical Machinery	.4899	-.0880	.3937	.8044	-.0259	-.7085	.8877
Heavy Electrical Machinery	-.2381	.1778	.1091	.7155	.1493	-.2760	.8678
Vehicles and Suppliers	.1446	-.0927	.1828	.2951	-.0833	.3178	.6000
Consumer Durables	.2220	-.2356	.3742	.4278	.1643	-.0934	.7148
Machine Tools	.0978	.0856	-.6892	-.1694	.3479	.6148	.8385
Basic Textiles	-.0977	.0100	-.0541	.0901	.6261	-.1806	.7120
Other Textiles	-.0187	-.4528	-.4615	.6465	.4037	.0629	.6943

APPENDIX B

ANNUAL RESULTS — SALES MODEL
PARTIAL AND MULTIPLE CORRELATIONS

1947

Industry	Depreciation Expense	Age	Change in Sales	Capacity	Liquidity Stock	Sales	Multiple Correlations
Pulp and Paper	.0105	-.2755	-.2608	.4405	.0869	.2168	.6008
Light Chemicals	-.0187	-.4528	-.4615	.6465	.4037	.0630	.6943
Heavy Chemicals	-.0548	-.3924	-.4025	.5683	-.1738	.1292	.6803
Petroleum	-.0469	-.3782	.3256	-.0387	.4124	-.1483	.6573
Rubber	-.2780	-.6979	-.6870	.9055	-.5394	-.6473	.9338
Heavy Steel	-.0632	-.0957	.3094	.4680	-.0994	-.0439	.7280
Metal Products	-.0906	-.2504	-.1145	.2131	-.1082	.2263	.5666
Other Machinery	.1490	-.2724	-.0255	.3536	.1396	.0967	.5235
Light Electrical Machinery	-.1897	-.4648	-.3302	.6000	.2619	.3271	.6921
Heavy Electrical Machinery	-.2748	-.0608	-.0253	.7099	.2296	.2298	.7849
Vehicles and Suppliers	.2152	.0758	-.2379	.3154	.4219	.2385	.6333
Consumer Durables	.3154	-.0936	.2114	.3123	.4183	-.1149	.7190
Machine Tools	.2919	.3661	-.4183	.6173	-.4074	.5805	.8408
Basic Textiles	.2243	-.0089	-.0960	.3606	.1741	-.1109	.7050
Other Textiles	.2462	-.4594	.0921	.6964	.6892	-.0901	.9033

1948

Industry	Depreciation Expense	Age	Change in Sales	Capacity	Liquidity Stock	Sales	Multiple Correlations
Pulp and Paper	.0803	.0089	-.1517	.3010	-.0740	.4382	.4909
Light Chemicals	.2236	-.2243	.2555	.3847	.3256	-.1196	.6504
Heavy Chemicals	.2864	-.1349	-.0373	.3089	-.0290	.1749	.4919
Petroleum	.1257	.0398	.5385	.2225	.6834	-.3647	.7301
Rubber	-.4243	-.0718	.2492	.0965	-.1044	.6406	.7497
Heavy Steel	-.1171	.3225	-.1718	.4494	-.1685	.2552	.5950
Metal Products	.0080	.0919	-.0642	-.1714	-.1868	.4455	.5263
Other Machinery	.0000	-.0593	-.3071	.3317	.0305	.1998	.4025
Light Electrical Machinery	.0568	-.1688	-.1652	.2356	-.1269	.2040	.4393
Heavy Electrical Machinery	.6450	-.0219	-.1670	.2458	-.0351	-.0245	.7382
Vehicles and Suppliers	.2506	-.0575	-.0856	.0032	.0796	.1794	.4025
Consumer Durables	-.1375	-.1473	.1269	.0000	-.1237	.4313	.6878
Machine Tools	.3106	.4111	-.2598	.3089	-.1530	.1634	.5450
Basic Textiles	.4279	.2105	-.3592	.5639	-.1193	.2839	.7918
Other Textiles	.0295	-.3564	.0615	-.4472	.2095	.1942	.6768

APPENDIX B

ANNUAL RESULTS — SALES MODEL
PARTIAL AND MULTIPLE CORRELATIONS

1949

Industry	Depreciation Expense	Age	Change in Sales	Capacity	Liquidity Stock	Sales	Multiple Correlations
Pulp and Paper	.0423	-.1584	-.2559	.1600	.2851	.2027	.6550
Light Chemicals	.6066	.0883	.0559	.1411	.3647	.4171	.7576
Heavy Chemicals	.5404	.0400	-.1175	.5404	-.2561	.0346	.7085
Petroleum	.2135	-.3015	-.2724	.0439	-.0984	.2343	.5099
Rubber	.7043	-.1903	.8391	-.4207	-.0784	.2577	.8843
Heavy Steel	-.0690	-.0561	-.0537	.0831	-.3103	.2943	.4336
Metal Products	.3030	.0561	-.2642	.1578	.0138	.3606	.6325
Other Machinery	.0866	-.1556	-.0420	.2081	.1749	.0655	.4207
Light Electrical Machinery	.1507	-.3127	.0444	-.0123	.1480	.0676	.3834
Heavy Electrical Machinery	.1634	-.1631	.3018	.1127	.3162	-.1732	.5496
Vehicles and Suppliers	.1540	-.0321	.2737	-.2828	.1171	.3674	.5727
Consumer Durables	-.0071	-.2366	.1783	-.0712	.0983	.5468	.7369
Machine Tools	.2943	-.0323	.0879	.2818	-.1183	.1308	.6481
Basic Textiles	-.0245	.0000	.4207	-.7396	-.3495	.7668	.8742
Other Textiles	.4517	-.2694	.0315	-.0530	-.0522	.2550	.6205

1950

Industry	Depreciation Expense	Age	Change in Sales	Capacity	Liquidity Stock	Sales	Multiple Correlations
Pulp and Paper	.2433	-.2152	-.0612	-.3012	.3988	-.0487	.6716
Light Chemicals	.4528	-.0167	.1030	-.0739	-.0488	.2425	.5577
Heavy Chemicals	.3150	.0138	-.0148	.2285	.0000	.0966	.4427
Petroleum	.3008	-.4025	-.5263	.2672	.1836	.2379	.7200
Rubber	.7797	.2878	.1357	-.1296	-.1389	.2956	.8234
Heavy Steel	-.1096	.0972	.1957	-.1300	-.1655	-.0290	.3860
Metal Products	.1483	.0313	.3000	-.0395	-.0684	.2429	.6465
Other Machinery	.3286	.0439	-.0506	.1453	-.1229	.1726	.5167
Light Electrical Machinery	.7043	.4000	.1315	-.1005	-.1792	-.1225	.8432
Heavy Electrical Machinery	-.0480	-.3860	.0469	.5040	.4316	.0148	.7356
Vehicles and Suppliers	.1375	-.1897	-.2627	.1814	.0356	.3507	.6419
Consumer Durables	.0836	-.3209	.1655	.1543	.1808	.2530	.7301
Machine Tools	.5099	.0332	.1619	.0359	-.0447	.2328	.8056
Basic Textiles	.7969	.5891	.3578	.6269	.1568	.2081	.8798
Other Textiles	-.1726	-.4123	-.4909	.0706	.5020	.5613	.9311

APPENDIX B

ANNUAL RESULTS — PROFIT MODEL
PARTIAL REGRESSION COEFFICIENTS IN STANDARD UNITS *
1946

Industry	Depreciation Expense	Age	Change in Sales	Capacity	Liquidity Stock	Profits
Pulp and Paper	.0334 (.0250)	-.3228 (1.8034)	.1063 (.6111)	.2928 (1.5091)	.0525 (.2354)	.2548 (1.1375)
Light Chemicals	-.0679 (.3031)	-.3625 (1.2205)	.0829 (.1880)	.4552 (1.5588)	.0596 (.5846)	.1771 (.5984)
Heavy Chemicals	-.0662 (.2273)	.2104 (1.0264)	.0652 (.5214)	.8800 (3.7930)	-.1300 (1.2385)	.0489 (.3674)
Petroleum	-.1900 (.8261)	.0081 (.0346)	.2026 (.9423)	.2693 (1.0644)	.0768 (.3268)	.4306 (1.8402)
Rubber	-.3728 (2.4051)	-.6634 (4.1721)	1.1649 (1.1310)	.7910 (4.5723)	.1453 (.8972)	-1.3176 (.9797)
Heavy Steel	.0934 (.5307)	-.0650 (.3801)	-.2663 (1.4877)	.5493 (2.7193)	-.1785 (.9346)	.0297 (.1421)
Metal Products	.2714 (1.3303)	-.2435 (1.3835)	-.1923 (.9567)	.3040 (1.7572)	-.0824 (.3924)	.2461 (1.2182)
Other Machinery	.1172 (.7371)	-.3833 (2.6618)	-.1689 (.9877)	.5210 (3.0291)	.0451 (.2987)	.1403 (.7086)
Light Electrical Machinery	.1551 (.8206)	-.0484 (.2767)	.2104 (.7881)	1.1888 (4.0851)	.1702 (.9672)	-.7267 (6.1586)
Heavy Electrical Machinery	.4232 (2.8597)	-.2623 (1.9868)	-.6188 (5.1999)	-.1073 (.7151)	.2858 (2.1985)	.2439 (1.6036)
Vehicles and Suppliers	.1504 (.7556)	-.1398 (.6656)	.0479 (.2249)	.4981 (1.9379)	-.1263 (.5444)	-.0351 (.1348)
Consumer Durables	.2552 (1.0206)	-.1705 (.7349)	.6157 (2.0799)	.7181 (6.7115)	.2861 (1.0556)	-.6496 (4.7766)
Machine Tools	.4046 (3.3717)	.2869 (.9563)	-.2077 (1.3757)	.6012 (6.0122)	-.3585 (3.1448)	.2903 (2.2506)
Basic Textiles	-.2284 (1.4101)	.1238 (.7036)	.0051 (.0405)	.7566 (4.9448)	.0339 (.2093)	-.1757 (.9551)
Other Textiles	-.1782 (1.1347)	.0186 (.1591)	-.0907 (.7498)	.1310 (.7237)	.7449 (5.8198)	-.0913 (.6340)

*Each regression coefficient has been divided by its standard error and the resulting quotient placed underneath in parentheses. The quotient is exactly the same when the coefficients are expressed in original units. The signs of the regression coefficients have not been recorded with the quotient.

APPENDIX B

ANNUAL RESULTS — PROFIT MODEL
PARTIAL REGRESSION COEFFICIENTS IN STANDARD UNITS*

1947

Industry	Depreciation Expense	Age	Change in Sales	Capacity	Liquidity Stock	Profits
Pulp and Paper	.0979 (.4047)	-.3157 (1.5706)	-.1280 (.5162)	.3930 (2.1127)	.2899 (1.3938)	-.0240 (.0932)
Light Chemicals	.0431 (.1669)	-.4979 (4.7874)	-.6278 (5.5555)	.8264 (2.6320)	.4621 (3.6104)	.0254 (.0837)
Heavy Chemicals	-.1321 (.5621)	-.3164 (1.7385)	-.6568 (2.1256)	.8558 (3.0348)	-.2326 (1.0920)	.1524 (.8106)
Petroleum	-.1574 (.6477)	-.2983 (1.2970)	.3064 (1.3802)	.0066 (.0265)	.2427 (2.2472)	.2238 (1.9632)
Rubber	-.0420 (.3185)	-.2979 (2.0401)	-.2151 (1.3043)	1.4300 (12.3274)	-.2496 (1.0710)	-.5527 (.3692)
Heavy Steel	-.1116 (.4000)	-.0683 (.4215)	.4131 (2.0554)	.4540 (2.4543)	-.0668 (.2384)	-.0607 (.2930)
Metal Products	-.1301 (.6135)	-.2199 (1.3744)	.0865 (.3863)	.1765 (.9386)	-.2045 (.8928)	.5530 (2.0107)
Other Machinery	.1261 (.9072)	-.3421 (2.3593)	-.0425 (.2724)	.3884 (2.6067)	.0946 (.5987)	.1559 (.9012)
Light Electrical Machinery	-.0625 (.3858)	-.4177 (3.8321)	-.3160 (1.6289)	.6575 (5.3455)	.1473 (1.4029)	.0921 (.2961)
Heavy Electrical Machinery	-.1595 (1.4112)	-.1182 (1.0372)	.0280 (.1764)	.7680 (6.5088)	.1548 (1.1905)	.0841 (.5530)
Vehicles and Suppliers	.1574 (.8462)	.0004 (.0022)	-.2671 (2.3848)	.2660 (2.6337)	.3975 (2.0812)	.3131 (2.9538)
Consumer Durables	.2992 (1.0961)	-.0659 (.3008)	.2406 (2.0560)	.3278 (1.0854)	.3914 (1.3449)	-.0652 (.2182)
Machine Tools	.2368 (.8804)	.2902 (2.6381)	-.4020 (2.5935)	.3788 (3.3526)	-.4924 (3.5678)	.9491 (4.3738)
Basic Textiles	.7480 (3.1168)	.0221 (.1826)	.2092 (.6748)	1.0452 (5.5304)	.1885 (1.6981)	-1.2127 (.9647)
Other Textiles	.0614 (.3696)	-.1984 (1.6128)	.0024 (.0181)	.5221 (4.1769)	.5476 (4.7613)	.1146 (.7392)

*Each regression coefficient has been divided by its standard error and the resulting quotient placed underneath in parentheses. The quotient is exactly the same when the coefficients are expressed in original units. The signs of the regression coefficients have not been recorded with the quotient.

APPENDIX B

ANNUAL RESULTS — PROFIT MODEL
PARTIAL REGRESSION COEFFICIENTS IN STANDARD UNITS*

1948

Industry	Depreciation Expense	Age	Change in Sales	Capacity	Liquidity Stock	Profits
Pulp and Paper	-.0267 (.1527)	-.1200 (.6857)	.0537 (.2952)	.0646 (.3457)	-.0739 (.4199)	.7042 (4.0473)
Light Chemicals	.1863 (.7796)	-.1578 (.6024)	.2109 (.8174)	.3963 (1.4841)	.2426 (.8696)	.1085 (.4447)
Heavy Chemicals	.0326 (.1113)	-.0891 (.5244)	-.2079 (.8486)	.4940 (2.0671)	-.2396 (1.0417)	.6578 (5.9798)
Petroleum	-.1910 (.6495)	.1311 (.6012)	.3461 (1.2867)	.1912 (.8279)	.2426 (2.1468)	.4426 (3.7195)
Rubber	-.0280 (.2256)	.0548 (.4061)	.0604 (.2903)	-.1067 (.4987)	-.0526 (.3605)	.9891 (6.5503)
Heavy Steel	-.0501 (.2895)	.2467 (1.4424)	-.0490 (.2460)	.4716 (2.5217)	-.1490 (.7926)	-.0407 (.2045)
Metal Products	.0459 (.2623)	.0282 (.1808)	.0591 (.3094)	-.1493 (.8834)	-.1458 (.7477)	.5540 (2.6381)
Other Machinery	.0682 (.4871)	-.1332 (.8940)	-.3047 (1.6560)	.3804 (2.2643)	.1273 (.6735)	.0223 (.1083)
Light Electrical Machinery	.1831 (1.5514)	-.2661 (2.0008)	-.0807 (.4717)	.4946 (3.0346)	.2136 (.9536)	-.3811 (1.6215)
Heavy Electrical Machinery	.7018 (2.2420)	-.0110 (.0564)	-.2849 (1.4683)	.4152 (2.1186)	-.0006 (.0046)	-.0541 (.3655)
Vehicles and Suppliers	.3288 (1.6859)	-.0416 (.7825)	-.1521 (.5156)	.0260 (.0907)	.1283 (.5886)	.0102 (.0462)
Consumer Durables	-.0242 (.0988)	-.2207 (.8900)	.2228 (1.2588)	-.3101 (1.6944)	-.4859 (4.8594)	.9109 (6.1549)
Machine Tools	.4078 (2.9548)	.5036 (4.5785)	-.4050 (2.3545)	.4106 (2.9972)	-.1689 (1.4557)	.1954 (1.7445)
Basic Textiles	.4188 (3.7730)	.1906 (1.8152)	-.5345 (2.6460)	.9838 (4.4117)	-.1842 (1.4736)	.0001 (.0006)
Other Textiles	-.0382 (.2894)	-.2335 (.7484)	.0718 (.4787)	-.6917 (5.1620)	.1357 (1.2119)	.2800 (2.0440)

*Each regression coefficient has been divided by its standard error and the resulting quotient placed underneath in parentheses. The quotient is exactly the same when the coefficients are expressed in original units. The signs of the regression coefficients have not been recorded with the quotient.

APPENDIX B

ANNUAL RESULTS — PROFIT MODEL
PARTIAL REGRESSION COEFFICIENTS IN STANDARD UNITS *

1949

Industry	Depreciation Expense	Age	Change in Sales	Capacity	Liquidity Stock	Profits
Pulp and Paper	.0977 (.4174)	-.0867 (.4953)	.0098 (.0418)	.1018 (.4991)	.3836 (1.5657)	.4149 (1.9477)
Light Chemicals	.6164 (2.3348)	-.0111 (.0426)	.0269 (.0939)	.2599 (.9806)	.2741 (1.0460)	-.0126 (.3950)
Heavy Chemicals	.5836 (2.0264)	.0256 (.1539)	-.1525 (.7027)	.6196 (2.8163)	-.2519 (.8627)	.0470 (.3703)
Petroleum	.1568 (.5808)	-.2059 (.9150)	-.2610 (.9321)	-.0023 (.0079)	-.2874 (1.0413)	.6362 (2.5758)
Rubber	.3579 (2.5561)	.0965 (.6843)	-.2050 (.1770)	-.1570 (1.0399)	-.3070 (1.9184)	1.2959 (1.0954)
Heavy Steel	-.1246 (1.0130)	-.1236 (.7923)	-.0634 (.4403)	.0112 (.0404)	-.2889 (1.8401)	.2764 (1.4860)
Metal Products	.3560 (2.3118)	-.0194 (.1286)	-.2199 (.9646)	.2319 (1.0214)	.0676 (.3734)	.3304 (1.7670)
Other Machinery	.1099 (.7687)	-.0862 (.6070)	-.0891 (.5094)	.0820 (.4205)	-.1524 (.7814)	.5836 (2.6525)
Light Electrical Machinery	.2428 (.7757)	-.5839 (3.6726)	.1704 (1.4944)	.0085 (.0276)	.3603 (2.3245)	-.1882 (1.4151)
Heavy Electrical Machinery	.1946 (1.7222)	-.1092 (.9834)	.7431 (3.4243)	-.0980 (.5570)	.3861 (2.7380)	.1965 (1.3011)
Vehicles and Suppliers	.2862 (1.5222)	.0767 (.3567)	.7330 (2.4514)	-.1787 (.7091)	.3664 (1.8504)	-.3180 (1.1734)
Consumer Durables	.1930 (.7753)	-.2136 (.8718)	.0571 (.5195)	-.3331 (2.2509)	-.0381 (.1434)	1.0383 (8.0488)
Machine Tools	.3184 (1.0140)	-.0274 (.2514)	.0146 (.1304)	.3367 (3.0333)	-.1532 (1.2983)	.1613 (1.5362)
Basic Textiles	.5242 (3.5904)	-.0061 (.0194)	-.0993 (.8788)	-.8660 (5.8121)	-.1434 (.8744)	.7043 (3.9791)
Other Textiles	.3856 (3.0848)	-.1762 (.5684)	.0365 (.1197)	-.3863 (2.8404)	-.1296 (1.2000)	.6389 (4.5636)

*Each regression coefficient has been divided by its standard error and the resulting quotient placed underneath in parentheses. The quotient is exactly the same when the coefficients are expressed in original units. The signs of the regression coefficients have not been recorded with the quotient.

APPENDIX B

ANNUAL RESULTS — PROFIT MODEL
PARTIAL REGRESSION COEFFICIENTS IN STANDARD UNITS *

1950

Industry	Depreciation Expense	Age	Change in Sales	Capacity	Liquidity Stock	Profits
Pulp and Paper	.2255 (2.0318)	-.1793 (.6016)	-.1429 (1.4288)	-.2599 (.8330)	.4040 (3.5129)	.0318 (.1063)
Light Chemicals	.4670 (1.9378)	-.0491 (.1729)	.0641 (.2233)	-.1278 (1.2780)	-.1269 (1.2320)	.2785 (.9042)
Heavy Chemicals	.2096 (1.0532)	.0389 (.2286)	-.0801 (.9948)	.1616 (.9505)	-.4006 (1.4729)	.6776 (2.1579)
Petroleum	.3472 (1.2182)	-.3234 (1.4568)	-.4521 (2.0093)	.2054 (.7840)	.1158 (.4559)	.1828 (.6924)
Rubber	.7721 (5.1820)	.1680 (.5676)	.3630 (1.3011)	-.1809 (1.2303)	.0114 (.0372)	.0389 (.0300)
Heavy Steel	-.1126 (.6289)	.1129 (.6237)	.4137 (1.7756)	-.2035 (.6944)	-.2309 (1.0081)	.0444 (1.2340)
Metal Products	.1363 (.8017)	.0035 (.0218)	.5065 (2.6379)	-.0431 (.2406)	-.0774 (.5056)	.3130 (2.0730)
Other Machinery	.3686 (2.5597)	-.0091 (.0619)	-.0307 (.1377)	.3056 (1.1845)	-.0424 (.1919)	.0230 (.1031)
Light Electrical Machinery	.7268 (6.1597)	.4275 (2.7761)	-.2548 (.9004)	-.1245 (1.0376)	-.2168 (1.7628)	.3354 (1.1525)
Heavy Electrical Machinery	.0010 (.0099)	-.4205 (4.0048)	.1621 (1.0526)	.5647 (4.9973)	.5667 (2.8766)	-.2537 (1.1377)
Vehicles and Suppliers	.3411 (1.7404)	-.0467 (.2443)	-.1992 (1.0011)	.1792 (.6712)	.1364 (.6465)	.3146 (1.0999)
Consumer Durables	.0906 (.3974)	-.2238 (1.0129)	.3507 (1.2847)	.1107 (.4011)	.0823 (.3549)	.3612 (1.3530)
Machine Tools	.4401 (1.5124)	.0746 (.2383)	.3230 (2.9636)	-.0192 (.0677)	-.0947 (.3299)	.3016 (2.4922)
Basic Textiles	.7370 (6.8241)	.3181 (1.0783)	.2946 (2.6782)	.4939 (4.6159)	.0550 (.4867)	.2422 (1.8211)
Other Textiles	-.0238 (.0144)	.2029 (.9661)	-.1510 (.1148)	-.2871 (.1392)	.0455 (.4175)	1.4178 (.7590)

*Each regression coefficient has been divided by its standard error and the resulting quotient placed underneath in parentheses. The quotient is exactly the same when the coefficients are expressed in original units. The signs of the regression coefficients have not been recorded with the quotient.

APPENDIX B

ANNUAL RESULTS — SALES MODEL
PARTIAL REGRESSION COEFFICIENTS IN STANDARD UNITS*

1946

Industry	Depreciation Expense	Age	Change in Sales	Capacity	Liquidity Stock	Sales
Pulp and Paper	.0598 (.3496)	-.3077 (1.7001)	.0481 (.2734)	.2863 (1.4171)	.0214 (.0768)	.2445 (.8124)
Light Chemicals	-.0016 (.0052)	-.2214 (2.1088)	.0470 (.1808)	.3983 (1.3320)	.0235 (.0775)	.3291 (1.0935)
Heavy Chemicals	-.0665 (.3123)	.1449 (.6933)	-.2260 (1.9315)	.8517 (3.7687)	-.1662 (13.0835)	.3726 (1.1943)
Petroleum	-.4475 (1.8492)	.0759 (.3216)	.3392 (1.5631)	.2966 (1.1817)	.2170 (1.0046)	.3684 (1.5544)
Rubber	-.4289 (2.3568)	-.4648 (2.5538)	.0753 (.3087)	-.4902 (2.8665)	-.1088 (.7402)	.0675 (.0635)
Heavy Steel	.0891 (.5063)	-.0155 (.0856)	-.1843 (.9355)	.3876 (1.5504)	-.1499 (.8374)	.2427 (1.0155)
Metal Products	.2528 (1.1982)	-.2087 (1.1466)	-.2437 (1.1231)	.3086 (1.7635)	-.0302 (.1486)	.1848 (.8595)
Other Machinery	.2749 (1.6557)	-.4347 (2.9775)	-.0403 (.2683)	.7702 (3.8319)	.1286 (.8573)	-.3527 (1.5605)
Light Electrical Machinery	.5173 (2.3199)	-.0524 (1.0581)	.4359 (1.7647)	1.3909 (5.6084)	-.0200 (.6419)	-1.1634 (4.1404)
Heavy Electrical Machinery	-.1866 (1.2195)	.1344 (.8963)	.0747 (.5453)	.7318 (5.0820)	.1339 (.7483)	-.2696 (1.4341)
Vehicles and Suppliers	.1191 (.6201)	-.0838 (.3951)	.1771 (.7869)	.3051 (1.3093)	-.0769 (.3546)	.3220 (1.4184)
Consumer Durables	.1909 (.7124)	-.1833 (.7576)	.4187 (3.9875)	.4368 (1.4807)	.1305 (.5219)	-.1163 (.9306)
Machine Tools	.0915 (.6780)	.0739 (.5911)	-.5579 (2.0741)	-.1406 (1.1812)	.2331 (.8092)	.6884 (5.3783)
Basic Textiles	-.1176 (.6534)	.0089 (.0687)	-.0485 (.3620)	.1147 (.6038)	.7828 (5.3617)	-.2067 (1.2230)
Other Textiles	-.0248 (.1424)	-.5005 (3.8202)	-.6661 (3.9182)	.8415 (6.3751)	.4803 (3.3353)	.0800 (.4763)

*Each regression coefficient has been divided by its standard error and the resulting quotient placed underneath in parentheses. The quotient is exactly the same when the coefficients are expressed in original units. The signs of the regression coefficients have not been recorded with the quotient.

APPENDIX B

ANNUAL RESULTS — SALES MODEL
PARTIAL REGRESSION COEFFICIENTS IN STANDARD UNITS *
1947

Industry	Depreciation Expense	Age	Change in Sales	Capacity	Liquidity Stock	Sales
Pulp and Paper	.0105 (.0487)	-.2722 (1.3541)	-.3921 (1.2773)	.4515 (2.3154)	.1097 (.4125)	.3640 (3.3087)
Light Chemicals	-.0248 (.1863)	-.5005 (1.5938)	-.6661 (5.1636)	.8415 (8.4151)	.4803 (4.3662)	.0800 (.6251)
Heavy Chemicals	-.0548 (.2342)	-.3296 (1.8210)	-.5630 (1.8829)	.7999 (2.9517)	-.1584 (.7543)	.1035 (.5565)
Petroleum	-.0420 (.1728)	-.3422 (1.5142)	.5463 (4.0169)	-.0340 (.1429)	.3991 (1.6769)	-.2530 (1.7448)
Rubber	-.1157 (.8634)	-.4911 (2.9061)	-.4136 (2.8330)	1.4249 (6.3896)	-.3490 (1.9175)	-.6276 (2.5410)
Heavy Steel	-.0662 (.2817)	-.0709 (.4268)	.4354 (1.4463)	.4565 (.8067)	-.1062 (.4445)	-.0631 (.6185)
Metal Products	-.1183 (.4849)	-.2215 (1.3842)	-.2368 (1.9407)	.2206 (1.1672)	-.1412 (.9966)	.6919 (3.9315)
Other Machinery	.1328 (1.0797)	-.2779 (1.1624)	-.0258 (.1663)	.3801 (2.4364)	.1337 (.9499)	.1060 (.6273)
Light Electrical Machinery	-.2775 (1.5249)	.4491 (4.1583)	-.6361 (2.7657)	.7851 (5.9028)	.2331 (2.1388)	.3331 (2.7302)
Heavy Electrical Machinery	-.2278 (1.8669)	-.0486 (.3947)	-.0256 (.1651)	.7642 (6.5317)	.1988 (1.5290)	.2643 (.9554)
Vehicles and Suppliers	.1809 (.9940)	.0606 (.3441)	-.5808 (3.4990)	.4598 (1.5027)	.3978 (2.1048)	.4637 (3.5125)
Consumer Durables	.3419 (1.1320)	-.0700 (.3195)	.3157 (2.3215)	.3303 (1.1195)	.3809 (1.5739)	-.1447 (1.2472)
Machine Tools	.1836 (.6604)	.2832 (2.6971)	-.5170 (3.1523)	.5646 (5.3772)	-.3529 (3.0688)	.9121 (4.8773)
Basic Textiles	.3215 (1.6321)	-.0080 (.0655)	-.2198 (.2166)	.5371 (2.7401)	.1421 (1.2462)	-.2281 (.7891)
Other Textiles	.1518 (1.0845)	-.2602 (2.2235)	.0467 (.9970)	.5190 (4.1518)	.4993 (4.0925)	-.0499 (.3869)

*Each regression coefficient has been divided by its standard error and the resulting quotient placed underneath in parentheses. The quotient is exactly the same when the coefficients are expressed in original units. The signs of the regression coefficients have not been recorded with the quotient.

APPENDIX B

ANNUAL RESULTS — SALES MODEL
PARTIAL REGRESSION COEFFICIENTS IN STANDARD UNITS*

1948

Industry	Depreciation Expense	Age	Change in Sales	Capacity	Liquidity Stock	Sales
Pulp and Paper	.0761 (.4399)	.0084 (.0490)	-.1615 (.8367)	.3154 (1.7234)	-.0722 (.4055)	.4652 (2.6580)
Light Chemicals	.2285 (.8161)	-.2193 (.8213)	.2481 (.9397)	.3976 (1.4891)	.3239 (1.2317)	-.1243 (.4287)
Heavy Chemicals	.3532 (1.6054)	-.1239 (.7331)	-.0447 (.2006)	.4187 (1.7444)	-.0317 (.1560)	.1902 (.9559)
Petroleum	.1288 (.4155)	.0291 (.1304)	1.2048 (6.6197)	.1742 (.7477)	.6602 (3.0707)	-.7698 (4.0729)
Rubber	-.3314 (2.5892)	-.0535 (1.1457)	.3401 (1.5746)	.1135 (.5381)	-.0949 (.5821)	.8003 (4.6260)
Heavy Steel	-.1038 (.5933)	.2947 (1.7133)	-.1787 (.8761)	.4681 (2.5304)	-.1459 (.8584)	.2480 (1.3263)
Metal Products	.0087 (.0485)	.0874 (.5431)	-.0766 (.3794)	-.1746 (1.0212)	-.2237 (1.0966)	.7222 (2.9356)
Other Machinery	-.0017 (.0109)	-.0642 (.4167)	-.4682 (2.2730)	.4199 (2.4701)	.0330 (.2157)	.2916 (1.4365)
Light Electrical Machinery	.0753 (1.2987)	-.2054 (1.6839)	-.2460 (1.6511)	.3920 (2.3905)	-.1472 (1.0016)	.2297 (2.0512)
Heavy Electrical Machinery	.7010 (6.7403)	-.0177 (.1750)	-.2804 (1.3483)	.3955 (2.0283)	-.0268 (.0885)	-.0248 (.1950)
Vehicles and Suppliers	.2682 (1.4040)	-.0565 (.8645)	-.1256 (.4652)	.0039 (.0139)	.0934 (.4303)	.1814 (.9858)
Consumer Durables	-.1095 (.4508)	-.1178 (.4826)	.2363 (1.3129)	.0037 (.0216)	-.0927 (1.2779)	.4859 (1.5525)
Machine Tools	.4392 (3.3530)	.5112 (4.6476)	-.4709 (2.7700)	.4465 (3.3317)	-.1871 (1.5992)	.1864 (1.6941)
Basic Textiles	.3434 (3.0123)	.1424 (1.3825)	-.4510 (2.4645)	.8321 (4.3795)	-.3486 (2.6211)	.2934 (1.2477)
Other Textiles	.0289 (1.0567)	-.2882 (.9737)	.0778 (.4953)	-.5827 (4.0184)	.1999 (1.7234)	.1690 (1.5945)

*Each regression coefficient has been divided by its standard error and the resulting quotient placed underneath in parentheses. The quotient is exactly the same when the coefficients are expressed in original units. The signs of the regression coefficients have not been recorded with the quotient.

APPENDIX B

ANNUAL RESULTS — SALES MODEL
PARTIAL REGRESSION COEFFICIENTS IN STANDARD UNITS *
1949

Industry	Depreciation Expense	Age	Change in Sales	Capacity	Liquidity Stock	Sales
Pulp and Paper	.0469 (.2004)	-.1310 (.7571)	-.2438 (.7372)	.1661 (.7652)	.3705 (1.4036)	.2238 .9772
Light Chemicals	.5428 (2.2806)	.0665 (.2649)	.0468 (.1671)	.1206 (.4262)	.3023 (1.1718)	.3473 (1.3728)
Heavy Chemicals	.5948 (2.7410)	.0297 (.7585)	-.1285 (.5079)	.6154 (2.7473)	-.2344 (1.1379)	.0349 (.1473)
Petroleum	.2467 (.9205)	-.2952 (1.3295)	-.3324 (1.1915)	.0546 (.1852)	-.1107 (.4163)	.2340 (1.0172)
Rubber	.5130 (3.8860)	-.1007 (.7574)	.9178 (6.0379)	-.2696 (1.8091)	-.0427 (.3071)	.1543 (1.0427)
Heavy Steel	-.1567 (1.3060)	-.0549 (.3366)	-.1388 (1.0132)	.1192 (.9172)	-.3068 (1.9544)	.3057 (1.8416)
Metal Products	.2858 (1.7641)	.0491 (.3108)	-.3465 (1.5132)	.2014 (.9711)	.0142 (.6174)	.4289 (2.1443)
Other Machinery	.0902 (.6220)	-.1634 (1.1270)	-.0525 (.3000)	.2855 (1.5184)	.1941 (1.2685)	.0804 (.4700)
Light Electrical Machinery	.1715 (1.6026)	-.4284 (3.4830)	.0559 (.4693)	-.0125 (.0410)	.2011 (1.5709)	.0856 (.7129)
Heavy Electrical Machinery	.1849 (1.0167)	-.1862 (1.0190)	.5522 (3.1376)	.1756 (1.1183)	.4394 (1.0483)	-.2011 (.9574)
Vehicles and Suppliers	.1499 (.7570)	-.0315 (.1558)	.3792 (1.3791)	-.3455 (1.4336)	.1103 (.5717)	.4233 (1.9153)
Consumer Durables	-.0050 (.0211)	-.1799 (.7373)	.1961 (1.7354)	-.0967 (.6808)	.0769 (.2991)	.6581 (6.2671)
Machine Tools	.3038 (2.9786)	-.0340 (.3092)	.0916 (.8485)	.3340 (2.8301)	-.1331 (1.1472)	.1464 (1.2731)
Basic Textiles	.0646 (.3963)	-.0111 (.0359)	.2979 (2.3643)	-.7917 (5.6149)	-.2839 (1.9054)	1.2654 (6.0837)
Other Textiles	.5243 (4.3331)	-.2330 (.7613)	.0262 (.0854)	-.0515 (1.3403)	-.0478 (.4512)	.2164 (.7165)

*Each regression coefficient has been divided by its standard error and the resulting quotient placed underneath in parentheses. The quotient is exactly the same when the coefficients are expressed in original units. The signs of the regression coefficients have not been recorded with the quotient.

APPENDIX B

ANNUAL RESULTS — SALES MODEL
PARTIAL REGRESSION COEFFICIENTS IN STANDARD UNITS*

1950

Industry	Depreciation Expense	Age	Change in Sales	Capacity	Liquidity Stock	Sales
Pulp and Paper	.2433 (1.1317)	-.1716 (.9918)	-.0858 (.2760)	-.2529 (1.4210)	.4281 (1.9639)	-.0783 (.6930)
Light Chemicals	.4503 (1.8841)	-.0185 (.3988)	.1088 (.3846)	-.0824 (.2757)	-.0519 (.1814)	.2464 (.9262)
Heavy Chemicals	.3594 (1.8149)	.0128 (.0747)	-.0188 (.0819)	.2349 (1.2768)	-.0019 (.5147)	.1602 (.5304)
Petroleum	.3184 (1.0942)	-.3331 (1.5280)	-.6189 (2.1490)	.2443 (.9618)	.1558 (.6492)	.2590 (.8520)
Rubber	.7526 (5.4931)	.1837 (1.3212)	.1403 (.6022)	-.0867 (.5703)	-.1138 (.6151)	.3143 (1.3605)
Heavy Steel	-.1056 (.6521)	.1071 (.5758)	.4918 (3.7260)	-.2009 (.7755)	-.2068 (.9896)	-.0656 (.5418)
Metal Products	.1502 (.8393)	.0281 (.1756)	.3792 (1.7636)	-.0397 (.2217)	-.0606 (.3835)	.2794 (1.4042)
Other Machinery	.3398 (2.3276)	.0426 (.2939)	-.0691 (.3385)	.2170 (.9819)	-.1377 (.8293)	.2230 (1.1736)
Light Electrical Machinery	.8127 (.8110)	.2898 (2.5650)	.2853 (.2474)	-.0605 (.5933)	-.1203 (1.0744)	-.2880 (1.5036)
Heavy Electrical Machinery	-.0382 (.1261)	-.3579 (3.4748)	.0154 (.1242)	.5680 (4.8547)	.3603 (1.2554)	.0485 (.3911)
Vehicles and Suppliers	.1521 (.6473)	-.1809 (.9002)	-.2565 (1.2697)	.1925 (.8595)	.0362 (.1661)	.4831 (1.7440)
Consumer Durables	.0608 (.7116)	-.2482 (1.0837)	.2184 (.9252)	.1407 (.5007)	.1360 (.5886)	.3608 (2.6530)
Machine Tools	.4521 (1.5326)	.0259 (.0857)	.2124 (1.3445)	.0266 (.0928)	-.0312 (.1157)	.3152 (1.9575)
Basic Textiles	.7519 (6.8355)	.3526 (1.1993)	.2736 (1.9967)	.4821 (4.1919)	.0944 (.8284)	.1761 (1.1077)
Other Textiles	-.3832 (.2022)	-.3622 (1.6539)	-1.9706 (.6499)	.1593 (.0817)	.3809 (2.1159)	3.0492 (2.4810)

*Each regression coefficient has been divided by its standard error and the resulting quotient placed underneath in parentheses. The quotient is exactly the same when the coefficients are expressed in original units. The signs of the regression coefficients have not been recorded with the quotient.

APPENDIX B

ANNUAL RESULTS — PROFIT MODEL
PARTIAL REGRESSION COEFFICIENTS

1946

Industry	Depreciation Expense	Age	Change in Sales	Capacity	Liquidity Stock	Profits
Pulp and Paper	.2215	-.8485	.2682	.0927	.0448	.8688
Light Chemicals	-.4810	-1.8242	.2512	.0161	.0182	.0659
Heavy Chemicals	-.2722	.5683	.8850	.0188	-.1110	.0366
Petroleum	-.3319	.0063	.0812	.0323	.0335	.6578
Rubber	-.2891	-.8322	.5256	.0078	.0780	-.8231
Heavy Steel	.1860	-.0790	-.1375	.0336	-.0380	.0140
Metal Products	.0772	-.3642	-.1234	.0093	-.0097	.2050
Other Machinery	1.0336	-2.4693	-1.0706	.0624	.0430	.2456
Light Electrical Machinery	.1596	-.1096	.6315	.0041	.0360	-.1790
Heavy Electrical Machinery	1.3120	-.3546	-.0483	-.0204	.0818	.1291
Vehicles and Suppliers	.6570	-.5654	.4934	.0042	-.0493	-.0340
Consumer Durables	.9417	-.3191	.2544	.0331	.0764	-.1434
Machine Tools	.7420	.4001	-.1728	.0055	-.0824	.1333
Basic Textiles	-.6837	.0840	.2989	.0002	.0064	-.0365
Other Textiles	-.9632	.0163	-.0423	.0136	.2396	-.0332

1947

Industry	Depreciation Expense	Age	Change in Sales	Capacity	Liquidity Stock	Profits
Pulp and Paper	.8822	-.9534	-.4736	.0527	.2592	-.0376
Light Chemicals	.1518	-2.4351	-.3985	.0624	.0972	.0091
Heavy Chemicals	-.7798	-.4035	-.4927	.0472	-.1330	.1025
Petroleum	-.8672	-.3900	.0035	.0163	.4054	.4253
Rubber	-.2993	-.7413	-1.3488	.0334	-.1083	-.2402
Heavy Steel	-.1707	-.1135	.1831	.0427	-.0124	-.0262
Metal Products	-.6042	-.4246	.0382	.0148	-.0336	.2999
Other Machinery	.2689	-.4932	-.2031	.0054	.0152	.0482
Light Electrical Machinery	-.0266	-.6562	-.3021	.0180	.0204	.0278
Heavy Electrical Machinery	-.9332	-.1727	.5489	.0029	.0268	.0198
Vehicles and Suppliers	.4710	.0015	-.0593	.0165	.1662	.1630
Consumer Durables	.8602	-.1728	.1441	.0160	.1092	-.0188
Machine Tools	.4315	.2477	-.1916	.0338	-.0737	.2366
Basic Textiles	5.2908	.0282	.7055	.0181	.0494	-.2868
Other Textiles	.4021	-.2273	.3533	.0006	.5777	.0576

APPENDIX B

ANNUAL RESULTS — PROFIT MODEL
PARTIAL REGRESSION COEFFICIENTS

1948

Industry	Depreciation Expense	Age	Change in Sales	Capacity	Liquidity Stock	Profits
Pulp and Paper	-.1569	-.2470	.0374	.0164	-.0659	.3665
Light Chemicals	.5195	-.7697	.1198	.0439	.0484	.0300
Heavy Chemicals	.0752	-.1404	-.1075	.1640	-.0934	.2820
Petroleum	-1.0176	.2312	.1988	.1033	.2203	.7929
Rubber	-.1726	.1423	.0830	-.0123	-.0256	.5978
Heavy Steel	-.2637	.3130	-.2463	.0088	-.0463	-.0319
Metal Products	.2187	.0566	.0634	-.0101	-.0320	.2422
Other Machinery	.2461	-.2212	-.2355	.0269	.0231	.0060
Light Electrical Machinery	.9242	-.6550	-.2850	.0135	.0519	-.2078
Heavy Electrical Machinery	4.5895	-.0205	-.2036	.0306	-.0002	-.0131
Vehicles and Suppliers	2.4210	-.3073	-.0292	.0162	.0699	.0082
Consumer Durables	-.0879	-.8979	.1548	-.0118	-.1225	.2005
Machine Tools	.9609	.4902	-.1455	.0379	-.0216	.0526
Basic Textiles	4.7169	.3530	-.2966	.1709	-.0629	.0000
Other Textiles	-.3184	-.3955	.4033	-.0183	.1046	.1697

1949

Industry	Depreciation Expense	Age	Change in Sales	Capacity	Liquidity Stock	Profits
Pulp and Paper	.4106	-.2989	.0466	.0030	.2431	.2951
Light Chemicals	3.1072	-.0690	.1352	.0050	.0560	-.0057
Heavy Chemicals	2.1780	.0937	-.4566	.0780	-.1639	.0450
Petroleum	.7646	-.4180	-.0018	-.1173	-.3474	.7076
Rubber	1.4160	.1193	-.0613	-.0371	-.1087	.3848
Heavy Steel	-.1431	-.2122	-.0056	.0142	-.0088	.1567
Metal Products	5.2652	-.1527	-.3302	.1068	.0753	.4255
Other Machinery	.3449	-.1591	-.0394	.0128	-.0261	.1653
Light Electrical Machinery	.9652	-1.1906	.0906	.0010	.0697	-.1426
Heavy Electrical Machinery	1.1425	-.3028	.0355	-.0523	.0829	.0764
Vehicles and Suppliers	.7016	.1002	.0554	-.0399	.0770	-.0985
Consumer Durables	.5279	-.9222	.1227	-.0036	-.0075	.2393
Machine Tools	.8193	-.0470	.0034	.0022	-.0245	.0868
Basic Textiles	4.8626	.0226	-.4380	-.0267	-.0321	.4354
Other Textiles	2.5224	-.3495	.2109	-.0078	-.0968	.7088

APPENDIX B

ANNUAL RESULTS — PROFIT MODEL
PARTIAL REGRESSION COEFFICIENTS
1950

Industry	Depreciation Expense	Age	Change in Sales	Capacity	Liquidity Stock	Profits
Pulp and Paper	1.5580	-1.1450	-.2000	-.1057	.3969	.0639
Light Chemicals	3.5862	-.2419	.0607	-.0135	-.0453	.1715
Heavy Chemicals	.2805	.0184	-.0521	.0167	-.0827	.2944
Petroleum	.8114	-.3186	-.0346	.1110	.0561	.1728
Rubber	2.0054	.1213	.0561	-.0211	.0180	.0184
Heavy Steel	-.2091	.1408	.0305	-.0062	-.0577	.0293
Metal Products	.5451	.0069	.0096	-.0578	-.0124	.1310
Other Machinery	.7748	.0097	-.0843	.0017	-.0042	.0054
Light Electrical Machinery	3.8615	.9539	-.0511	-.0174	-.0623	.1650
Heavy Electrical Machinery	.0032	-.8529	.1283	.0137	.0770	-.0877
Vehicles and Suppliers	1.7508	-.3838	-.0885	.0260	.0768	.2078
Consumer Durables	.2672	-.7688	.0305	.0273	.0157	.0982
Machine Tools	1.1323	.0962	.0060	-.0222	-.0132	.1193
Basic Textiles	7.8947	2.1007	.3379	.0675	.0148	.2403
Other Textiles	-.0489	-.4127	-.0255	-.0124	.0130	.4768

ANNUAL RESULTS — SALES MODEL
PARTIAL REGRESSION COEFFICIENTS
1946

Industry	Depreciation Expense	Age	Change in Sales	Capacity	Liquidity Stock	Sales
Pulp and Paper	.3963	-.8088	.2623	.0419	.0183	.0344
Light Chemicals	-.0111	-1.1143	.2198	.0091	.0072	.0066
Heavy Chemicals	-.2736	.3913	-.8565	.0653	-.1419	.0292
Petroleum	-.7818	.0589	.1195	.0542	.0947	.0436
Rubber	-.3327	-.5831	.3257	-.0064	-.0584	.0041
Heavy Steel	.1775	-.0188	-.0971	.0233	-.0319	.0122
Metal Products	.0719	-.3121	-.1252	.0118	-.0036	.0089
Other Machinery	2.4240	-2.8006	-1.5827	.0149	.1226	-.0955
Light Electrical Machinery	.5323	-.1185	.7388	.0085	-.0042	-.0244
Heavy Electrical Machinery	-.5784	.1818	.3297	.0025	.0384	-.0178
Vehicles and Suppliers	.5202	-.3388	.3022	.0156	-.0300	.0406
Consumer Durables	.7046	-.3431	.1548	.0225	.0348	-.0058
Machine Tools	.1678	.1030	-.0404	-.0147	.0536	.0487
Basic Textiles	-.3520	.0060	-.0453	.0023	.1466	-.0051
Other Textiles	-.1340	-.4391	-.2716	.0098	.1545	.0065

ANNUAL RESULTS — SALES MODEL
PARTIAL REGRESSION COEFFICIENTS

1947

Industry	Depreciation Expense	Age	Change in Sales	Capacity	Liquidity Stock	Sales
Pulp and Paper	.0944	-.8220	-.5442	.1614	.0981	.0480
Light Chemicals	-.0873	-2.4477	-.4057	.0662	.1010	.0032
Heavy Chemicals	-.3235	-.4203	-.4605	.0405	-.0906	.0062
Petroleum	-.2314	-.4474	.0180	-.0290	.6667	-.0408
Rubber	-.8237	-1.2224	-1.3440	.0642	-.1515	-.0425
Heavy Steel	-.1013	-.1178	.1821	.0449	-.0198	-.0027
Metal Products	-.5496	-.4276	-.0973	.0198	-.0232	.0213
Other Machinery	.2831	-.4005	-.1987	.0033	.0215	.0062
Light Electrical Machinery	-.1180	-.7055	-.3607	.0362	.0322	.0086
Heavy Electrical Machinery	-1.3314	-.0709	-.5462	.0026	.0344	.0112
Vehicles and Suppliers	.5413	.2214	-.1026	.0359	.1663	.0208
Consumer Durables	.9827	-.1836	.1451	.0209	.1063	-.0058
Machine Tools	.3345	.2417	-.2856	.0434	-.0528	.0262
Basic Textiles	2.2741	-.0102	-.3625	.0190	.0373	-.0069
Other Textiles	.9949	-.2981	.3512	.0110	.5268	-.0054

1948

Industry	Depreciation Expense	Age	Change in Sales	Capacity	Liquidity Stock	Sales
Pulp and Paper	.4468	.0173	-.1825	.0494	-.0644	.0406
Light Chemicals	.6370	-1.0694	.2258	.0275	.0647	-.0053
Heavy Chemicals	.8150	-.1951	-.2166	.0149	-.0123	.0114
Petroleum	.6863	.0513	.1811	.3597	.5995	-.1075
Rubber	-2.0447	-.1389	.0883	.0694	-.0461	.0842
Heavy Steel	-.5467	.3740	-.2445	.0322	-.0454	.0188
Metal Products	.0414	.1754	-.0740	-.0131	-.0490	.0336
Other Machinery	-.0060	-.1066	-.2600	.0414	.0060	.0145
Light Electrical Machinery	.3803	-.5057	-.2259	.0411	-.0358	.0171
Heavy Electrical Machinery	4.5845	-.0330	-.1940	.0301	-.0070	-.0011
Vehicles and Suppliers	1.9749	-.4169	-.0044	.0134	.0509	.0153
Consumer Durables	-.3977	-.4790	.0019	.0125	-.0234	.0184
Machine Tools	1.0351	.4976	-.1582	.0440	-.0239	.0055
Basic Textiles	3.8677	.2637	-.4618	.0784	-.1189	.0210
Other Textiles	.2411	-.4882	.3397	-.0199	.1541	.0222

APPENDIX B

ANNUAL RESULTS — SALES MODEL
PARTIAL REGRESSION COEFFICIENTS

1949

Industry	Depreciation Expense	Age	Change in Sales	Capacity	Liquidity Stock	Sales
Pulp and Paper	.1971	-.4517	-.0761	.0745	.2349	.0195
Light Chemicals	2.7362	.4131	.0628	.0087	.0618	.0199
Heavy Chemicals	2.2199	.1089	-.4536	.0658	-.1525	.0054
Petroleum	1.2028	-.5953	-.0432	.1494	-.1339	.0319
Rubber	2.0298	-.1246	.1052	-.1660	-.0151	.0096
Heavy Steel	-.1800	-.0942	-.0594	..0211	-.0093	.0198
Metal Products	4.2266	.3862	-.2868	.1683	.0158	.0820
Other Machinery	.2829	-.3017	-.1371	.0075	.0333	.0041
Light Electrical Machinery	.6818	-.8735	.0066	-.0063	.0389	.0051
Heavy Electrical Machinery	1.0854	-.5164	.0635	.0389	.0944	-.0120
Vehicles and Suppliers	.3675	-.0411	.1072	-.0207	.0232	.0167
Consumer Durables	-.0136	-1.0949	.0356	-.0123	.0151	.0344
Machine Tools	.8071	-.0583	.1707	.0137	-.0213	.0069
Basic Textiles	-.5992	-.0410	.1507	-.2125	-.0636	.0905
Other Textiles	3.4297	-.4621	.0281	-.0056	-.0357	.0303

1950

Industry	Depreciation Expense	Age	Change in Sales	Capacity	Liquidity Stock	Sales
Pulp and Paper	1.6820	-1.0958	-.1946	-.0635	.4206	-.0120
Light Chemicals	3.4579	-.0909	.0391	-.0230	-.0185	.0192
Heavy Chemicals	.4809	.0267	-.0757	.0039	-.0004	.0086
Petroleum	.7441	-.3282	-.0411	.1520	.0755	.0174
Rubber	1.9546	.1325	.0269	-.0081	-.0018	.0108
Heavy Steel	-.1962	.1336	.0301	-.0074	-.0517	-.0027
Metal Products	.6009	.0553	.0089	-.0432	-.0159	.0133
Other Machinery	.7143	.0455	-.0599	.0039	-.0137	.0076
Light Electrical Machinery	4.3178	.6467	.0248	-.0195	-.0346	-.0113
Heavy Electrical Machinery	-.1222	-.7259	.0035	.0482	.0489	.0020
Vehicles and Suppliers	.7808	-1.4885	-.0951	.0334	.0204	.0343
Consumer Durables	.1794	-.8524	.0388	.0170	.0260	.0131
Machine Tools	1.1632	.0334	.0083	.0146	-.0043	.0099
Basic Textiles	8.0544	2.3285	.3298	.0627	.0254	.0155
Other Textiles	-.7875	-.7368	-.0142	.1622	.1090	.1061

APPENDIX B

AVERAGED DATA RESULTS — PROFIT MODEL
PARTIAL AND MULTIPLE CORRELATIONS

Industry	Depreciation Expense	Age	Capacity	Liquidity Stock	Profits	Multiple Correlations
Pulp and Paper	.5859	-.1163	.2922	.3994	.2467	.7701
Light Chemicals	.4461	-.5745	.2970	.4985	.0230	.7676
Heavy Chemicals	.6466	-.0571	.4515	.0134	-.1369	.8735
Petroleum	.3503	-.3764	.1772	-.4825	.5657	.7829
Rubber	-.0338	.0213	.1350	-.3127	.7891	.8721
Heavy Steel	.1681	-.2102	.1757	-.0566	.5292	.6866
Metal Products	.3203	-.0735	.0617	.0743	.2107	.4736
Other Machinery	.1387	-.0881	.2803	-.1651	.1688	.4425
Light Electrical Machinery	.3095	-.2917	.4775	.0737	.2385	.6723
Heavy Electrical Machinery	.7053	.0401	-.1634	.6317	.0746	.8503
Vehicles and Suppliers	-.7980	-.6680	.7546	-.1028	.5647	.9042
Consumer Durables	.2663	-.0214	.4627	-.0155	.1122	.7598
Machine Tools	.7496	.2509	.7301	-.4488	.1404	.9270
Basic Textiles	.0480	-.1389	.5158	.0114	.5381	.6763
Other Textiles	.3805	-.0934	.2619	.6953	.3358	.8921

AVERAGED DATA RESULTS — SALES MODEL
PARTIAL AND MULTIPLE CORRELATIONS

Industry	Depreciation Expense	Age	Capacity	Liquidity Stock	Sales	Multiple Correlations
Pulp and Paper	.5756	-.0925	.2508	.2142	.1900	.7631
Light Chemicals	.4675	-.5966	.2508	.5783	.2944	.7905
Heavy Chemicals	.3193	-.0315	.2771	-.2193	.5263	.7969
Petroleum	.3450	-.2625	.2145	-.2946	.3420	.7052
Rubber	-.3493	-.5234	.6317	-.3550	.8540	.8386
Heavy Steel	-.0100	-.0786	-.1497	.0391	.7348	.8135
Metal Products	.2619	-.0434	.0385	.0427	.3092	.5157
Other Machinery	.0780	-.0803	.1673	-.1646	.2110	.4572
Light Electrical Machinery	.2383	-.3715	.5753	.1783	.3491	.6833
Heavy Electrical Machinery	.6404	.0674	-.1741	.6357	.1130	.8515
Vehicles and Suppliers	-.7483	-.5670	.4990	.0205	.4090	.8815
Consumer Durables	.0720	.0192	.4722	-.1882	.5465	.8129
Machine Tools	.7681	.2704	.6054	-.3882	.5474	.9367
Basic Textiles	.0785	-.0665	.5805	.0114	.6542	.7504
Other Textiles	.4450	-.1490	.2650	.6434	.1005	.8792

APPENDIX B

AVERAGED DATA RESULTS — PROFIT MODEL
PARTIAL REGRESSION COEFFICIENTS IN STANDARD UNITS*

Industry	Depreciation Expense	Age	Capacity	Liquidity Stock	Profit
Pulp and Paper	.4900 (3.0578)	-.0797 (.4983)	.2041 (1.2931)	.3210 (1.8432)	.1814 (1.0776)
Light Chemicals	.3425 (1.7474)	-.1844 (1.2049)	.2543 (1.0865)	.5089 (2.0193)	.0058 (.0252)
Heavy Chemicals	.9330 (2.6389)	-.0296 (.1784)	.2590 (1.5794)	.0120 (.0417)	-.1187 (.4309)
Petroleum	.2263 (1.2525)	-.3106 (1.3610)	.1313 (.6037)	-.4714 (1.8449)	.5335 (2.2979)
Rubber	-.0180 (.0468)	.0467 (.2959)	.0740 (.1886)	-.1751 (.4551)	.8885 (1.7770)
Heavy Steel	.1299 (.8676)	-.1708 (1.0936)	.1601 (.9081)	-.0542 (.2886)	.5800 (3.1782)
Metal Products	.3175 (2.3468)	-.0682 (.5112)	.0570 (.4287)	.0803 (.5621)	.2151 (1.4948)
Other Machinery	.1405 (1.0812)	-.0944 (.6864)	.2881 (2.2703)	-.1779 (1.3009)	.1816 (1.3312)
Light Electrical Machinery	.2615 (1.0502)	-.2464 (.9842)	.4436 (1.7480)	.0615 (.2386)	.1987 (.7921)
Heavy Electrical Machinery	.6132 (1.6567)	.0257 (.0667)	-.1257 (.2756)	.5632 (1.3581)	.0430 (.1247)
Vehicles and Suppliers	-.7516 (4.0759)	-.4013 (2.7690)	.7427 (3.5409)	-.0561 (.3187)	.4338 (2.1092)
Consumer Durables	.2525 (.9159)	-.0181 (.0715)	.4095 (1.7306)	-.0132 (.0519)	.3377 (1.2594)
Machine Tools	.4989 (2.0367)	.1348 (.4662)	.5268 (1.9209)	-.2394 (.9035)	.2271 (.8907)
Basic Textiles	.0358 (.1580)	-.1094 (.5089)	.4517 (1.9846)	.0268 (.1186)	.4852 (2.1036)
Other Textiles	.3778 (.6944)	-.0549 (.1583)	.2453 (.4572)	.5417 (1.6334)	.2430 (.6020)

*Each regression coefficient has been divided by its standard error and the resulting quotient placed underneath in parentheses. The quotient is exactly the same when the coefficients are expressed in original units.

AVERAGED DATA RESULTS — SALES MODEL
PARTIAL REGRESSION COEFFICIENTS IN STANDARD UNITS*

Industry	Depreciation Expense	Age	Capacity	Liquidity Stock	Sales
Pulp and Paper	.4877 (3.0186)	-.0649 (.3983)	.1738 (1.1103)	.2469 (1.0312)	.1973 (1.4475)
Light Chemicals	.3353 (1.8320)	-.4678 (2.5753)	.1967 (.8979)	.5198 (2.4557)	.1998 (1.0677)
Heavy Chemicals	.2906 (1.3061)	-.0236 (.1219)	.2357 (1.1150)	-.1766 (.8699)	.5328 (2.3973)
Petroleum	.3062 (1.4035)	-.2430 (1.0407)	.1846 (.8389)	-.2773 (.1770)	.2933 (1.3906)
Rubber	-.2441 (.5737)	-.3726 (.9465)	.5030 (1.2535)	-.2342 (.5855)	.6934 (2.3180)
Heavy Steel	-.0064 (.0421)	-.0517 (.3210)	-.1081 (.6158)	.0280 (.1594)	.7472 (4.4105)
Metal Products	.2570 (1.8312)	-.0394 (.2930)	.0346 (.2586)	.0413 (.2883)	.3331 (2.1965)
Other Machinery	.0811 (.6025)	-.0853 (.6203)	.1957 (1.3075)	-.1681 (1.2853)	.2596 (1.6619)
Light Electrical Machinery	.1736 (.7810)	-.2501 (1.2712)	.4203 (2.2402)	.1309 (.5768)	.2625 (1.1882)
Heavy Electrical Machinery	.5825 (1.9558)	.0454 (.1585)	-.1349 (.4144)	.5432 (1.9301)	.0914 (.2673)
Vehicles and Suppliers	-.7091 (3.8797)	-.3514 (2.3475)	.5806 (1.9606)	.0119 (.0700)	.4589 (1.5287)
Consumer Durables	.0647 (.2143)	.0144 (.0572)	.3711 (1.5925)	-.1558 (.5694)	.6495 (1.9408)
Machine Tools	.4930 (2.0160)	.1344 (.4712)	.4025 (1.2778)	-.1861 (.7071)	.3338 (1.0981)
Basic Textiles	.0528 (.2328)	-.0474 (.1971)	.4798 (2.1080)	.0077 (.0342)	.6016 (2.5582)
Other Textiles	.4623 (.8836)	-.0915 (.2669)	.2807 (.4895)	.5260 (1.4986)	.0684 (.1789)

*Each regression coefficient has been divided by its standard error and the resulting quotient placed underneath in parentheses. The quotient is exactly the same when the coefficients are expressed in original units.

APPENDIX B

AVERAGED RESULTS — PROFIT MODEL
PARTIAL REGRESSION COEFFICIENTS

Industry	Depreciation Expense	Age	Capacity	Liquidity Stock	Profits
Pulp and Paper	2.2511	-.2497	.0094	.1368	.1538
Light Chemicals	2.1855	-.0707	.0114	.0809	.0023
Heavy Chemicals	2.1253	-.0578	.0176	.0013	-.0452
Petroleum	.1024	-.7343	.0101	-.1719	.4639
Rubber	-.0550	.2655	.0074	.0824	.4555
Heavy Steel	.7201	-1.4976	.0120	-.0211	.4437
Metal Products	1.2575	-.4657	.0035	.0112	.0888
Other Machinery	.7327	-.9447	.0164	-.0388	.0990
Light Electrical Machinery	.4553	-1.5706	.0338	.0078	.0798
Heavy Electrical Machinery	6.0934	-.2894	.0090	.1883	.0341
Vehicles and Suppliers	1.2371	-1.0236	.0141	-.0086	.1314
Consumer Durables	1.1635	-.2055	.0411	-.0037	.1123
Machine Tools	1.2766	.9098	.0229	-.0468	.0958
Basic Textiles	.0687	-.5510	.0416	.0076	.1795
Other Textiles	6.8378	.9127	.0364	.0985	.0100

AVERAGED RESULTS — SALES MODEL
PARTIAL REGRESSION COEFFICIENTS

Industry	Depreciation Expense	Age	Capacity	Liquidity Stock	Sales
Pulp and Paper	2.2403	-.2034	.0080	.1052	.0157
Light Chemicals	2.1396	-1.7941	.0088	.0826	.0097
Heavy Chemicals	.6620	-.0462	.0160	-.0192	.0284
Petroleum	1.1777	-.5743	.0142	-.1011	.0225
Rubber	-.7463	-2.1188	.0505	-.1103	.0545
Heavy Steel	-.0353	-.4529	-.0080	.0109	.0584
Metal Products	1.0180	-.2692	.0021	.0058	.0171
Other Machinery	.0423	-.8537	.0112	-.0367	.0249
Light Electrical Machinery	.3022	-1.5937	.0320	.0167	.0075
Heavy Electrical Machinery	5.7885	-.5119	.0096	.1816	.0087
Vehicles and Suppliers	1.1678	-.8963	.0110	.0018	.0127
Consumer Durables	.2979	.1633	.0372	-.0433	.0271
Machine Tools	1.2616	.9073	.0175	-.0364	.0117
Basic Textiles	.1014	-.2387	.0442	.0022	.0279
Other Textiles	4.5857	1.5190	.0456	.1003	.0046

Appendix C

Correlation and Regression Estimates When the Data Are Ratios[1]

INTRODUCTION

Our concern is with a question which has arisen frequently in recent econometric work: What is the correct interpretation of correlation and regression parameters when the observations are ratios? This question can be broken down into two parts: (1) What is the nature of the correlation coefficients obtained from deflated observations? Are such correlations likely to be, in some sense or other, spuriously high or spuriously low? (2) What are the properties of the regression coefficients obtained from deflated observations? Are these coefficients more or less biased and efficient than those obtained from undeflated values?

In obtaining answers, we shall be concerned with the following tasks:

1. Generalizing some results about spurious correlation which were first established by Karl Pearson;
2. Showing under what circumstances the simple correlation between ratios is an unbiased estimate of the partial correlation between

[1] This is a condensed version of a paper with the same title which appeared in *Econometrica*, XXIII (October 1955), 400–416. We wish to thank Professors Carl Christ, University of Chicago, and Guy Orcutt, Harvard University, for many helpful suggestions.

undeflated variables, the influence of the deflating variable eliminated or held constant;

3. Generalizing the above correlation results to instances involving more than two deflated series and thereby showing when each higher order partial correlation between ratios is an unbiased estimate of the corresponding partial correlation between undeflated variables;[2]

4. Indicating necessary and sufficient conditions for the least-squares ratio-data estimates of regression parameters to be the best in the sense of most efficient unbiased estimates.

THE SPURIOUS CORRELATION PROBLEM

In his pioneer work on spurious ratio correlation, Karl Pearson's primary objective was to observe what happens to the correlation between ratios having a common deflator when the true correlation between the undeflated series is zero.[3] More generally, he made the well-known point that correlations between ratios can often be larger than the simple correlation between the numerator series. Thus, the ratio correlations can be "spuriously" high estimates of the true relationship between the numerators.

The question of spurious correlation quite obviously does not arise when the hypothesis to be tested has initially been formulated in terms of ratios, for instance in problems involving relative prices. Similarly, when a series such as money value of output is divided by a price index to obtain a "constant dollar" estimate of output, no question of spurious correlation need arise. Thus, spurious correlation can only exist when a hypothesis pertains to undeflated variables and the data have been divided through by another series for reasons extraneous to but not in conflict with the hypothesis framed as an exact, i.e., non-stochastic, relation.

Using the first two terms of a series expansion in order to express the correlation of the ratios in terms of moments of the original series, Pearson derived the following relation:[4]

---

[2] Furthermore, it then follows that the multiple correlation coefficient for the ratios is an unbiased estimate of the equivalent multiple correlation for the absolute values when these conditions have been met.

[3] Karl Pearson, "On a Form of Spurious Correlation which May Arise when Indices Are Used in the Measurement of Organs," *Proceedings of the Royal Society of London,* LX (1897), 489–496.

[4] In order for this relation to be a good approximation of the index correlation, V_z must be small so that the third and higher order terms of the series expansion are inconsequential. The analogue to the usual product-moment correlation coefficient is obvious: The numerator of P is the covariance of X/Z and Y/Z while the denominator is the product of the standard deviations of the ratio variables.

$$P = \frac{r_{xy}V_xV_y - r_{xz}V_xV_z - r_{yz}V_yV_z + V_z^2}{(V_x^2 + V_z^2 - 2r_{xz}V_xV_z)^{\frac{1}{2}}(V_y^2 + V_z^2 - 2r_{yz}V_yV_z)^{\frac{1}{2}}} \quad (1)$$

where

P is the correlation between the ratios X/Z and Y/Z (usually called the ratio correlation hereafter);

X, Y are the variables to be deflated;

Z is the deflating variable;

V_x, V_y, V_z are the coefficients of variation for X, Y, and Z respectively, i.e., the ratio of the standard deviation to the mean;

r_{xy}, r_{yz}, r_{xz} are simple correlation coefficients.

Working with this general formulation, Pearson made the simplifying assumptions that all coefficients of variation are equal while the intercorrelations, r_{xz} and r_{yz}, are assumed equal to each other but different from the correlation r_{xy} between the main series. To simplify, we will use the new symbol r' where $r' = r_{xz} = r_{yz}$. Under this set of assumptions Pearson derived the following results from (1):

$$P = .5\left(\frac{1 + r_{xy} - 2r'}{1 - r'}\right) = .5 + .5\left(\frac{r_{xy} - r'}{1 - r'}\right). \quad (2)$$

Because the results will be strongly influenced by relations among the coefficients of variation, the usefulness of (2) can be immediately extended by assuming that the coefficients of variation for the main series X and Y are equal while that of the deflating series Z is some multiple of this value, i.e., if $V_x = V_y$, then $V_z = aV_x = aV_y$. Thus, remembering that $r_{xz} = r_{yz} = r'$,

$$P = \frac{r_{xy} + a^2 - 2ar'}{1 + a^2 - 2ar'}. \quad (3)$$

From this formulation, the extent of so-called spurious correlation can be easily found by setting r_{xy} equal to zero and observing how much the ratio correlation P exceeds or falls short of zero for different values of r' and a. In other words, given the underlying assumptions, relation (3) with r_{xy} set equal to zero becomes the appropriate alternative hypothesis of no relation when ratios are used instead of the original series. Further, a cursory examination of (3) indicates a wide variety of possible relations between P and r_{xy}. P will: (1) equal r_{xy} when $a = 0$ or $2r'$; (2) be greater than r_{xy} when a is greater than $2r'$;[5] and (3) be less than r_{xy} when a is greater than zero but less than $2r'$.

The main point can be simply summarized: correlating ratio vari-

[5] The limit of (3) as a approaches infinity is unity.

ables and making inferences from these to the simple correlations between the series in the numerator is an extremely hazardous business. A possibly unexpected result is that in the context of spurious correlation the ratio correlations may just as well be spuriously low as spuriously high. Consequently, if primary interest centers on the simple correlation between the numerator series, it would usually be appropriate to proceed in a straightforward manner by relating these values to one another. The subject of Pearsonian spurious correlation thus has more historical than practical relevance and is included here primarily because it conveniently introduces more important aspects of the ratio correlation problem.

RATIO CORRELATIONS AS ESTIMATES OF PARTIAL CORRELATIONS

Thus far, we have developed certain elements of the spurious correlation problem on the basis of restrictive assumptions concerning the intercorrelations and coefficients of variation. We shall now take up the distinctly different and econometrically more relevant problem of what happens when deflation has been undertaken to control or eliminate unwanted influences without the previously employed restrictive assumptions. Explicitly, we shall consider the relationship between P and the partial correlation $r_{xy.z}$ rather than the relationship between P and the simple correlation r_{xy} as we did in the context of Pearsonian spurious correlation.

To begin, we must discover how the ratio correlation varies when V_z varies and so we shall differentiate P partially with respect to V_z. Holding the other five variables constant is appropriate because their magnitudes will be determined by economic influences. Clearly, the coefficients of variation for X and Y, as well as r_{xy}, will be determined by the series chosen to test the hypothesis under consideration. Further, taking the intercorrelations r_{xz} and r_{yz} as fixed is reasonable because the strength of these relations will be determined by economic considerations that underlie any choice of deflator. For example, size deflators for firms can be chosen in a manner that will eliminate secular, cyclical, and seasonal variations as well as size effects. Just how many of these influences should be eliminated depends on the nature of the hypothesis under test. The more such influences that are eliminated, the larger will r_{xz} and r_{yz} be. Thus, all the elements of the ratio correlation except V_z will be largely determined on economic grounds. Consequently, if there are several deflators with equal properties from the economic standpoint, the statistician should choose that one with a V_z value that minimizes the possibility of spurious results.

Differentiating (1) with respect to V_z we find that

APPENDIX C

$$\frac{\partial P}{\partial V_z} = \frac{1}{B^{\frac{2}{3}}C^{\frac{2}{3}}}\{(-r_{xz}V_x - r_{yz}V_y + 2V_z)(V_x^2 + V_z^2 - 2r_{xz}V_xV_z)$$
$$(V_y^2 + V_z^2 - 2r_{yz}V_yV_z) - [r_{xy}V_xV_y - r_{xz}V_xV_z - r_{yz}V_yV_z$$
$$+ V_z^2][(V_z - r_{yz}V_y) \cdot (V_x^2 + V_z^2 - 2r_{xz}V_xV_z)$$
$$+ (V_z - r_{xz}V_x)(V_y^2 + V_z^2 - 2r_{yz}V_yV_z)]\} \qquad (4)$$

where B equals the variance of the ratio X/Z and C the variance of Y/Z. The term outside the bracket does not contain a root of the derivative since it is the reciprocal of the product of the cube root of the squared variance of the ratios X/Z and Y/Z which will always be positive and finite except under trivial circumstances. Within the large brackets several possibilities appear. A particular case arises when the covariance of the ratios equals zero when r_{xy} is zero. In this case the derivative equates to zero, but, since the covariance of the ratios will not in general be zero, this root is not pertinent. We are left with only one relevant possibility, $r_{xz}V_x = r_{yz}V_y = V_z$, which results in the first derivative being equal to zero. That this is also a minimum value of P with respect to V_z has been established by using different numerical values of the variables in the neighborhood of the stationary value. Further, when we substitute this minimizing value for V_z into equation (1) the ratio correlation is equal to the partial correlation. That is, given that $V_z = r_{xz}V_x = r_{yz}V_y$,

$$P = \frac{r_{xy}V_xV_y - V_z^2}{(V_x^2 - V_z^2)^{\frac{1}{2}}(V_y^2 - V_z^2)^{\frac{1}{2}}} = \frac{r_{xy} - r_{xz}r_{yz}}{(1 - r_{xz}^2)^{\frac{1}{2}}(1 - r_{yz}^2)^{\frac{1}{2}}} = r_{xy.z}. \quad (5)$$

So, at its minimum with respect to V_z, where $V_z = r_{xz}V_x = r_{yz}V_y$, P is equal to the partial correlation between X and Y with the influence of Z held constant, while at any other value P will be greater than $r_{xy.z}$.

To indicate the significance of this result we shall describe necessary and sufficient conditions for V_z to equal $r_{xz}V_x$ and $r_{yz}V_y$ and therefore for the correlation of ratios to yield correct estimates of the undeflated partial correlations. By definition,

$$\frac{V_z}{V_x} = \frac{S_z/\overline{Z}}{S_x/\overline{X}} \qquad (6)$$

where the S's denote standard deviations and barred variables are means.

In addition, simple linear deflation is based on the maintained hypothesis that there is a linear relation $X = k + bZ + v$ where k

APPENDIX C

is the regression intercept, b the regression slope, and v the error term. X is the dependent variable because deflation constitutes an effort to explain variations in X caused by Z. So, $\overline{X} = k + b\overline{Z}$ and substituting back into (6)

$$V_z/V_x = S_z(k + b\overline{Z})/\overline{Z}S_x. \qquad (7)$$

Furthermore, by definition, $b = r_{xz} S_x/S_z$ which when substituted into (7) yields:

$$V_z/V_x = (kS_z + r_{xz} S_x \overline{Z})/\overline{Z}S_x = (kS_z/\overline{Z}S_x) + r_{xz}. \qquad (8)$$

Therefore

$$V_z = V_x (kS_z/\overline{Z}S_x) + V_x r_{xz} = k (V_z/\overline{X}) + V_x r_{xz}. \qquad (9)$$

From (9) it is clear that $V_z = r_{xz} V_x$ only when $k = 0$ since S_z and V_x must be greater than zero except in the trivial case when Z and X are constants. By the same reasoning we can show that $r_{yz} V_y = V_z$ only when the regression of Y on Z is also a linear homogeneous function. Thus it is necessary as well as sufficient for $V_z = r_{xz} V_x = r_{yz} V_y$ that each of the main variables be linear homogeneous functions of the deflating variable. It follows, then, that in the general case necessary and sufficient conditions for P to be at a minimum with respect to V_z and to equal $r_{xy.z}$ approximately are: (1) that V_z be small so that the series expansion yields a good approximation of P; and (2) that the variables deflated, X and Y, be linear homogeneous functions of the deflator, Z.

Furthermore, this conclusion can be generalized to the case of more than two main series since all higher order partial correlations can be derived in terms of the next lower order correlations. Consider the case involving the partial correlation between X and Y with W a third main series, and Z again the deflator. We wish to show that $P_{xy.w} = r_{xy.wz}$.

When both of the previous assumptions are met, i.e., when V_z is small and when X and Y and W are linear homogeneous functions of Z, it follows that $P_{xy} = r_{xy.z}$, $P_{xw} = r_{xw.z}$ and $P_{yw} = r_{yw.z}$. Using definitions of partial correlations in terms of next lower order correlations and making appropriate substitutions, it then follows that:

$$r_{xy.zw} \equiv \frac{r_{xy.z} - r_{xw.z} r_{yw.z}}{(1 - r_{xw.z}^2)^{\frac{1}{2}}(1 - r_{yw.z}^2)^{\frac{1}{2}}} = \frac{P_{xy} - P_{xw} P_{yw}}{(1 - P_{xw}^2)^{\frac{1}{2}}(1 - P_{yw}^2)^{\frac{1}{2}}} \equiv P_{xy.w}, \qquad (10)$$

proving the desired equivalence. Since all higher partial correlations could be expressed in a similar manner, we need proceed no further.

In addition, the multiple correlation coefficient can be defined in terms of partial correlations. It can be readily shown, therefore, that the multiple correlation coefficient involving ratios equals the multiple correlation coefficient involving undeflated variables (including the deflating variable entered into the estimating equation separately) when the same assumptions are met.

The econometric relevance of these results lies in the fact that in most cases of size deflation with cross-section data, although certainly not all, the economic relationships will come close to satisfying the homogeneity requirement. Where linear relations exist, small firms will have values for most variables which will be in the vicinity of the origin. Barring unusual values for larger firms, these small firm observations will tend to guarantee that the simple regression of a particular variable on a size variable will in fact go through the origin. This is particularly likely with variables whose observations are always positive, like sales, depreciation expense, and liquid assets. But for variables which can assume negative values, such as change in sales or profits, small firms may often have a higher proportion of negative values than large firms so that the simple regression on size will have a negative intercept. In this case the partial correlation estimate will be biased upward. The bias should not be very large, however, since the smaller firms cannot, relative to the larger firms, have values very far from the origin. Thus, under a wide range of circumstances, the ratio estimates should not be greatly biased in applications to cross-section data.

Furthermore, deviations from homogeneity will lead to greater or less bias depending upon the relation of r_{xy} to r_{xz} and r_{yz}. If r_{xz} and r_{yz} are small relative to r_{xy} and the coefficients of variation are not too large, the ratio correlation will differ little from the correct partial correlation value while if r_{xz} and r_{yz} are large compared to r_{xy}, comparatively small deviations from the minimum value of P will lead to quite different values for the partial correlation and the ratio correlation. In economic terms, this means that when the influence of size is weak relative to the relation between the main series, bias is likely to be negligible. On the other hand, when the influence of size is relatively important, minor deviations from homogeneity can lead to comparatively large bias.

It was indicated at the beginning of this section that the strength of intercorrelations between the deflator and the deflated series would be largely determined by economic considerations. When we view deflation as a method to eliminate trend (either in the context of size in cross sections or the more usual time series framework), as frequently occurs, it becomes apparent that actual success in removing trend depends upon the homogeneity condition being satisfied. When the trend influence is powerful, it follows from what we have just pointed out that the elimination of trend by deflation will be unsuccessful even if only moderate deviations from homogeneity exist.

EFFICIENCY AND BIAS IN REGRESSION ESTIMATES

Until now we have been dealing with a Pearson-Yule correlation model of the straightforward least-squares variety. In both this and the usual regression model it is assumed that the error variance is constant. If this homoscedasticity assumption was met in the undeflated series, deflation would then lead to heteroscedasticity since the true error term, just like the included variables, is transformed by deflation. In this situation, least squares would not lead to the most efficient unbiased estimates. However, with undeflated cross-section data the assumption of constant error variance usually is not appropriate. Just as small firms have small observations, they may also have small shocks — while the opposite is true for large firms. In such cases, David and Neyman[6] have shown that least squares will yield the most efficient unbiased [7] estimates only if the sum of squares to be minimized is appropriately weighted. Explicitly, say that $s_i^2 = s^2/w_i$ where s^2 is the unknown but constant population variance, s_i^2 is the variance of the conditional distribution of the dependent variable, X, and w_i is some known series of positive constants. Then, if the other Markoff assumptions are also met,[8] in the simple linear bivariate case the most efficient unbiased estimates of the regression parameters will be found by minimizing

$$\Sigma(X_i - k - bY_i)^2 w_i. \qquad (11)$$

Obviously the usual application of least squares is a special case of (11) in which w_i is always equal to unity.

Likewise it can readily be seen that simple deflation is a special case of (11) in which $w_i = 1/Z_i^2$ and k, the regression intercept, is zero. Thus if the error variance increases as the square of the size factor (i.e., if $s_i^2 = Z_i^2 s^2$ or $s_i = Z_i s$), then deflation will yield the most

---

[6] "Extension of the Markoff Theorem of Least Squares," *Statistical Research Memoirs,* II (1938), 105–116.

[7] "Unbiased" is here used in the conventional sense, i.e., when the expected value of the estimator equals the true population value to be estimated.

[8] These are linearity, independence, and a sufficient number of independent relationships so that the parameters can be uniquely determined. It should be noticed that normality is not necessary.

efficient unbiased estimates when least-squares techniques are applied. While the proportionality in the error variance may not hold exactly, in most economic cross sections such a relationship would appear to be a reasonable approximation. At the very worst, deflation should usually be superior to arbitrarily assuming that a constant unitary weight is appropriate.[9,10] As for the homogeneity assumption, we have already argued that in many circumstances, particularly when observations pertain to firms, most of the bivariate interrelations between the main and deflating series will be homogeneous. The last section of this appendix shows that this is a sufficient although not a necessary condition for the regression plane to have a zero intercept. In short, ratio models will tend to be more appropriate in cross-section applications than the simple regression model based on undeflated values.

Two other important properties of the weighted least-squares regression model should also be noted. First, one of the greatest practical advantages of ratio or weighted regression is that extreme observations will have a minor effect on parameter estimates. This is not true in many cross-section applications when unweighted data are used. As a consequence, the deflated findings are less subject to capricious variation due to the inclusion or exclusion of a few extreme values.[11] Second, in samples of firm data, deflation will often remove trend elements. Therefore, if several cross sections are pooled over time into one sample or if one compares parameters estimated from cross-section data drawn from different time periods, the necessary assumption of independence in sample draws is more likely to be satisfied when the data are deflated.

A SUFFICIENT CONDITION FOR A REGRESSION EQUATION TO HAVE A ZERO INTERCEPT

When $n - 1$ bivariate regressions between any one independent variable and the remaining variables are linear and homogeneous, the n variable regression will have a zero intercept. The converse is not necessarily true.

[9] From a statistical standpoint, a logarithmic transformation will sometimes be as appropriate as deflation for correcting heteroscedasticity but in many situations the economic interpretation of a logarithmic model will be more difficult to ascertain.

[10] Lawrence R. Klein, *Econometrics* (Evanston, 1953), pp. 311–313, in a discussion of weighted regressions using cross-section data sets up a similar model.

[11] The work of J. W. Brown, M. Greenwood, Jr., and F. Wood, "A Study of Index Correlations," *Journal of the Royal Statistical Society*, LXXVII (1914), 317–346, lends convincing empirical support to this proposition.

APPENDIX C

Let: M be the moment matrix; M_{ij} be the i,j cofactor; m_{ij} be the i,j element in M; $\bar{X}_i$ be the ith variable's mean, $i = 1, 2, \cdots j, \cdots n$; $b_{1j \cdot 23 \cdots (j) \cdots n} = -\dfrac{M_{1j}}{M_{11}}$ be the regression coefficient of dependent variable 1 with independent variable j.

Given: $$\bar{X}_i = \frac{m_{in}}{m_{nn}} \bar{X}_n.$$

This is the homogeneity relation of variables X_i, $i = 1, 2, \cdots j \cdots (n-1)$ with the nth variable.

To prove: $$\bar{X}_1 = \sum_{j=2}^{n} b_{1j \cdot 23 \cdots (j) \cdots n} \bar{X}_j.$$

1. An elementary theorem in determinants is that:

$$\sum_{j=1}^{n} M_{ij} m_{nj} = 0 \quad \text{for} \quad i \neq n.$$

2. $$M_{11} m_{n1} = -\sum_{j=2}^{n} M_{ij} m_{nj}.$$

3. Multiplying both sides of (2) by $\dfrac{\bar{X}_n}{M_{11} m_{nn}}$ we obtain:

$$\frac{m_{n1}}{m_{nn}} \bar{X}_n = -\sum_{j=2}^{n} \frac{M_{1j}}{M_{11}} \cdot \frac{m_{nj}}{m_{nn}} \cdot \bar{X}_n.$$

4. Since $\bar{X}_i = \dfrac{m_{in}}{m_{nn}} \bar{X}_n$, we can substitute this and the values of regression coefficients in terms of cofactors into (3) to obtain:

$$\bar{X}_1 = \sum_{j=2}^{n} b_{1j \cdot 2 \cdots (j) \cdots n} \bar{X}_j.$$

List of Works Cited

Adelman, Morris A. "The Measurement of Industrial Concentration," *Review of Economics and Statistics,* 33:269–296 (November 1951).
Andrews, Philip Walter Sawford. "A Further Inquiry into the Effects of Rates of Interest," *Oxford Economic Papers,* No. 3:33–73 (February 1940).
——— and Elizabeth Brunner. *Capital Development in Steel; a Study of the United Steel Companies, Ltd.* Oxford, 1951.
Arrow, Kenneth J. "Alternative Approaches to the Theory of Choice in Risk-Taking Situations," *Econometrica,* 19:404–437 (October 1951).
Bain, Joe S. "Economies of Scale, Concentration and Entry," *American Economic Review,* 44:15–39 (March 1954).
——— "Pricing in Monopoly and Oligopoly," *American Economic Review,* 39:448–464 (March 1949).
——— "The Relation of Economic Life of Equipment to Reinvestment Cycles," *Review of Economic Statistics,* 21:79–88 (May 1939).
Boulding, Kenneth E. "An Application of Population Analysis to the Automobile Population of the United States," *Kyklos,* 8, Fasc. ii:109–124 (1955).
——— *A Reconstruction of Economics.* New York, 1950.
Brems, Hans. "A Discontinuous Cost Function," *American Economic Review,* 42:577–586 (September 1952).
Bridge, Lawrence. "The Financing of Investment by New Firms," in *Conference on Research in Business Finance,* Universities — National Bureau Committee for Economic Research. New York, 1952.
——— "Capital Expenditures by Manufacturing Industries in the Postwar Period," *Survey of Current Business,* 31:15–22 (December 1951).

Brill, Daniel H. "Financing of Capital Formation," in *Problems of Capital Formation,* ed. Franco Modigliani, Conference on Income and Wealth, Volume 19, Princeton, 1957.

Brown, Edgar Cary. *Effects of Taxation: Depreciation Adjustments for Price Changes.* Division of Research, Graduate School of Business Administration, Harvard University. Boston, 1952.

Brown, J. W., M. Greenwood, Jr., and F. Wood. "A Study of Index Correlations," *Journal of the Royal Statistical Society,* 77:317–346. 1914.

Business Week, January 22, 1949, page 55.

Butters, J. Keith and John Lintner. *Effect of Federal Taxes on Growing Enterprises.* Boston, 1945.

———— "Effect of Mergers on Industrial Concentration, 1940–47," *Review of Economics and Statistics,* 32:30–48 (February 1950).

Chamberlin, Edward H. *The Theory of Monopolistic Competition.* 5th ed. Cambridge, Mass., 1947.

Chawner, Lowell J. "Capital Expenditures in Selected Manufacturing Industries," *Survey of Current Business,* Part I, 21:19–26 (December 1941); Part II, 22:14–23 (May 1942).

Chenery, Hollis. "Overcapacity and the Acceleration Principle," *Econometrica,* 20:1–28 (January 1952).

Chernoff, Herman. "Rational Selection of Decision Functions," *Econometrica,* 22:422–443 (October 1954).

Clark, John M. "Business Acceleration and the Law of Demand; A Technical Factor in Economic Cycles," *Journal of Political Economy,* 25:217–235 (March 1917).

Cochran, William G. "The Chi-Square Test of Goodness of Fit," *Annals of Mathematical Statistics,* 23:315–345 (September 1952).

———— *Sampling Techniques.* New York, 1953.

Cooper, William W. "Theory of the Firm — Some Suggestions for Revision," *American Economic Review,* 16:1204–1232 (December 1949).

David, F. N. *Tables of the Ordinates and Probability Integral of the Distribution of the Correlation Coefficient in Small Samples.* London, 1938.

———— and Jerzy Neyman. "Extension of the Markoff Theorem of Least Squares," in *Statistical Research Memoirs,* 2:105–116 (1938).

Dean, Joel. *Capital Budgeting.* New York, 1951.

———— "Department Store Cost Functions" in *Studies in Mathematical Economics and Econometrics,* ed. Oscar Lange, Francis McIntyre, and Theodore O. Yntema. Chicago, 1942.

────── *The Relation of Cost to Output for a Leather Belt Shop.* National Bureau of Economic Research. New York, 1941.

────── *Statistical Cost Functions of a Hosiery Mill.* Studies in Business Administration, Vol. XI, No. 4. Chicago, 1941.

────── *Statistical Determination of Cost with Special Reference to Marginal Costs.* Studies in Business Administration, Vol. VII, No. 1. Chicago, 1936.

Domar, Evsey David. "Depreciation, Replacement and Growth," *Economic Journal,* 63:1–32 (March 1953).

────── and Richard A. Musgrave. "Proportional Income Taxation and Risk-Taking," *Quarterly Journal of Economics,* 58:388–422 (May 1944).

Durbin, J. "A Note on Regression when there Is Extraneous Information about One of the Coefficients," *Journal of the American Statistical Association,* 48:799–808 (December 1953).

Ebersole, J. Franklin. "The Influence of Interest Rates upon Entrepreneurial Decisions in Business — A Case Study," *Harvard Business Review,* 17:35–39 (Autumn 1938).

Eckaus, Richard S. "The Acceleration Principle Reconsidered," *Quarterly Journal of Economics,* 67:209–230 (May 1953).

Edwards, Corwin D., George W. Stocking, Edwin B. George, and Adolph A. Berle, Jr., "Four Comments on 'The Measurement of Industrial Concentration,'" *Review of Economics and Statistics,* 34:156–174 (May 1952).

Einarsen, Johan. *Reinvestment Cycles and Their Manifestation in the Norwegian Shipping Industry.* Oslo, 1938.

Eisner, Robert. "Expectations, Plans and Capital Expenditures: A Synthesis of *Ex-Post* and *Ex-Ante* Data." (Mimeo.) Paper presented at joint meeting of the American Economic Association, Econometric Society and American Statistical Association, December 1953.

────── "Interview and Other Survey Techniques and the Study of Investment." (Mimeo.) Paper presented at Conference on Research in Income and Wealth. National Bureau of Economic Research, Inc. October 9–11, 1953.

Evans, G. Heberton. "Comment on Historical Series on Sources and Uses," in *Conference on Research in Business Finance.* Universities — National Bureau for Economic Research. New York, 1952.

Ezekiel, Mordecai. *Methods of Correlation Analysis.* 2nd ed. New York, 1950.

Fabricant, Solomon. *Capital Consumption and Adjustment.* National Bureau of Economic Research, Inc. New York, 1938.

Fellner, William. *Competition Among the Few; Oligopoly and Similar Market Structures.* New York, 1949.

Firestone, O. J. "Investment Forecasting in Canada," in *Short-Term Economic Forecasting: Studies in Income and Wealth, Vol. XVII,* ed. Lawrence R. Klein. Princeton, 1955.

Fisher, Ronald A. *Statistical Methods for Research Workers.* Edinburgh, 1936.

Friend, Irwin and Jean Bronfenbrenner. "Business Investment Programs and Their Realization," *Survey of Current Business,* 30:11-22 (December 1950).

Frisch, Ragnar. "The Interrelation between Capital Production and Consumer-Taking," *Journal of Political Economy,* 39:646-654 (October 1931).

Goodwin, Richard M. "The Nonlinear Accelerator and the Persistence of Business Cycles," *Econometrica,* 19:1-17 (January 1951).

Gordon, Robert A. *Business Leadership in the Large Corporation.* Washington, 1945.

Gort, Michael. "The Planning of Investment: A Study of Capital Budgeting in the Electric Power Industry," *The Journal of Business of the University of Chicago,* 24:79-95, 181-202 (April 1951; July 1951).

Harberger, Arnold C. [*The Measurement of Consumers' Expenditure and Behaviour in the United Kingdom 1920-1938: Volume I* by Richard Stone.] (Review), *Econometrica,* 23:217-218 (April 1955).

Hart, Albert G. *Anticipation, Uncertainty, and Dynamic Planning.* Chicago, 1948.

Heflebower, Richard B. "Full Costs, Cost Changes, and Prices," in *Business Concentration and Price Policy.* A Conference of the Universities — National Bureau Committee for Economic Research. Princeton, New Jersey, 1955.

Heller, Walter. "The Anatomy of Investment Decisions," *Harvard Business Review,* 29:95-103 (March 1951).

Henderson, Hubert D. "The Significance of the Rate of Interest," *Oxford Economic Papers,* No. 1:1-13 (October 1938).

Hicks, John R. *A Contribution to the Theory of the Trade Cycle.* Oxford, 1950.

Hood, William C. "Empirical Studies of Demand," *The Canadian Journal of Economics and Political Science,* 21:309-327 (August 1955).

LIST OF WORKS CITED

Hoover, Edgar M. "Some Institutional Factors in Business Investment Decisions," *American Economic Review*, 44:201–213 (May 1954).

Hotelling, Harold and Margaret R. Pabst. "Rank Correlation and Tests of Significance Involving No Assumption of Normality," *Annals of Mathematical Statistics*, 12:29–43 (1936).

Hurwicz, Leonid. "Theory of the Firm and of Investment," *Econometrica*, 14:109–136 (April 1946).

Jung, C. R. "Business Expectations and Plant Expansion with Special Reference to the Rubber Industry." Unpublished Ph.D. Dissertation, The Ohio State University, Columbus, Ohio, 1953.

Kalecki, Michael. "A New Approach to the Problem of Business Cycles," *Review of Economic Studies*, 16:57–64 (1949–50).

——— "The Principle of Increasing Risk," *Economica*, N. S., 4:440–447 (November 1937).

——— *Studies in Economic Dynamics*. London, 1943.

Katona, George and James N. Morgan. "The Quantitative Study of Factors Determining Business Decisions," *Quarterly Journal of Economics*, 66:67–90 (February 1952).

Kaysen, Carl. "A Dynamic Aspect of the Monopoly Problem," *Review of Economics and Statistics*, 31:109–113 (May 1949).

——— "Dynamic Aspects of Oligopoly Price Theory," *American Economic Review*, 42:198–210 (May 1952).

Kendall, Maurice G. *Rank Correlation Methods*. London, 1948.

Kimmel, L. H. *Depreciation Policy and Postwar Expansion*. Washington, 1946.

Kisselgoff, Avram. "Investment in Plant and Equipment in Private Electrical Utilities in the U. S." (Summary), *Econometrica*, 19:58–59 (January 1951).

Klein, Lawrence R. *Economic Fluctuations in the United States, 1921–1941*. New York, 1950.

——— *Econometrics*. Evanston, 1953.

——— "Studies in Investment Behavior," in *Conference on Business Cycles*. National Bureau of Economic Research, Inc. New York, 1951.

Koch, Albert R. and Charles H. Schmidt. "Financial Position of Manufacturing and Trade in Relation to Size and Profitability, 1946," *Federal Reserve Bulletin*, 33:1091–1102 (September 1947).

Kuznets, Simon. "Relation Between Capital Goods and Finished Products in the Business Cycle," in *Economic Essays in Honour of Wesley Clair Mitchell*. New York, 1935.

Leontief, Wassily. "A Comment on Klein's Studies in Investment Behavior," in *Conference on Business Cycles*. National Bureau of Economic Research, Inc. New York, 1951.

——— *Studies in the Structure of the American Economy*. New York, 1953.

Lintner, John. "The Determinants of Corporate Savings," in *Savings in the Modern Economy (A Symposium)*. Minneapolis, 1953. Edited by Walter W. Heller, Francis M. Boddy, and Carl L. Nelson.

——— "Distribution of Incomes of Corporations among Dividends, Retained Earnings and Taxes," *American Economic Review*, 46:97–113 (May 1956).

Liu, Ta-Chung and Ching-Gwan Chang. "U. S. Consumption and Investment Propensities: Prewar and Postwar," *American Economic Review*, 40:565–582 (September 1950).

Lutz, Friedrich A. and Vera C. Lutz. *The Theory of Investment of the Firm*. Princeton, 1951.

McHugh, Loughlin F. "Financing Small Business in the Postwar Period," *Survey of Current Business*, 31:17–24 (November 1951).

——— and Leonard G. Rosenberg. "Financial Experience of Large and Medium Size Manufacturing Firms, 1927–51," *Survey of Current Business*, 32:7–13 (November 1952).

Mack, Ruth. *The Flow of Business Funds and Consumer Purchasing Power*. New York, 1941.

Manne, Alan S. "Some Notes on the Acceleration Principle," *Review of Economics and Statistics*, 27:93–99 (May 1945).

Marschak, Jacob. "Money and the Theory of Assets," *Econometrica*, 6:311–325 (October 1938).

——— "On Combining Market and Budget Data in Demand Studies: A Suggestion," *Econometrica*, 7:332–335 (October 1939).

Mason, Edward S., ed. *Price Behavior and Cost Policy*. Conference on Price Research. New York, 1943.

Meade, James E. and Philip Walter Sawford Andrews. "Summary of Replies to Questions on Effects of Interest Rates," *Oxford Economic Papers*, No. 1:14–31 (October 1938).

Milnor, John. "Games Against Nature," in *Decision Processes*, ed. R. M. Thrall, C. H. Coombs, and R. C. Davis. New York, 1954.

Nutter, G. Warren. *The Extent of Enterprise Monopoly in the United States, 1899–1939*. Chicago, 1951.

Orcutt, Guy H. and D. Cochrane. "Application of Least Squares Regression to Relationships Containing Autocorrelated Error

LIST OF WORKS CITED

Terms, *Journal of the American Statistical Association,* 44:32–61 (September 1949).

Pearson, Karl. "On a Form of Spurious Correlation which May Arise when Indices Are Used in the Measurement of Organs," *Proceedings of the Royal Society of London,* 60:489–496. 1897.

Robinson, Joan. *An Essay in Marxian Economics.* London, 1942.

Roos, Charles F. "A Dynamical Theory of Economics," *Journal of Political Economy,* 35:632–656 (October 1927).

Rosenbluth, Gideon. "Measures of Concentration," in *Business Concentration and Price Policy.* Conference of Universities — National Bureau Committee for Economic Research. Princeton, 1955.

Ruggles, Richard. "The Nature of Price Flexibility and the Determinants of Relative Price Changes in the Economy," in *Business Concentration and Price Policy.* A Conference of the Universities — National Bureau Committee for Economic Research. Princeton, 1955.

Schmidt, Charles H. "Analyzing the Effects of Business Size on Sources and Uses of Funds," in *Conference on Research in Business Finance.* Universities — National Bureau Committee for Economic Research. New York, 1952.

Schroeder, Gertrude G. *The Growth of Major Steel Companies, 1900–1950.* Baltimore, 1953.

Segal, Martin. "Some Economic Aspects of Adjustment to Technological Change." Unpublished Ph.D. Dissertation, Harvard University, Cambridge, Massachusetts, 1953.

Shackles, G. L. S. *Expectations in Economics.* New York, 1949.

Smith, Caleb A. "The Cost-Output Relation for the U. S. Steel Corporation," *The Review of Economic Statistics,* 24:166–176 (November 1942).

Smith, Dan T. *Effects of Taxation: Corporate Financial Policy.* Boston, 1952.

Snedecor, George. *Statistical Methods.* 4th ed. Ames, 1946.

Somers, Harold M. *Public Finance and National Income.* Philadelphia, 1949.

Standard and Poor's Corporation. *Standard and Poor's Trade and Securities Statistics: Security Price Index Record, 1952 Edition.* New York, 1952.

——— *Standard and Poor's Trade and Securities Statistics: Security Price Index Record, 1954 Edition.* New York, 1954.

Stone, Richard. *The Measurement of Consumers' Expenditure and Behavior in the United Kingdom 1920–1938; Volume I.* Cambridge, Eng., 1954.

Stuart, Alan. "Asymtotic Relative Efficiencies of Distribution-Free Tests of Randomness against Normal Alternates," *Journal of the American Statistical Association,* 49:147–157 (March 1954).

——— "The Efficiencies of Tests of Randomness against Normal Regression," *Journal of the American Statistical Association,* 51: 285–287 (June 1956).

Terborgh, George. *Amortization of Defense Facilities.* Chicago, 1952.

——— *A Dynamic Equipment Policy.* New York, 1949.

——— "Estimated Expenditures for New Durable Goods 1919–1938," *Federal Reserve Bulletin,* 25:731–736 (September 1939).

Tinbergen, Jan. "Statistical Evidence on the Acceleration Principle," *Economica,* N. S. 5:164–176 (May 1938).

——— *Statistical Testing of Business Cycle Theories.* Geneva, 1938.

——— and J. J. Polak. *The Dynamics of Business Cycles, a Study in Economic Fluctuations.* Chicago, 1950.

Tintner, Gerhard. "A Contribution to the Non-Static Theory of Production," in *Studies in Mathematical Economics and Econometrica.* Chicago, 1942.

Tobin, James. "A Statistical Demand Function for Food in the U. S. A.," *Journal of the Royal Statistical Society,* Series A, 113:113–141 (Part II, 1950).

Tsiang, S. C. "Accelerator, Theory of the Firm, and the Business Cycle," *Quarterly Journal of Economics,* 65:325–341 (August 1951).

Tukey, John W. "Comparing Individual Means in the Analysis of Variance," *Biometrics,* 5:99–114 (June 1949).

U. S., Congress, House, Committee on the Judiciary, *Hearings, Study of Monopoly Power,* 81st Congress, 1st Session, 1949, Serial No. 14, Part 2–B. Washington, 1950.

U. S. Department of Commerce. *Business Statistics, 1953 Bi-Annual Edition: Statistical Supplement to the Survey of Current Business.* Washington, 1953.

——— *National Income, 1954 Edition: A Supplement to the Survey of Current Business.* Washington, 1954.

——— *Survey of Current Business, 31* (July 1953).

——— *Survey of Current Business: 1942 Supplement.* Washington, 1942.

U. S. Federal Trade Commission and U. S. Securities and Exchange Commission. *Quarterly Financial Report, United States Manufacturing Corporations,* 1948–49.

U. S. Securities and Exchange Commission. *Sales Record of Unseasoned Registered Securities, 1933–39.* Washington, 1941.

────── Statistical Series Release No. 1202, December 10, 1953.
U. S. Treasury Department, Bureau of Internal Revenue. *Bulletin F: Income Tax Depreciation and Obsolescence Estimated Useful Lives and Depreciation Rates.* Washington, 1942.
────── *Statistics of Income,* 1926–1952.
Von Neumann, John and Oskar Morganstern. *Theory of Games and Economic Behavior.* Princeton, 1947.
Weckstein, R. S. "On the Use of the Theory of Probability in Economics," *Review of Economic Studies,* 20:191–198 (1952–53).
Weston, J. Fred. *The Role of Mergers in the Growth of Large Firms.* Berkeley and Los Angeles, 1953.
Wilcox, Clair. *Competition and Monopoly in American Industry,* Investigation of Concentration of Economic Power, Temporary National Economic Committee, Monograph No. 21. Washington, 1940.
Wold, Herman and Lars Jureen. *Demand Analysis.* New York, 1953.
Yntema, Dwight B. "Measures of the Inequality in the Personal Distribution of Wealth or Income," *Journal of the American Statistical Association,* 28:423–433 (December 1933).
Yntema, Theodore O. *An Analysis of Steel Prices, Volume and Costs Controlling Limitations on Price Reductions: Pamphlet No. 6* in *United States Steel Corporation T. N. E. C. Papers: Comprising the Pamphlets and Charts Submitted by United States Steel Corporation to the Temporary National Economic Committee.* 3 vols. Vol. I: Economic and Related Studies. New York, 1940.
Yule, G. Udny and Maurice G. Kendall. *An Introduction to the Theory of Statistics.* 14th ed. London, 1950.

Index

Accelerated amortization, arguments for, 102; in recession, 109; and tax policy, 101
Accelerated amortization effects, previous tests of, 103–104
Accelerator, alternative statements of, 16, 121; assumptions, 124–125; and financial restraints, 15; irreversibilities of, 14; and liquidity assumptions, 130; long-run, and pricing, 193–194; and postwar cycle, 124–125, 190. *See also* Capacity variable; Change in sales variable
Adelman, M., 159, 160
Age of capital stock, in declining industry, 94. *See also* Depreciation reserve variable; Echo effect; Replacement investment
Andrews, P. W. S., 17, 26, 29, 33
Arrow, K. J., **13**
Averaged data, models, 76; statistical problems of, 80

Bain, J. S., 192, 201
Berle, A. A., Jr., 160
Beta coefficients, explanation of, 75
Boulding, K. E., 10, 15
Bowman, M. J., 23
Brems, H., 193
Bridge, L., 45, 70, 172
Brill, D. H., 137, 141
Bronfenbrenner, J., 29, 33, 167
Brown, E. C., 102
Brown, J. W., 266
Brunner, E., 29, 33
Butters, J. K., 17, 19, 29, 160, 163, **167**

Capacity variable, averaged data performance, 132–133; data properties of, 67–68; and financial restraints, 134; identification properties of, 82; postwar performance, 123–126, 191. *See also* Accelerator; Sales variable
Capacity pressures, long-run force, 192
Capital markets and real investment, 198
Causation direction, tests of, 125
Chamberlin, E. H., 201
Chang, C.-G., 28, 33
Change in sales variable, data properties of, 68; identification properties of, 82; measures expectations, liquidity flows, 123; postwar performance, 123–125. *See also* Accelerator; Capacity variable
Chawner, L. W., 69, 70, 71
Chenery, H., 15, 30, 35
Chernoff, H., 11
Christ, C., 258
Clark, J. M., 14, 15
Cochran, W. G., 46, 85
Cochrane, D., 185
Concentration indices, 147–150; "experts' index," 150–153; external finance, 149-150; industry composition of, 147; limitations of, 150; and Lorenz curves, 149
Consumer credit, 199
Cooper, W. W., 10
Correlation, and causation, 75; by size groups, 176
Correlation techniques, advantages of, 74; differences from regression, 74
Cost-plus pricing, 193, 195
Cross-section estimates, cyclical variability of, 184; and disaggregation, 54; as long-run behavior measure, 183; stability of, 53
Cross-section sample, coverage, 39
Cross-section and time series estimates combined, 182–187; choice

of cross-section parameters for, 184, 186-187; hazards of, 184; interest rates in, 187; regression models, 182; stock prices in, 187; why relative cost of labor excluded from, 187

David, F. N., 84, 85
Dean, J., 17, 19, 60, 193
Deflation and gross fixed assets, 59
Depreciation, short-run determinants, 197
Depreciation expense, cause of within industry variations in, 104–108
Depreciation expense variable, actual liquidity characteristics, 109, 118–119; correlations with investment, 110–112, 118–119; data properties of, 66; measure of liquidity, replacement needs, 112–113; relation to durability range, 113–114
Depreciation reserve variable, and adequacy of echo effect test, 92–93; change in, as growth measure, 143–147; correlation with investment, 63; curvilinear form, 61; data properties of, 68; and net quick liquidity, 97. See also Age of capital stock
Depression, effects on external financing, 17
Disaggregation and cross-sections, 54; outside information, 77
Dividend payout variable, data properties of, 69; and growth postwar, 138, 191; and growth rate, 156–157; and short-run investment correlations, 153–155
Dividends and profits, and short-run investment, 196
Domar, E. D., 10, 102
Durability range, rank correlation with depreciation expense, 113–114
Durbin, J., 78, 182

Ebersole, J. F., 26
Echo effect and depreciation reserve variable, 92–93; theory unconfirmed, 91; and time series, 93
Eckaus, R. S., 16
Edwards, C. D., 160

Einarsen, J., 15, 91
Eisner, R., 12, 23, 31, 32, 33
Evans, G. H., 172
Expectations, extrapolation of recent experience, 11; and game theory, 13; subjective nature of, 11; theories of, and investment, 10
"Experts' concentration index," 150–153; and external funds, 152
External finance, aversion to, postwar, 137–138; equity market decline and depression, 18–19; by sample industries, 141; restrictions and Securities and Exchange Act, 19; use of, in recession year 1949, 173. See also Capital markets; internal finance; liquidity flows and stocks
External finance, and growth, 143–147; growth industries postwar, 191; postwar access by growth industry large firms, 175
External funds, and concentration indices, 149–150; "experts' concentration index," 152; long-run equilibrium, 203; in residual funds investment theory, 198–199, 203–204; and trade position rivalry, 147
Extraneous estimators, and multicollinearity, 183; use with time series, 77. See also Cross-section and time series estimates combined
Ezekiel, M., 59, 60, 86

Fabricant, S., 70
Fellner, W., 21
Finance, 17–19. See also External finance; Internal finance
Firestone, O. J., 33
Firm, as unit of observation, 53
Firm size, see Size of firm
First differenced data and trend, 185
Fisher, R. A., 92, 95, 98, 132
Friend, I., 29, 33, 167
Frisch, R., 15

Game theory, and business behavior, 12–13
George, E. B., 160
Goodwin, R. M., 14

INDEX

Gordon, R. A., 19
Gort, M., 26, 33, 60
Greenwood, M., Jr., 266
Gross fixed assets, as deflator, 59; as measure of firm size, 163
Growth and dividend payout postwar, 191
Growth industries and external funds postwar, 143-147, 191
Growth, internal, of large and small firms postwar, 163; of large and small firms in recession, 166–167; measure of, 163
Growth rate and dividend payout, 157
Growth, measured by change in age variable, 143–147; by net investment rate, 143–147

Harberger, A. C., 183
Hart, A. G., 10
Heflebower, R. B., 193
Heller, W., 12, 17, 29, 60
Hicks, J. R., 14
Homoscedasticity and ratio deflation, 83–84
Hood, W. C., 183
Hoover, E., 17
Hotelling, H., 87
Hurwicz, L., 10
Hypotheses, clusters of, and selection process, 58; limits on sample, 52

Identification properties of, capacity variable, 82; change in sales variable, 82; profit variable, 82; sales variable, 82
Industry stratification, and capital intensity, 49; problems of, 48
Institutional findings on investment, preference for internal financing, 16–17. *See also* Trade position
Interest rates, in combined cross-section, time series models, 187; empirical importance of, and capital markets, 8–9; and marginalist theories, 8
Internal finance, comparative reliance of large and small firms on, 169; and managerial debt aversion, 19; preference for, 19, 142; relative access to by large and small firms postwar, 172; trend toward, 140–142; use postwar, 138. *See also* Capital markets; External finance; Liquidity flows; Liquidity stocks
Inventories, short-run, and investment, 196–197
Investment hypotheses, limits on, 4
Investment motivation, complexities of, 3–4, 6; and oligopoly pressures, 20
Investment, net rate, as growth measure, 143–147; theories of, and expectations, 10; variable, data properties of, 64–65

Jung, C. R., 10
Jureen, L., 78, 182

Kalecki, M., 10, 20
Katona, G., 12, 33
Kaysen, C., 20
Kendall, M. G., 84, 85, 128, 130
Kimmel, L. H., 102
Kisselgoff, A., 23, 29, 32, 35
Klein, L. R., 10, 12, 25, 26, 27, 28, 33, 34, 35, 266
Koch, A. R., 169, 170
Kuznets, S., 15, 20, 32, 33

Large firms, influenced by capacity variable, 178; recession sales decline less than for small firms, 167
Large and small firms, access to external funds, 172; comparative reliance on internal and short-term funds, 169; internal growth postwar, 163; use of external funds in recession year 1949, 173–175
Leontief, W., 15, 33
Lintner, J., 17, 19, 29, 160, 163, 167, 195-196
Liquidity flow, depreciation as a postwar fund source, 109; short-run force, 192
Liquidity flows, depreciation expense and profits postwar, 191; and postwar cycle, 118–119, 190; and senility effect, 98–99
Liquidity and investment, different theories of, 117

Liquidity restraint, profit and depreciation expense behavior in 1949–1950, 118–119
Liquidity stock variable, contrast with liquidity flow variables, 120; data properties of, 68–69; and depreciation reserve variable, 97; postwar behavior, 120; and senility effect, 98
Liquidity stock excess, from wartime, 112; eliminated by 1949 and 1950, 119
Liu, T.-C., 28, 33
Lutz, F. A., 10
Lutz, V. C., 10

McHugh, L. F., 137, 138, 139
Mack, R., 17, 20, 26, 29, 60
Manne, A. S., 32, 35
Marginal cost functions, linearity, 192; pricing and short-run investment, 193
Marginal costs, pricing, long-run investment and accelerator, 193–194
Marginalist investment theories, and interest rates, 8; standard statement of, 7–9; for tests of, *see* Interest rates and Stock prices
Market structure, oligopolistic, and residual funds investment theory, 201–203; and trade position, 20. *See also* Concentration indices
Markoff theorem of least squares, 265
Marshall, A., 5
Marschak, J., 10, 77, 182
Marx, K., 91
Meade, J. E., 17, 26
Milnor, J., 11
Models, averaged data, 76; cross-section, 78; time series, 78, 186
Modigliani, F., 23
Morgan, J. N., 12, 33
Morganstern, O., 13
Multicollinearity, 59, 185; and extraneous estimators, 183
Musgrave, R. A., 10

Neyman, J., 84
Non-parametric methods, effects of difference in sample sizes on, 85; efficiency of, 87

Nutter, G. W., 150
Oligopoly pressures, and investment motivation, 20; and residual funds investment theory, 201–203. *See also* Trade position
Orcutt, G. H., 185, 258

Pabst, M. R., 87
Pearson, K., 259
Polak, J. J., 12, 20
Profit, and accelerator performance, 126–128; liquidity restraint in 1949–50, 118–119; and transition, 1948–49, 125–126
Profit theories, expectations, 11–12; liquidity and expectations behavior, 125
Profits, and dividends, 196; retained, advantages of to professional management, 19–20; and postwar cycle, 118–119, 190; short-run investment determinant, 191, 195, 197
Profit variable, data properties of, 65; different behavior from sales, 131; identification properties, 82; and sales, 76

Ratio deflation, and skewness, 83–84; and spurious index correlation, 84
Recession, internal growth of large and small firm in, 166–167; small firm and large firm sales reactions during, 167; year 1949, external funds, use by large and small firms, 173
Regression, and biased estimates, 74; and causation, 74–75; models in combined cross-section and time series estimates, 182–185; models, extraneous estimates, 77–78; by size groups, 176; and time series, 75, 77
Regression techniques, advantages of, 74; differences from correlation, 74
Relative cost of labor, why excluded from combined cross-section, time series estimates, 187
Replacement investment, determinants of, 15; measurement of, 93;

INDEX

theory of, and echo effect, 91, 93
Residual funds investment model, 200–204; assumptions of, 200; external funds and competitive markets, 203; long-run equilibrium, 202; oligopoly market structure, 201–203; relation to financing investment, 197; short-run equilibrium adjustments, 201; technological change, 202
Robinson, J., 91
Roos, C. F., 10
Rosenberg, L. G., 137
Rosenbluth, G., 149
Ruggles, R., 193

Sales and capacity as long-run determinants of investment, 191
Sales variable, collinearity with profits, 76, 120; data properties of, 65; different behavior compared with profits, 131; identification properties of, 82; measures liquidity, acceleration concepts, 120–121; relation to profits, 120
Sample, accounting characteristics, 40; biases and significance tests, 47; data properties of, 64–70; exclusions, extremely rapid growth, 44; exclusions, special firm experiences, 41; exclusions, time heterogeneity, 44; limits set by hypothesis, 52; statistical basis for, 53
Schmidt, C. H., 169, 170
Schroeder, G. G., 160, 163
Securities and Exchange Act, strictness of, and external financing, 19
Securities and Exchange Commission and sample, 44–46
Segal, M., 60
Selection process, empirical basis of, and simple correlations, 59–64
Senility effect, and cross-section investment, 94–97; and liquidity flows, 98–99; and net quick liquidity, 98; and trade position, 96
Shackles, G. L. S., 10
Significance tests and sample biases, 47
Size of firm, capacity variable postwar, 191; comparisons, size and liquidity flows postwar, 191; correlation comparisons, 178; definition by industry, 161–162; gross fixed assets, as measure of, 163; liquidity flows, depreciation expense and profits postwar, 191; regression and correlation results, 176
Skewness and ratio deflation, 83–84
Small firm, decline of sales much larger than for large firm in recession, 167; growth aided by general prosperity, 167–168; influenced by liquidity flow variables, 178
Smith, C. A., 193
Smith, D. T., 18
Snedecor, G., 92, 95, 98, 109
Somers, H. M., 16
Spurious index correlation and ratio deflation, 84, 261
Stock prices, 192; in combined cross-section, time series, 187–188
Stocking, G. W., 160
Stone, R., 78, 182, 183, 184, 185
Stratification, statistical problems of, 80
Stuart, A., 87

Tax policy and accelerated amortization, 101
Technological change and long-run equilibrium, 202
Time series variables, data properties of, 69–70; *See* cross-section and time series estimates combined
Terborgh, G., 17, 29, 70, 102, 103
Tinbergen, J., 12, 20, 25, 27, 28, 29, 30, 181, 188
Tintner, G., 10
Tobin, J., 77–78, 182
Trade position, market structure and institutional theories, 20–22; and postwar cycle, 190; and senility effect, 96–97
Transition, 1948–1949, and discrimination among theories, 125–126; rank correlation tests, 126–128
Trend and first differenced data, 185
Tsiang, S. C., 15, 20
Tukey, J. W., 52

Utility maximization and marginalism, 9; and uncertainty, 10

Variables, list chosen for study, 60; in models, 78
Von Neumann, J., 13

Weckstein, R. S., 10

Weston, J. F., 160, 163
Wilcox, C., 150
Wold, H., 78, 182
Wood, F., 266

Yntema, D. B., 149
Yntema, T., 192
Yule, G. U., 84